Parents Should Be Heard

Parents Should Be Heard

An Exploration of the Interpersonal
Dynamics of Communication, Teaching and Learning

Daphne Nicholson Bennett

HUTCHINSON OF LONDON

HUTCHINSON EDUCATIONAL LTD
3 Fitzroy Square, London W1

London Melbourne Sydney Auckland
Wellington Johannesburg Cape Town
and agencies throughout the world

First published 1972

*This book has been set in Bembo type, printed in Great Britain
on antique wove paper by Anchor Press, and
bound by Wm. Brendon, both of Tiptree, Essex*

ISBN 0 09 108960 3

To

WENDY, BRENDA and FAY

CONTENTS

ACKNOWLEDGMENTS

A first expression of appreciation goes to all the people—parents, husbands, wives, students, and professional people who have not only permitted material from their lives to be used for publication but have asked that it be shared with others to make better known methods of resolving problems of human communication in family and other social groups, and have gone to great trouble to convey what the methods meant to them. Diverse settings over the years have provided opportunities to work with a developing philosophy, beginning with Dudley College of Education (an affiliate of the Department of Education, University of Birmingham) in England and continuing in the United States in University of Southern California, private practice in Los Angeles, the University of North Dakota, and Mount St Mary's College, Los Angeles. Thanks go to persons and organisations who supplied encouragement and financial support in early research days: Chancellor R. B. von Klein Smid of the University of Southern California, the Audiology Foundation, Phi Beta Kappa Alumni of Southern California through their international grants, the Fulbright Commission through their travel grants. A particular debt of thanks goes to Mrs Spenser Tracy for her generosity in supplying material and research opportunities at the John Tracy Clinic during her administration, especially the opportunities to work with Mrs Alathena Johnson Smith, Ph.D., outstanding teacher and therapist, dynamic practitioner of the preventive philosophy described in this book. It is a privilege now to be able to incorporate practical illustrations of her work, notably included in the lecture excerpts and in half the cases in Chapter 4 (concentrated in the latter part of the chapter), in the group interchanges which are the main substance of Chapter 6 and a proportion of Chapters 7 and 8, and in the first three cases in Chapter 10.

D.N.B.

PREFACE

This book is concerned essentially with the preservative and preventive aspects of psychological health. Since each person's emotional capacity to handle his life-demands originates in the family, this book is about parents. It is also about ways of assisting parents to become the kind of people who can help their children grow up to realise their potential both in using the gifts with which they were born and in being able to make satisfying and enduring relationships within and beyond the family.

There is an implied philosophy in the book which is far from defeatist—that we can make live a viewpoint which respects individuals and human commitments, and that education can lead to personal growth as well as to advancement of knowledge. As mothers and fathers are very important people both from the point of view of handing on cultural values and producing the heirs to solve the world's problems, the education of parents must be explored in the light of possibilities for personal growth, rather than just information gathering.

This book is offered as one contribution to human relationships and one approach to solving the personal and social problems that still challenge and plague us.

1 Prologue

'*Prevention is better than cure*' in matters of physical well-being is a truism nowadays. In general we take for granted that there are measures which contribute towards good health—proper nutrition, sufficient rest and exercise, a balance between work and recreation.

In relation to specific diseases prevention is now the rule rather than the exception—the use of X-rays at regular intervals to detect tuberculosis, vaccines to achieve increased immunity from smallpox, diphtheria, poliomyelitis, tetanus and many other diseases. Travel to certain parts of the world is prohibited without a quota of 'shots' to build up resistance against possible infections.

We are not unaware today that prevention is better than cure in matters of mental health also. We recognise that for children a good home is an insurance against behaviour problems and difficulties with relationships later in life. Precisely what constitutes a good home and ways of achieving it in reality are perhaps less widely recognised in spite of the popularisation of psychological concepts originally made available to the general public in Freud's *Psychopathology of Everyday Life*. The use of psychological terms relating to complexes, neuroses, psychoses, is widespread. Yet the incidence of physical disorders with psychological components, the increase of family break-up, drug addiction, alcoholism, delinquency, even the suicide rate, seem to indicate a continuing need for the effective use of psychology for the improvement of human relationships and the realisation of human potential. The continuing problems of social tension raise questions about how psychological knowledge may be used to improve the ability of social groups to live together with understanding and tolerance.

Perhaps the biggest challenge of the age lies in closing the gap between technological advance and man's apparently more slowly developing ability to solve social and national problems by peaceful and rational means. The race for survival is not only concerned with the H-bomb. Huxley's *Brave New World* and Orwell's *1984* are warnings of the ultimate possibilities of the manipulative uses of psychology and biology and the abolition of present human relationships with their values of affection and personal loyalty.

. . . . .

Imagine a group of people—men and women—gathered in a room, which can be a college or school classroom, a room in a clinic or hospital, an office or a private house. There may be ten or twelve, or over thirty. They have one thing in common—they are parents, and they all want to be better parents. They happen to be in the United States, but they could be anywhere.

There are many immediate reasons why parents join a group. Some want to find ways of improving their own ability to communicate. Another reason for joining can be the birth of a handicapped child, behaviour problems or learning difficulties in physically normal children. Alternatively, the immediate problem can be anything related to either family or social problems. How is one to cope with husband and children when mother-in-law is living in the house? What can be done about the child who runs away? What is the best way to cope with childish nightmates and sleeplessness? Just how does one keep the peace and reject relatives' unwanted advice? What does one do when one just does not approve of a child's boy- or girl-friend? Parents are concerned with the problems of discipline and academic achievement, their own marital problems, about the reasons why young people take to drugs, the generation gap, above all with preventing these problems arising in their own families.

The parent groups include people from many different social groups and professions: lawyers, bus-drivers, professional engineers, mechanics, educators, business executives and factory workers. Some possess higher degrees and some left school at fourteen, there are those who were popular and successful at school and those who just managed to scrape through, the beauty who had many admirers and the quiet, plain girl who married the boy next door. Rich or poor, they all want to understand their children better and to find ways of satisfying their children's needs as effectively as possible. However, the solution to the immediate problem is only the first step in dealing with more far-reaching problems.

The experience of the parent group and its significance both then and afterwards to the members are the subject of these pages. The author, a psychotherapist, trained in psychology and communication, has for many years studied and worked with the philosophy and methods described here, with many parents and students of human relations. The purpose of the book is to share the experiences with others—with those who are parents or who may become parents, with all who have had parents—and to understand them better. Parents are people. This book is for people, irrespective of their background or education. It is a human document.

There is an old maxim: 'Children should be seen and not heard.' In this book we say not only should children be heard, but parents should also be heard. The hearing tells its own story.

First let us look at some of the problems that may confront parents, discuss some necessary background for understanding people, and consider some of the difficulties in answering questions about human relationships.

2 *Happily Ever After?*

Parents can't give what they haven't learned.

Bruno Bettelheim

Once upon a time a beautiful princess was imprisoned in a tower by her wicked, jealous stepmother and by her father who was bewitched by his wife. But a handsome prince from another country outwitted the stepmother and rescued the princess. The angry stepmother fell from the tower and was killed, and the king, having discovered her stratagems to take over his kingdom, was reconciled with his daughter. The prince and the princess married and lived happily ever after and had beautiful children to reign after them.

Here we have an encapsulated fairy-tale, but the problems and hopes it expresses seem contemporary. Certainly in the story the younger generation is trying to do better than the older. A bad parent—in the traditional archetype of a wicked stepmother—is destroyed in her own trap; a good parent freed from bad influences survives to bestow blessings on his child. Reconciliation is the keynote.

But where the fairy-story ends—they married and lived happily ever after—our concern starts by raising questions. Do people outside the story-books live happily ever after? And do their children have hopes of continuing happiness? Or is real life fraught with unresolved problems like those of some of Dostoevsky's characters? Are the sins of the fathers inevitably visited on the children?

Marriage and children certainly raise problems to which there are no easy solutions. The parents we shall now meet have unresolved difficulties. Do they seem remote from us, rather unpleasant people, not worth much attention or understanding? Or in some ways and to a much lesser extent, perhaps, could any one of them be us or our children?

SOME UNANSWERED QUESTIONS

An absentee father. Andrew Smith married his wife Jane when he was twenty-one and she was eighteen, just finishing school. They had been going out together for two years; everyone said they were crazy about each other. Jane's mother objected to the marriage and wanted her to wait, but Jane insisted that she could not be happy unless she married Andrew. He worked as a junior buyer in a department store and she found a job as a typist so that they could afford to move immediately into their own house in the suburbs. They planned to take evening classes towards a degree. As a part-time student Andrew had now completed one year towards a qualification in business administration, but he found that a house and garden and a wife made it harder to study. There were always bills to pay, as well as jobs to be done at home, and he began to feel tied down. Within three years he was the father of a son and a daughter and, after his first interest in the new babies wore off, they seemed like a millstone and he wanted to escape with his friends. He tended to leave more and more to Jane and during her mother's frequent visits he felt his life was not his own. He found himself increasingly antagonistic to Jane's family because he felt they all thought him a poor prospect who had spoiled Jane's chances. Jane did not feel comfortable with his family either and especially disliked his sister, whom she thought overbearing. For Andrew home seemed a place of conflict from which he escaped as often as he could. Business trips were an excuse to stay away from home and he also began to go drinking after work.

Outings with the family were fewer. Jane felt neglected and concentrated on the children. She became sadder, quieter, and seemed to withdraw from other people except for occasional bursts of irritation at the children, Andrew and her mother. Every night she waited for her husband, never knowing when he would get home. He was moody and the children seemed to be afraid of him when he was at home.

A nagging wife. Jim Allen seemed to be another kind of person: an attentive husband who always stayed at home in the evenings. He had a steady position in a local engineering firm and hopes of promotion. More than anything else he wanted to please his wife, so he said. But Mary always seemed to be critical of him. She said he spent too much time in the garden and messing around with the car. She wanted some shelves made and the kitchen painted. But Jim began to feel discouraged because Mary constantly found small faults with what he did, or the way he did it. She always seemed to want something more. He felt 'torn down'. He'd wanted to marry an intelligent woman and

Mary had both 'brains and beauty'. But why did she nag him so? And why did he do little things that annoyed her, like not hanging up his clothes or forgetting to do the errand she asked on the way from work? He felt at times she was difficult to 'live up to'. He changed his job to please her, he bought the home she wanted, and she still drove him on. But he felt he was losing his drive. Then their son began to be a battle ground: Jim was indulgent and Mary strict.

A teenage rebel. Jack and Maxine Crane worked hard. They decided they were going to give their daughter Ann the best education money could buy. They themselves did not go to college and always regretted it, so they were going to make sure that Ann would have the opportunities they missed. Maxine worked to pay for their daughter's fees at private school, where they thought that she would meet better people than at the local high school. They made sure that she had all the clothes and all the spending money she needed. If she had difficulty with any class, Maxine paid for private lessons to make sure she would get through. Finally, when she was ready for college, her parents thought she should begin at a small local college as preparation for going away to a larger university. They were concerned because she was not sleeping well and seemed tense and unsure of herself, but thought this was a temporary period of adjustment. Her mother was pleased that she seemed popular with the boys but worried about the kind of boys she chose. Maxine said to her husband that the boys seemed 'unstable and on the make'. There was one drug party and the parents were called in by the college counsellor. Then things seemed to improve. But suddenly one day Ann came home and said that she had left college and had decided to go to work and make her own way, 'I just can't meet your standards,' she said. 'I want to live in my own place and run my own life.' Maxine and Jack felt that everything they had worked for had been destroyed. They said they would try to give her more independence and be less demanding if she would please return to college, but she said she had to do what she had decided. She left home and college and went out to work. The parents were devastated. They felt they had devoted their lives to her and she had not even finished one college term. Something had gone wrong with their relationships.

A handicapped child. Children, like everyone else, have their limitations. In this sense everyone starts with his own handicap. Children with major physical handicaps which require special compensatory training have more obvious limits than physically normal children. Programmes for the blind, the deaf, the cerebral palsied and other handicapped children require parents to help with early language training or physiotherapy which must begin in the crucial formative pre-school years if language and social skills are not to be lost. However, children do not seem to learn skills of relating to others in speech or behaviour if the emotional climate at home does not give them a sense of security. For parents the birth of any child is a challenge and if he does not seem to be an 'easy baby' he may create a stress for parents. Discovery of a handicap can be such a stress—a parent may be in a state of shock and find it very difficult to face the demands of this frightening and unknown situation. 'Everything money can buy' does not help; nor does the parents' 'formal education'. Thus one successful professional man and his wife seemed unable to lose their sense of stigma in having a deaf child and the child made little progress even with private tuition. The teacher said he seemed to react to the atmosphere; his parents never seemed able to show pleasure in his progress; they were so worried because he was handicapped that he did not even develop what potential he had.

At other times children seem able to learn, but troubles develop later, as they did with Ann Crane, who had no physical handicap. What is the criterion of success for parents' efforts. Nora Kalman was deaf. When her mother, Janet, learned that compensatory training was possible she made it her life's work to be sure that Nora would learn to speak. But at eighteen her daughter refused to use the language acquired with such hard work on the part of both parent and child. 'I spent every hour *to teach her*,' the mother explained. 'People said, "How do you do it?" But I made up my mind that through the years I'd have a better frame of mind and she'd come out better if she had speech. I devoted my life to it. Nora graduated from the school for the deaf and then finished normal high school with very high grades. Her ambition was to be like everyone else. She was in the best clubs or none. They all treated her wonderfully. She was accepted in college and began required courses in summer school. It was then that she decided to do what she wanted. The college was not like high school and she seemed tired. She said, "Maybe I'm not as smart as you think.

B

You want me to do what you want." She began using signs and going more with the deaf children. I got so angry and then I just cried and cried. I can't understand why she uses sign language when she can talk. She wants me to learn the sign language but I can't make myself use it. She feels I don't like the deaf children because I won't learn the sign language. "You don't understand, Mother," she says. I think it's a psychological thing with her. We've lost so much. I've worked so hard with this. I feel she's missing so much. I can't accept it.'

Everyday problems. With the best intentions, any of us may find ourselves in little pockets of disappointment, irritation or just a general sense of dissatisfaction. A wife wonders if she can retain her husband's interest in her; keeping house seems insufficiently satisfying. A husband is under pressure to make his way in a career; there are problems in the firm and he wonders if he can provide for the needs of his family. There may be anxiety about losing a job or getting one. Husband and wife do not agree about bringing up the children; even when they agree they may wonder if they are doing the right thing. Teenagers stay out until all hours no matter what parents say, yet everywhere people blame parents. 'If parents put their foot down we wouldn't have delinquency. We wouldn't have all this early marriage and divorce if children could talk to parents.' Children blame their parents and authority becomes the enemy. Parents wonder if they can avert these problems with their children. Is it possible to ensure enduring and satisfying relationships in the family and give one's children a foundation for emotional satisfaction in their own families?

FAMILY SOLUTIONS

All family members have their own ideas about the reason for things going wrong and can usually suggest improvements or solutions and a child can be very definite about cures for parents, especially if he feels as upset as Andrew Smith's daughter felt about her father. 'The way my father treats my mother makes me feel terrible. He has moods when he won't talk to anybody for days. He doesn't seem to understand anything. People said when I got a scholarship, "Your father must be proud of you." It doesn't seem real. I don't care whether he's proud or not. He can turn on you and something you care about with brutal little remarks. And then he's nice for a while—and especially when he's been drinking he expects you to be nice to him. But you can't depend on him. If he had stood by my mother she wouldn't be the isolated unhappy person she is.'

Mary Allen's son was just as definite about his mother. 'My mother always criticised when I was a kid. I don't remember her ever praising anything. She was always on at you. My father, I think, gave up in despair of ever really pleasing her. If Mother had encouraged him he'd have had that promotion. And she seems to have had such an effect on me that I'm so scared I won't come up to scratch I hardly dare open my mouth. My mother's the problem in our family.'

For parents a child may be *the* problem, as in Janet Kalman's case. Jack and Maxine Crane felt that their daughter had laid waste their lives. 'If she had finished college, all our efforts would have paid off. Everything would have been all right but for her.'

But for . . . Everything would be all right 'but for' him or her, but for this or that situation. The variations are legion on the ways of saying if you could change someone or something, *all* would be well. 'If my wife were different, if my husband had more drive, if my daughter were as pretty as the kid next door, if my son were half as bright as George's boy, if only I had a son instead of another daughter, if only I had one more child . . .'

But the problems that may arise from the multiple transactions in family life cannot be dispensed with on one level, or with one solution. A person's expectations may be so great that he is always disappointed, since those expectations cannot in reality be satisfied. His disappointed expectations may then demand a scapegoat—someone to blame: 'But for . . .' Even when he gets what he wants he may still feel unaccountably disappointed. It does not seem to solve the problem.

CRUCIBLES OF BECOMING

We know that each person has a backlog both of remembered and forgotten experience through which he views his world, which determines his attitudes and exerts an important influence on his behaviour. In human relationships we are not consciously aware of an overwhelmingly important part of the experience that determines our attitudes and the way we perceive others. The analogy of the iceberg has become a cliché: the largest and most important part is beneath the surface. We also need to remind ourselves of two major features of human growth, inseparable features, whether we are boy or girl and whatever our potential. First, growth is psychosomatic; that is the mind (psyche) and the body (soma) are one and we cannot separate the part from the whole. The child's physical growth, learning to walk and talk, do not proceed separately from his emotional development. Secondly, development is continuous and takes place in stages; each stage is necessary to the growth of the whole.

Throughout life, there seem to be three constant emotional needs which arise from the nature of being human, and are in practice interrelated: needs for *self-worth, adequacy* and *belonging*. The child develops emotionally as these needs are satisfied. He learns attitudes towards himself and others while attempting to meet these needs through interpersonal relationships with parents, brothers and sisters, relatives, friends and acquaintances in a widening environment of peer groups and adults. But the social learning most important for later relationships takes place in infancy and early childhood. The human being reveals three constant emotional needs which are in practice interrelated: needs for *self-worth, adequacy* and *belonging*.

One needs a sense of *self-worth*, a sense that one is lovable rather than rejectable, no matter what one is; boy or girl, head of the class or bottom, a magazine cover baby or a child limited by physical handicap or deformity, one needs to feel that one is worthy in oneself. For such a sense of self-worth one needs to feel that none of the biological functions is shameful: that elimination is as vital as eating but neither should be a battle ground for parent and child, that an interest in one's body and the meaning of sex is normal. The sense of self-worth may be impaired if any human attribute becomes a source of fear or guilt —tenderness or anger, a need to depend or to move into greater autonomy should not be distorted by the necessity of measuring up to someone else's expectations. Another constant need is a sense of *adequacy* in that a person needs confidence that he can meet the demands that the important people in his life seem to place upon him as well as find recognition for himself. A sense of *belonging* as a person is the third constant need: as a person feels he belongs, it contributes to feelings of both self-worth and adequacy.

At different stages the constant needs are met in different ways. In infancy, touch is the first kind of communication and conveys belonging and self-worth. Just being cuddled and fed is a good feeling, being hungry and in pain is not, but it is adequacy to cry and succeed in having someone come and relieve the pain.

If a young child could put his experience into oral language he might express himself in these words: 'Going to the bathroom and having Mother be pleased with what I do is both adequacy and self-worth, and when she hugs me then I really belong. But why do they get mad when I have an accident and Mother scowls and smacks and drags me off? In that case, I won't have any accidents anywhere. They don't like that either and seem worried because I hold things in. But at least they fuss around me then and I like that. Why did Mother laugh when I pulled that sheet off the bed and we had such fun putting it in the washing machine? But today why was she furious when I pulled the sheet off the table? Every time I touch anything these days Mother says "No," and if I don't stop she hits me. Sometimes she hits me without warning me at all. I'd just better keep still, play it safe. Now they keep wanting me to look at this picture-book, but Mother hit me when I pulled that other picture-book off that shelf. They keep wanting me to say things. I don't want to talk. I don't know what they want so I won't say anything.'

Children need a measure of consistency in the way their adults meet their efforts, otherwise they feel that their world is too arbitrary to handle. 'Where will the next blow come from?' Feelings about early attempts at exploration may be equated with feelings about learning anything. Talking is touching others and having them touch you. All kinds of explorations may be equated with pain, and letting others know how one feels may be terrifying rather than inviting if early attempts made them so. In this way, children hesitate to learn and talk. They develop learning and speech problems. Even in adulthood people have talents which they do not utilise—they feel inhibited and cramped. Anyone may develop feelings of inadequacy if individual tasks are too difficult and he does not achieve a sense of accomplishment. Equally he may come to feel he is inadequate as a person if he never knows how anything he does is going to be received.

He may deal with feelings that have brought him pain by denying their existence—'I just don't feel', 'I don't need anybody' or 'I don't care'; he may become secretive and fearful of biological functions that have brought him shame. Emotional crippling has begun. The inadequacy (I can't cope) and the denial of feeling (I don't have any feelings) are components of the impotence and frigidity that may block adult relationships. Denial is simply one of the defences against hurt.

OPEN TO REALITY OR BUILDING DEFENCES

A gradually developing discrimination is a normal part of physical growth. Muscles become capable of finer and finer movements and co-ordination. Objects in the environment also become differentiated

—people become individuals, animals become cats or dogs. There is also discrimination about appropriate ways of channelling feelings and satisfying needs. An adult may yell at a football game, or take the verbal lid off aggressions at a political rally. He absorbs the prohibitions of his culture and learns to use its acceptable outlets. If he becomes hungry he doesn't scream for Mother, he prepares a meal or goes to arestaurant. He has learned to postpone and plan for gratification of his needs. He can live from day to day, meeting the short-term goals of everyday necessities while working for a long-term goal such as becoming qualified for a profession or bringing up children.

A child must feel a sense of security that his basic physical and emotional needs will be met, if he is to learn to discriminate and make relevant rational distinctions about the real world and the people in it, if he is to learn about his own capabilities and learn to accept his limitations. It is of paramount importance for his sense of adequacy, and his ability to make realistic distinctions and to find realistic solutions to his problems, that he is permitted to live through each stage of his growth, grappling with its meaning and enjoying it. He has to discover for himself what he can do at each stage and the experience is vital if he is to go soundly into the next stage. A chicken has to get itself out of the shell—unless it is able to be adequate to that task it does not survive to the next stage. You cannot tear open a bud and expect a flower to grow more quickly. The baby needs to be utterly dependent. When he is ready to crawl after six months, he needs an opportunity to do so safely. In the adventures of walking and talking, normal mistakes should not be made to seem calamities otherwise the child does not simply learn to correct mistakes but learns to feel that he has failed as a person. Then, instead of discriminating, he *generalises*. Instead of saying: 'I made a mistake but I can learn from it,' he concludes, '*I* am a mistake, *I* am bad, unworthy, inadequate; they cast me out—*I* don't belong because I had a bathroom accident, because I got mad.' If parents seem to be enemies, he may generalise that *all* people in authority are against him.

Generalisation like denial is a defence. By generalisation the little child attempts to defend himself from all possible dangers. He and his feelings, that is his internal world, are bad and will bring pain, so he must be on guard against expressing them.

However, though feelings and needs may be pushed out of awareness and their existence denied, they still persist in indirect ways in adult life. Originally the child wants his mother to cuddle him, but she spends time with the baby. He gets angry and throws the baby's bottle on the floor. Then his mother hits him. He would like to hit her back but his anger at those who cause him pain will invite more pain from them in punishment so the child is in a difficult dilemma: he wants the love of those for whom he feels anger. Both the desire for love and his anger seem to bring pain so he represses them both. But he does not lose them; later on, the child-within-the-adult is expressing these repressed feelings when the adult is conscious of a vague anxiety, a feeling of shakiness or lack of confidence. He may be irritable, impatient for no apparent reason, or he may feel that neither achievement nor affection give real satisfaction.

Now he may call into play another defence—the defence of *projection*. He may project on to the external world his own feared feelings. Other people may appear antagonistic to him rather than he to them. He may also use *rationalisation*, that is, use acceptable reasons to substantiate for otherwise unacceptable feelings to justify his version of events. Thus he will say, 'The business world is ruthless. Everyone is out to get everyone else. It's dog eat dog. Only the boss's son gets the top job.'

Meanwhile he has made many other equations, *personal synonyms*, from the context of his own experience: 'It is not worth trying to communicate with anyone because contact with those I needed brought despair.' 'All men are out for what they can get.' 'All women want to dominate you.'

In spite of all the defences that a child may build to protect himself and his world, he still identifies with those important adults who were his source of physical and emotional sustenance. *Identification* is an unconscious and necessary process. Where the child has felt love and feelings of belonging and adequacy, he becomes like his important adults and acquires a sense of inner security and the confidence to use his talents. Where there has been conflict and pain, an awareness of harsh demands and rejection, identification still takes place in the inevitable unconscious process of emotional learning. But the identification is hostile. A boy or girl may consciously hate a mother or father as a defence against depending on or making demands on a harsh parent. Yet the boy or girl may also resemble the hated parent even in the attitudes he or she has found most intolerable. For example, the child may find that he has all the irritability and unresponsiveness of a hated father or mother for whom he denies any affection, but for whose love he unconsciously still feels a desperate need. A child internalises parental attitudes and they become part of his personality and of his spontaneous reaction to his environment.

Where there is conflict between parents and between parents and child, the phenomenon of *splitting* may occur. In this case the child sees the parent who seems to give less pain as the 'good parent' and the parent who seems to give more pain as the 'bad parent'. There is nothing to like or admire in the bad parent. He or she is *the* problem. This may be the case with an overtly rejecting harsh father and a protective mother who also appears to be the victim of the father. In fact the mother's feelings of anger and rejection may be concealed and find expression in protectiveness; she may readily rationalise her feelings as depression and anxiety caused by a harsh mate. Both mother and child may thus relieve themselves of the necessity for looking at the deeper causes of their irritations or despairs. 'My father is to blame.' 'My husband's to blame.'

Through all the defences of *generalisation, personal synonym, projection, hostile identification, denial, splitting,* and *rationalisation* with which a person protects himself, unresolved emotional problems from the childhood past find indirect expression. To reduce anxiety produced by conflict about real needs a child may resort to symbolic behaviour which may then persist into adult life as his way of handling his internal world and indirectly trying to meet its imperatives and its warnings. For example, learning problems at school may imply: 'I'm avoiding learning anything from books because learning means realising that my mother didn't like me.' Symbolic behaviour telling of unmet needs and unresolved conflicts may range from alcoholism and drug addiction to sexual frigidity or promiscuity in which troubled people express variations on their personal synonyms. The body may express rebellion as well as need through the vital organs. Thus the little boy who was never allowed to cry gets constant colds or asthma. The little girl who was the centre of attention, as long as she did not express what she really felt, becomes the woman who suffers from 'blinding' headaches. The seemingly independent man with constant digestive problems says he can't 'stomach' his life situation and expresses his need to depend. The outwardly frugal and careful housewife, in hoarding every cast-off from old clothes to rubber bands and matchboxes, mistakenly seeks, by saving things, to gain the store of love she felt deprived of by a critical and demanding mother; then there is the man with hesitant speech who reveals deeply ambivalent feelings about contact with others. The apparently careless person who never picks things up, leaving it to others to clear them away, indirectly expresses a childlike need to be taken care of. Even seemingly 'senseless' behaviour has its underlying personal motivations—no one ever does anything for no reason.

LOOKING BEHIND THE LABELS

A *label* may document behaviour or one aspect of behaviour by selecting its most obvious feature, as in the phrases 'a *nagging* wife', 'a teenage *rebel*'. Such self-limiting tags present a superficial caricature of a human being and obscure implications and motivations underlying behaviour. However, negative epithets may enable the labeller to project his anger and inadequacy in a situation on to someone else, as when one mother shouted, 'My son's wife is a witch of the first order', expressing similar feelings to Desdemona's father in *Othello*: 'O, thou foul thief, where hast thou stowed my daughter? Damned as thou art, thou hast enchanted her.' Negative labels may simply assert, 'The case is closed' and, in effect, categorise the labelled person in a catch-all condemnation. They imply for the speaker, 'I don't have to look further either to understand this person or myself.' Categorising of this kind metaphorically kills. Thus, when Jane's mother labelled Andrew Smith 'a no-good who put a spell on my daughter', his reaction, 'I felt annihilated', responded to a metaphorical annihilation.

But what are some of the deeper transactions that had for one of its outward manifestations an absentee father?

'Overwhelming love' was overwhelming need. Andrew fell in love with Jane. It seemed that they were so overwhelmingly in love that they could successfully make up through each other for the disappointments in their own families. They were both children who were unwanted accidents in their parents' lives. But when they were born they were both attractive babies and became the centre of attention of admiring relatives and friends.

In both cases older brothers and sisters were disturbed and jealous of the new arrival. Both had older sisters who also resented them because they had to take care of the baby.

Andrew and Jane had a great deal of experience in common and tended to see the world with similar eyes. It seemed to them that they had a good basis for a partnership.

But in fact Andrew was repeating his father's experience. An emotionally needy and angry man, he had married Andrew's mother to make up for the deprivations in his relationship with his own parents. But Andrew's mother was not very happy about being a woman—she was resentful that her father gave her brothers a college education but would not educate a girl, and she felt that her mother ignored her. She was very hesitant about getting married and then felt that children deprived her of her last opportunity to get an education. Guilty about her rejecting feelings, she was an overly protective mother and became a slave in the house. Andrew's father at first made a pet of the sister, seven years Andrew's senior, then he rejected her. He was completely unpredictable, one day engulfing her with attention, the next pushing her away. After she was two her father spent an increasing amount of time away from home on fishing trips or at his club. Home was too demanding. His wife and daughter were frightened of his bad moods when he would be either explosive or surly. He did not want a second child but Andrew's birth filled him with pride which temporarily brought him a new sense of adequacy. Andrew's sister was extremely jealous as it seemed to her that her brother had removed her last hope of being close to her father. She could not attack her father because he was too big but she did attack her brother. She whacked him with a ruler, pulled his hair, and, when he learned to stand, she trod on his foot. When her mother asked her to feed the baby, she tried to choke him. So, by attacking Andrew, she was also able to hurt her mother.

From Andrew's point of view the world was overwhelmingly full of arbitrary knocks and kicks. The cuddling and attention he had as a baby were reassuring, but when he wanted to crawl around and explore he met painful obstacles. His sister soon became identified as an enemy; one day she pushed him into the bath and he nearly drowned. On another occasion she pushed him off the swing and he cut his head open so that it had to be stitched. Each time her father smacked her and told her how wicked she was to hurt a harmless child. There was no doubt that she did want to get rid of her rival, so desperately did she long for her father's love. Andrew felt that she was the bigger one and that he was the loser. He also felt overwhelmed by his father's possessiveness. He was unable to cope with this world and his sense of adequacy shrivelled, although people still called him a nice child. He soon learned to annoy his sister, 'accidentally' tearing her library book, breaking her records or messing up her homework. As soon as he was able to go out and play with other boys in the neighbourhood, he stayed away from home except for brief appearances for meals.

When he married, both he and his wife unconsciusly attempted to reconcile conflicting and irreconcilable purposes. Each wanted to depend on the other for the emotional support they had not had in childhood. It became apparent that their overwhelming love was overwhelming need and neither had the resources to meet the needs of the other. In their very choice of partner both were trying to get in touch with their own unfinished learnings, to meet their childhood needs through the other. In the logic of unconscious emotional choice both were also seeking a punishment for their 'badness' by marrying an unsatisfactory partner. Jane's possessiveness overwhelmed Andrew in the same way as his father's possessiveness had done, and it seemed as threatening as his sister's childhood attacks. It justified his escaping and his wife's reproaches served as his conscience. At the same time to Jane, Andrew's neglect seemed to justify as well as cause her anxieties and depressions.

In fact, even if her husband had been able to 'stand by her', all would not have been well, as Jane's daughter asserted. Jane had a chronic feeling of being unwanted; hurt and angry, she found it impossible to accept affection or help. She so desperately needed it that she could not trust it; and no matter what she was given, it was not enough, her emotional hunger was so great. It was much easier to have a 'real reason', for her despairs than to look at their deeper meaning—an unsatisfactory husband provided a reason, someone to blame. Really to find the understanding she said she wanted would have meant looking at the meaning of her own anger and needs and that was too painful and too threatening.

Whipping posts wanted. Andrew and Jane each provided a whipping post for the other, a necessary defence against the pain of looking at their unworthy selves. As so often happens when there appears to be a persecuted and persecutor, the children split their parents into the good and the bad. Andrew, overtly the aggressor, was 'all bad,' and Jane, the attacked and neglected mother, always at home for them, was 'all good'.

They did not see that her anxiety and reproaches revealed in many ways a more insidious problem of rejection of themselves than their father's open aggression.

Re-making my father. The 'nagging wife' Mary was also trying to get in touch with unfinished learnings in her life when she married Jim Allen, but she was doing so in self-defeating ways. For her husband she chose the most unlikely mate of all her boy-friends. But she was going to remake him. In this way she was at last going to be closer to her father, now made into a good father, the idealised negation of all that her own harsh father had been. Jim appeared to be an ideal candidate as his main aim was to please his wife, but Mary's insatiability made it impossible to please her. Jim was also trying to solve his problems—of inadequacy—by marrying Mary: he wanted a strong, attractive and intelligent wife whose interests would extend beyond the household routine. He felt that he could not live without her but he also resented her because he felt that she made him look small. Mary's strength was only superficial, however. It was her way of hiding inner devastation; the hurt, lost child concealed its pain in nagging hostility. In fact, Jim, with every appearance of compliance, was doing everything but comply. He was her impossible father all over again and his indulgence of the children was one of his ways of attacking both *his* unsatisfactory mother as well as theirs.

I can't be your image. When children reject what seems to be their best interests rather than do what their parents wish, they are not rebelling 'for no reason'. Jack and Maxine Crane wanted status which they had been unable to attain in their own lives and their daughter was to achieve it for them. Ann did not feel accepted in her own right, nor did she feel free to choose. For her the best education that money could buy was tainted by the feeling that she was being used to live her parents' life for them rather than finding her own. She therefore rejected a college education and her parents' standards because they symbolised for her their rejection of herself. She was making a bid for autonomy.

Another parent and child, Janet Kalman and her adolescent, deaf, daughter, engaged in conflict about speech and sign language. It is generally agreed that if a deaf child begins language training early and can learn to speak, this will obviate psychological isolation and allow him to use his talents; there is also a point of view that the deaf should be allowed to relax from the strain of keeping pace by lip-reading with constant oral conversations and occasionally have recourse to sign language. However, a mother and daughter here were concerned with more than theory about teaching the deaf. In her lifelong effort to give her child speech, Janet Kalman had expressed her real wish for a hearing child. In all the language teaching there had been an undertone of rejection of the deafness and thus of her daughter as she was. Now Nora began to say in effect: 'I am not a hearing child. I am deaf. It is too much strain trying to pretend that I am a hearing person. I am *not* and you must accept that fact. I can talk but I want you to understand my world of deafness before I can come out of my world and use your language. I want you to accept me as I really am.'

Language itself had become contaminated because language had been used as a denial of a real limitation. In the same way, academic achievement can be contaminated for any child if he tries to do well *in order* to gain acceptance. Nora Kalman could be any one who tired of trying to live up to someone else's image; in this case, a parent's.

WHY DON'T WE TELL THEM?

If parents are making mistakes without knowing it, it would seem logical to tell them what they are really doing. An authority such as a doctor, or even a friend could explain what is really happening—that parents are taking out on their partners and their children their resentments to their own fathers and mothers, that they are handing on the same self-defeating purposes from their own disturbed childhood, to their children. It would then seem logically possible for them to understand their own parents' insecurities, the real need for love behind brothers' or sisters' jealous behaviour, so that then parents could change. Jane, for instance, would surely become more self-confident and realise that she was not to blame for her parents' rejection of her. She would see they were worried by the responsibility of bringing up another child when they were middle aged. She would surely begin to feel compassion for Andrew's sister when she realised what devastated experience led to her irritating 'superior behaviour'. She would surely realise that she disliked Andrew's sister because she reflected her own experience of rejection. If Andrew realised how irrelevant it really was to react in adult life in terms of a two-year-old's hurt and fright, he might find confidence in the present, understand his wife and children better and be able to express some of his repressed tender feelings. If someone explained to them surely Jim and Mary would stop tormenting each other and using their son as a battle ground. If parents only realised that a rebelling teenager really wants their understanding before following their wishes, surely this kind of knowledge would mean a lessening of conflict between the generations. Finally, if children realised that they could be denying their own needs and destroying their own potential in order to attack their parents, then they might find more reasonable routes to self-assertion.

STRATEGIES OF RESISTANCE TO CHANGE

A person may react in various ways when confronted with explanations of his behaviour intended to change him. First, he may not want to listen and secondly, he may not be able to hear even if he tries to listen. Janet Kalman felt that the devotion of a lifetime was probably misplaced, but she was unable to recognise the plea for acceptance behind her daughter's rebellion. Even when it was explained to her, she failed to see the girl's need for self-orientation and understanding which Nora expressed in her reversion to sign language and her demand that her mother also use it. Similarly, explanations of her mother's good intentions could not change Nora.

Ann Crane's parents felt ashamed, guilty and angry because Ann let them down after all that they had done for her. They could see no reason for her behaviour and did not wish to talk about it.

Andrew and Jane Smith also refused to listen.

Mary Allen did listen and tried to persuade her husband to understand their situation, but for the first time in their marriage he reacted with open violence. He was sick of his wife's attempts to change him for the better he said. He could see no value in self-contemplation. 'You want me to behave like a celibate monk contemplating his navel'.

Resistance to change uses many strategies. A person may deny any validity in the explanation presented to him. 'We know ourselves, you don't.' 'How can you know?' 'It simply isn't true that I'm dissatisfied—I like lots of things.' Alternatively, people may respond with hostility because they are affronted: 'You're taking sides.' 'You're trying to justify bitchy behaviour, brutal neglect.' 'He can stop drinking if he wants to.' They may justify their refusal to change on the basis of experience: 'This is the way I am. What do you expect with my background?'

Personality—a way of seeing. People, including parents, who have in common mistaken ways of trying to resolve their emotional problems also seem to suffer difficulty in admitting their mistaken ways. They also have in common an urge to fight to maintain those ways at all costs; it does not seem to matter how desirable in theory change may be.

Such a resistance to change is to do with the nature of personality—the definition of personality relevant to the problems we are discussing is a '*way of seeing*'. Personality is not a thing to be put on, or a collection of characteristics to be listed, but the eyes with which a person learned to see himself and his world as he experienced them for the first time. And as he saw, he did. His personality, his way of seeing, then, is a process by which he seeks to protect his private world. He carries his frame of reference, the context of his experience with him into every other situation in life.

Whatever happens he will resist contrary evidence to what he has felt and experienced already. He will select all the reasons why he should not change, such as 'I'm too old', or 'I'm beyond redemption'. He will seem to seek situations to justify his reactions, as we have seen in the choice of a marriage partner. He manages to choose friends who will make life difficult for him, or to say those things which will annoy his superiors.

So strongly does a person cling to his original emotional learning, that if, for example, an unsatisfactory husband changes for the better, his wife may not only remain dissatisfied, she may actually want to get rid of him. Thus one wife left her husband when he lost his craving for alcohol with the help of Alcoholics Anonymous because she did not feel needed. Moreover, she became an alcoholic herself. She had unconsciously chosen a husband who could act out for her a desire to let down defences which was what alcohol promised. By looking after her alcoholic husband, she vicariously satisfied her own needs. *Her* reproaches acted as his conscience while *his* alcoholism was a punishment for her 'badness' for which she could atone by taking care of him. In the same way, a man who resented his nagging wife, divorced and then married another who turned out to be as critical as the first—he married his need.

We have glanced at a few of the reasons why people resist change. It is painful to look at feelings in oneself one dreads and therefore denies. Even incapacitating difficulties such as ulcers, asthma, stuttering or obsessive cleanliness, may seem preferable to the overwhelming anxiety, the sense of devastation, which may result from examining the real problem. Some forms of symbolically acting out conflicted feelings have their own satisfactions: alcohol, drugs, sexual deviation and promiscuity, or delinquent behaviour which 'takes it out' on society. Looking at the meaning of such behaviours provokes anxiety, and the pain which may accompany change does not seem to be an attractive alternative to the 'satisfactions' of continuing the behaviours.

The personality, with all its idiosyncracies, may literally be a protection against emotional collapse. 'I feel that if I cry,' says one man, 'I'll never stop.' He has built a protective guard against any threat to the way he has learned to handle his world. Anyone who tries to tell him differently is an enemy. He needs his armour against all outside stimuli that can lead to emotional awareness. His 'way of looking' at the world is valid to him and *words* cannot alter what *experience* has taught him. Meanwhile, he may continue with impossible goals and self-defeating behaviour without being aware of it. He will use every stratagem to avoid awareness. He cannot afford to be aware of it. If he is to keep going at all he must protect himself by not letting out the flood of conflicting emotions he is repressing. He will aid the repression process by keeping busy, doing things in a hurry or impulsively and not allowing time for contemplation. He will take on impossible loads of work as if to justify his very existence. He will live a non-stop fast-moving social life. He will look to outside things to right the balance if he feels 'something is lacking'. So, 'My wife will make up for what I never had', 'My children will lead the life I never had a chance to live'.

Thus parents bring to their children the pervasive needs which already inform their lives. In countless ways they may burden the baby with their own unconscious expectations. All kinds of specifics carry the weight of 'Let him be what I need', rather than 'Let him he himself.' 'He must get good grades'. 'He's got to be good at sports—I couldn't stand a cissie in the family', 'I want him to be a lawyer', 'My daughter must be popular'.

There are countless ways, too, in which parents may express subtle rejection. 'If he were just a *little* different' leads to un-numbered variations of the '*But for*' theme, blaming someone or something for inner dissatisfactions.

We find in fact in the dynamics of family relationships, the kinds of prejudgement of others found in social prejudice and a similar use of the scapegoat, which, like the ancient sacrificial animal, relieves both individuals and social groups of their burden of guilt. We find a similar inability to improve the situation by reason, similar resistance to information and similar rationalisations necessary to provide acceptable reasons for otherwise untenable attitudes. Stating that the black man 'does commit more crimes' that the white man is 'always the exploiter' seems to justify hatred of social groups in the way, that labelling an 'unsatisfactory' family member seems to justify criticism and rejection of him.

Children absorb very early in life the dynamic processes with which their parents protect their private worlds. Then comes the boomerang for the 'unsatisfactory parents'. Their children rebel and refuse to do what is expected of them. Not only does the boy not become a lawyer but he joins the student sit-in. He blames authority, the establishment, 'The system is against you', he says. What is the solution then if people refuse to listen when they are told of their mistakes and when they fight change by every possible strategy? Must 'the sins of the fathers be visited on the children from generation to generation' indefinitely?

To sum up, one conclusion is overwhelmingly clear. The parents, of whom so much is demanded, who are blamed for children's deficiencies and uncontrolled teenagers as well as for a multitude of social ills, may themselves be in great emotional need. No child can ever fill the gap in his parents' unsatisfied childhood needs, however beautiful or intelligent he or she may be. Children must exist as people in their own right. How then can we recognise and meet the emotional needs of both parents and children?

3 *A Philosophy of Listening: Early Days*

Anxiety cries for an answer. The answer giver ties the asker. He who makes the asker answer, makes the asker answer master.

Anon

In this century, psychological and medical research has taught us a great deal about the basic needs of human beings and the meaning of behaviour, about the nature of children's development and about the causes of family and social tension. The responsibility for a child's emotional growth, his way of relating to his world and using his potential rests squarely on the significant adults who nurtured him for those most important first two to five years of his life. Parents have sought the knowledge that would give them the know-how. Experts have provided it. Books, articles, lectures, the advice of psychiatrists and paediatricians have attempted to give information. Parents learn that growth is a step-by-step process, and certain behaviours are normal at each stage. At five months (with help) sitting erect is achieved. All kinds of movement and exploration of the immediate environment are part of being two. At three a child may begin to make things with his blocks, but at two he will be more likely to get the feel of materials and tear things apart to find out, rather than to put them together. At two he is the possessor but he may begin to share at three and even trade things at four. Parents know that some angry feelings towards them are normal, that some jealousy of brothers and sisters should be cause for understanding rather than punishment; and an interest in his body and questions about sex are part of a child's search for identity. A shy child may seem good, but may be in more trouble from repressed angry feelings than a noisy child, and harsh repression of normal feelings may play havoc with a child's relation to himself and others. Parents hear that feelings need acceptance—and need acceptable channels, but feelings pushed out of awareness still remain a powerful influence and will find an indirect outlet because unconscious feelings may be more powerful than conscious ones. Experts remind parents, too, that with all our knowledge of the average child, we must remember that individual differences are as important as 'norms' and 'averages'.

Parents do need knowledge of child growth and of techniques of child care. They need knowledge of special training if their child is handicapped. But the central determinant of the personality of children lies not in the techniques but in the *attitudes* of parents. Techniques are peripheral. This means it is not what parents *do*, but how they *feel* that is the heart of the parent-child relationship. Influencing parents' feelings is more subtle, but more important, than influencing the the way thay act. Parents are more likely to become comfortable parents if they have experienced child care in a reasonably happy family. But 'accept your child's anger' is an impossible route to follow, if we are still unconsciously wrestling with our own angry feelings. If we are explosive and irritable ourselves, it will be harder to accept such behaviour in our child.

TELLING CAN MAKE TROUBLE

As we have seen, there is no power in facts about psychology, or advice on what to feel, to alter people's attitudes. It's not that people don't want to hear. They can't hear. But even more startling is the discovery that not only has information about the parent-child relationship *not* helped parents become better parents, it has hindered rather than helped them.

There is no power in information to change attitudes simply because attitudes cannot be reached on an intellectual level; they originate in unconscious sources. To load people with psychological knowledge without a means to use it, deepens the sense of inadequacy and guilt which is the trouble in the first place. But children are then the recipients of the increased confusion. Guilty parents see a frightening picture of their responsibility and they cannot accept a child because even his natural need increases their confusion and inadequacy about meeting it. Psychology then becomes a trouble maker, not a trouble solver. Not only does it *not* solve problems of delinquency, it can be a contributory factor in increasing them, by increasing the problems of parents.

If we are going to help parents we must discard illusions about the all-powerful effects of a little knowledge.

A conscientious parent sees an error and tries to alter his behaviour, but finds actual events making nothing of his efforts: 'I know I'm making a mistake with my daughter, I'm doing just what my mother did which I hated and swore I'd never do, yelling without even thinking.' Even when a person seems desperately to want to change he can't. But, as he has learned through his experience to see his world, he will respond. Therefore, the possibility for change of response seems to lie in changing the *seeing*. Such change in seeing would seem to lie in a changed experience of the self; and, in the changed experience of the self, attitudes change.

A basic hypothesis, then, in our work with parents, is that if attitudes change, behaviour will *spontaneously* change. Therefore parent education cannot afford to concentrate on content. Knowledge must have direct meaning to a person in terms of his own life and experience. Parent education must recognise process—emotional growth leading to changed attitudes. It becomes important then to hear what parents convey about their own life and experience.

What does all this mean in practice?

LISTENING A ROUTE TO CHANGE

It means that we *listen* to parents. We stop focusing on *telling* them.

Listening means starting where a person *is*, not where he ought to be. It means hearing his here-and-now, experience. For his here-and-now experience is pervaded by the influence of his childhood perceptions. If there is unfinished business from the past distorting his present relationships, we can hear it in his here-and-now, experience. Our listening is to give him a chance to hear it too, but to hear it in such a way that he can change.

The kind of listening which becomes an instrument for a changed way of seeing oneself and others is not a matter of hearing superficial factual content, but of sensitivity to underlying feelings in each individual's personal world—sensitivity to the way each person perceives his world.

The content says: 'I don't know which way to turn, there's so much to do.'

The underlying feeling suggests: 'I don't know how to handle the demands of my world.'

The content says: 'I can't stand children, I don't want any children, I don't want any grandchildren.'

The underlying feeling suggests: 'A child stands for something unbearable in my experience,' and perhaps as some of our parents have found, 'I don't want to invite the anguish that being a child meant to me, by having a child, by welcoming grandchildren.'

The principles of the special kind of listening that may lead to change of attitudes follow logically.

Listening without criticism. First we listen without critical evaluation to the personal meanings of each person, exactly as he experiences them. The aim is to receive uncritically and completely, wherever a person is in his perception of his world. We censor no verbal expression of feeling. We permit him to be where he actually is in his feelings, even if his perception is mistaken.

Listening offers a choice. Second in this uncritical listening, we offer each person an opportunity to re-experience himself, without condemnation for anything he may feel or be. In so doing, we offer him a chance to re-evaluate his original perceptions and to make a new choice.

An opportunity for responsibility. Third, a person can take responsibility on himself for his own choice of perception and must be allowed to do so.

No coercion. Fourth, then, just as we permit a person to be where he is and offer no censorship to verbal expression, neither do we place coercion on anyone to talk at all. We simply provide an opportunity. Here, too a person makes his own choice. He must weigh the issues from his point of view—he must consider that the risk of revealing aspects of himself is preferable to the continued experience of fighting and denying. But the possibility of self-revelation may stir great anxiety In making a choice to communicate honestly with another there has to be a sufficient trust, enough security that the reception will not entail further condemnation.

People have to go at their pace and come to their communications their way. As a child has to go step by step in his growth, a parent has to go step by step in picking up his unfinished learning and finding emotional growth. Coercion tends to arrest rather than to hasten growth. It tends to increase resistance, rather than to encourage self-discovery. We offer an opportunity. We do not compel its use.

Non-verbal communication. Fifth, we listen to the total communication of a person. Tears, smiles, muscle tensions and even silence, say something, as well as words. While changes in attitude derive from the experience which accompanies speech, non-verbal processes are operating all the time. Parents, in finding a listener who pays close and uncritical attention to them, show they are finding a new kind of parent for themselves. Attitudes of acceptance on the part of this new listener-parent are the non-verbal sub-soil of verbal response.

Listening to the looking: understanding. Sixth, verbal responses of the listener when they occur are to the way things *appear* to the speaker. In this way the verbal response is a way of conveying empathy with the world of the speaker, so that he may feel understood. But in focusing on the way things appear to the individual parent there is always implied the possibility of another way of looking. Herein lies the possibility of change in parent attitudes, and resulting change in behaviour.

A MOTHER TALKS

Mrs Green has five children. Her middle son, Tim, aged four, has not developed speech and language at the normal time, and has been diagnosed severely deaf. Now he has been accepted in a group of five pre-school deaf children who are to have one hour of speech therapy each day, on five afternoons a week. On the first day on which she brings her son, her face appears tense and her eyes brim with tears which she seems to be fighting to keep back. The parent counsellor, a psychologist, is present at the first meeting of the children's group. Part of the programme is an interview for one mother each day. Tim seems to be interested in his male speech therapist and in the other children's activities, and has begun to join in. The counsellor then asks Mrs Green if she would like to come to the office. There is a short silence, and the counsellor recognises the feelings of stress which the mother seems to be experiencing.

Counsellor. Sometimes things seem rough going in dealing with the problems of a little deaf child.

Mrs. Green, in response to this recognition of feeling, breaks down and weeps openly. The counsellor waits in silence for a short time before making a structuring statement pointing out the possibility of help.

Counsellor. We believe here that talking about difficulties can help.
Mrs Green. (Still weeping.) I'm so confused. I don't know which

way to turn. And I've no goals. I don't know where I'm going. I just seem to blame myself for everything. I tried to do a course to help parents of deaf children teach their kids language. But I couldn't get anywhere. I couldn't follow the instructions. It just didn't work. (Pause. Still weeping). But I am very difficult to please. I'm never satisfied with anything I get, no matter how much I seem to want it. And Tim's exactly the same. He wants a toy. And then he's not interested.

Counsellor. (Another recognition.) You feel he's like you in that—these things you ask for don't seem to be meeting what you need.

A silence follows. Mrs Green looks at the counsellor and continues to weep, though more quietly. Then she ventures to express a need for help for herself.

Mrs Green. Maybe I need to come to school rather than him. (Pause.) If I do anything I feel it'll go wrong. I'm just sure of it. Like doing the course. It makes me feel it's useless even to try. And then things just happen. You never know what's going to hit. My father died at the time Linda was born and then when I had Tim my sister died. Then Tim was deaf. It seems there's always something. I could just give up, it seems so useless.

The temptations of reassurance. Now, confronted with real difficulties in the parent's life—events that could be deeply disturbing to anybody, occasions of great family sorrow, disappointments beyond human control, a counsellor can be tempted to concentrate on difficult events, to offer condolence and reassurance. Mrs Green suggests deeply unsatisfied needs that the things she asks for do not reach, she feels that she herself is a stimulus for things to go wrong, she blames herself. We can guess at her experience with significant adults which left her emotionally hungry and with a feeling 'I can't win'. When real stress occurs, we know it is not the real cause of the deeper inner turmoil, but it may tie up with it, and activate old troubles. But present stress may be used as a scapegoat, a means of rationalisation—these *are* the things which are the trouble. If we use reassurance then, we may cut off the chance of looking deeper and of changing attitudes as effectively as if we were using a didactic approach. The challenge in listening and in responding is two-fold: first to convey compassion for present situational predicaments (we do not ignore them); second, to recognise the internal world of the parent and its perceptions. In this way, we imply the possibility of seeing differently even real stress of changing the internal world even though the external cannot be changed.

The counsellor then responds to Mrs Green's . . . 'it seems so useless' not with reassurance about real external difficulties, but with recognition of *both* those difficulties and the continuing inside world suggested by the mother, expressed in pervading 'pessimism'.

Counsellor. These things played into the feeling of hopelessness.

Mrs Green. I want to teach Tim. But every time I try he rejects it. (Pause. Throughout the interview Mrs Green does not cease weeping.) And yet he follows me around.

Counsellor. (Re-stating but not going beyond what Mrs Green has said.) He seems to want something.

Mrs Green. I get mad when he rejects it when I try to teach him. (Pause. Looks down, then at the counsellor, then looks down again.) Maybe it is that I don't accept it. (Looks at the counsellor.)

Although Mrs Green seems clearly to be talking about the handicap the counsellor goes no further in making response than the mother's immediate cue.

Counsellor. You don't accept.

Mother. No, I don't accept that he's deaf. (There is a long pause here as the mother sobs.) I don't accept anything. I'm supposed to wear glasses and I don't. I have diabetes. I eat sweets, though I know I shouldn't. Things like that.

The temptation of an authority here could be not just to reassure but to step in and point out that Mrs Green should not endanger her life, that her husband and her children need her, that she has a responsibility to herself and them. But she is already showing that she has difficulty following not just instructions of a course but even important medical advice. More advice would be useless. The mother seems to have a difficulty about accepting restrictions, about having her wants denied.

Counsellor. It's hard to accept these denials.

Mrs Green. If I can't get what I want, I get mad. (Pause.) I always had what I wanted. Everything I wanted. All the things I asked for.

Counsellor. All the *things*. (This response intends to imply there may be something else she wants which is not satisfied by things.)

Mrs Green. I've never said that I didn't accept the deafness before. (Pause.) My husband does better than I do. I've no patience. I want everything done immediately.

Counsellor. And here is something that is a slow long pull.

Mrs Green. I couldn't do the course to help teach him speech.

QUESTIONS AND ANSWERS

Parents may ask questions but we do not answer them directly. To do so tends to focus on content and to take responsibility for choice away from the person. It confirms dependence on authority. (We've done it for him, 'answered' his question.) It tends to cut off the possibility of emotional growth as a result of which he may answer his own questions. We listen, therefore, to the underlying feeling that prompts the question and respond to *that*. Our concern is the parent-child relationship and attitude change, and this is not at the expense of practical programmes of child care or of rehabilitation if a child is handicapped. For all such practical matters have already received attention.

Questions may seem to seek practical answers when they indirectly seek for new attitudes: 'What could I have done? What can I do? Is this the way it ought to be?' may be seen as a plea for confidence which cannot be granted by answering a single question. Thus Mrs Wills comes with many questions which really express her doubt and her seeking for security. She has a son and a daughter—her son was born deaf. To answer her questions singly and directly for their literal content could deprive her of the possibility of finding what the real questions are, questions of underlying attitudes. The therapist's response aims to re-focus the question, staying always with Mrs Wills' own here-and-now feeling.

Mrs Wills. Is there something that I could have done to help him more? Ought I to repeat myself so many times?

Counsellor. 'Could I help him to communicate with less cost to me?'

Mrs Wills. I don't know, it may be silly but I keep hoping his hearing will come. Can he get his hearing?

Counsellor. You wish he didn't have this loss.

Mrs Wills. Yes.

Counsellor. Realistically, we all would prefer that he didn't, but how are we going to accept it comfortably to help him?

Mrs Wills. When they gave me his hearing aid I just wept. I couldn't stand it. (Weeps.) I can't stand his loud talk. I could say that it's wonderful he's got a hearing aid. But I can't feel it. Ought I to?

Counsellor. You're tuned into this reminder of his hearing loss. (Accepting her actual feeling, not demanding what she ought to feel.)

Mrs Wills. I can't tell people. I can't go around telling people about his deafness and the way I feel. Hiding it is like a neurotic obsession. I can't even mention it.

Counsellor. You're afraid of all that might come out if you mention it at all.

Mrs Wills. What's he going to do? Can he hold his own?

Counsellor. The thing you're most sensitive about is this business of holding one's own.

There are times, however, when questions may seem so many and so urgent in reality that a listener may be side-tracked into dealing with practical issues. Mrs Murphy has such urgent questions. And her questions and the counsellor's response are typical of the re-focus away from external content to internal perception, a re-focusing which opens a door for a person to begin to see his external problems differently and to answer his own questions.

The baby who brings Mrs Murphy to a parent programme has a mild spastic condition and needs both physiotherapy and speech therapy. Practical prognosis is good but the hospital asks for parent help in getting the child started without incapacitating feelings of difference. 'He needs acceptance' the hospital pamphlet says. But Mrs Murphy has many problems about her own self-acceptance. Her husband has deserted her and she has to work so there are practical problems of child care.

Mrs Murphy. There are so many demands that it just seems impossible to meet them. I want to do my best for Clive but I just know I'm not giving him what he needs. I feel harrassed all the time and that's no good. I'm always overworked. And the thing is I just can't manage him. He's just out of hand with me. What's the best thing I can do? Shall I send him to a foster home or to a residential school? Should I get domestic help? But I don't have the money. I've wondered if Bill's folks could help. Do you think I should try to get help from *his* parents? I've wondered if I should ask them if we could stay with them. They weren't very happy about the divorce and I just haven't heard from them since. They have a big house, and a small town would be better than the city for Clive. Then don't you think he'd have the space to play in a house? What do you think? If that didn't work out, would a residential school be better than just having anybody take care of him? I'm dreadfully upset about this.

Counsellor. (Not side-tracked into 'answering' questions, yet taking into account both a real problem and the mother's perception of it.) It towers above everything as the most difficult problem.

Mrs Murphy. Well, as I said, there's always too much to do. I'm just exhausted. I feel as if I'm going downhill—working, shopping, picking him up from the nursery school, keeping up the apartment.

Counsellor. The demands are almost more than you can bear.

Mrs Murphy. It just seems there are too many things. First the divorce. And just after the divorce my mother died. She was absolutely shattered by the divorce. She had a heart problem. And while she was in the hospital after a heart attack I was having to go through the clinic for tests for the baby. He seemed to be ailing in so many ways after Bill left us. I could hardly get to the hospital to visit my mother. And I know she was hurt because I was run ragged . . . Bill never helped even before he disappeared. Everything fell on my shoulders, till I felt like cracking. It's the same now.

Counsellor. (Continuing to restate Mrs Murphy's perception of the problem.) The responsibility is a load that seems almost too great to carry.

Mrs Murphy. It isn't as though I'm succeeding, even halfway. Clive just won't do a thing for me. He won't get dressed. He won't go to bed without an absolute fight. And then he doesn't sleep. And he yells. We already had complaints from the people in the apartment above us. It goes from bad to worse.

Counsellor. The load just seems to grow bigger. (Again the focus is on the mother's perception . . . and uncritical reception of her feelings is paramount in the counsellor's responses.)

Mrs Murphy. I can't get anything done. I can't write a letter. I brought some work home from the office and it was impossible to do a single thing. He's always interrupting. There just isn't a moment day or night.

Counsellor. There's no time for you.
Mrs Murphy. Well, it isn't that I have time for him. He just whines. He wants to go out. Why can't a child learn to wait. He has to have everything at once.
Counsellor. That is, why can't *he* be a bit more patient with *you?*
Mrs Murphy. (Smiles.) I see the irony.

Seeing that she is implicitly making a demand on the baby to meet her needs leads her to state again her central dilemma. 'What am I to do? How can I give him what he needs?' Then the questions about external solutions recur as they do many times in her searching. ('Should I find a foster home? Do you think I should write to my in-laws?') She speaks of the way others can do better for her son than she can—her 'fourteen-year-old nephew plays with him; the nursery school-teacher is good for him' but Mrs Murphy rarely sees her nephew and most of the time Clive has to stay in the apartment with her. 'But I'm not giving him what he needs.'

The counsellor recognises the plea behind all her questioning.

Counsellor. You need some help
Mrs Murphy. Yes.

Then she reiterates her questions, especially re-emphasising: 'What do you think about a foster home? I'd like a nice foster home where they were interested in the children.'

The counsellor recognises that she is really expressing a crucial hope for her son.

Counsellor. You do want him to have what he needs.
Mrs Murphy. Oh yes. A child has to have what he needs or he'll run into trouble for the rest of his life. I haven't been able to give him anything. I don't seem to be able to let go and even play with him.
Counsellor. You haven't found the freedom in yourself to do that.

Mrs Murphy reiterates the many instances which feed her sense of incapacity in giving Clive what he needs. She says he can't sleep and he has nightmares, but she adds, 'I have nightmares, too.' Then she implies the possibility of changing herself rather than trying to change the environment.

Mrs Murphy. Maybe it's the way *I* react that makes the baby the way he is. Maybe if I *change*, *he* might change.

Counsellor. If you felt differently, he would respond differently?
Mrs Murphy. That's right.

For the rest of the meeting she switches between proposing external solutions and internal change. But she already reverses an earlier statement that she is burdened because she is overworked, suggesting that external things are not really the problem.

Mrs Murphy. I can hardly drag myself to the bus. But my work is *really light* and they're very nice to me in the office. At home I just can't *do anything*. I let the dishes pile up. Somehow I just can't get going. I just sit.
Counsellor. (Recognising the internal world, picking up the mother's cue.) There is something more than the work in this load.
Mrs Murphy. Am I just making things worse than they are? (Pause.) But you know I'm terrified I'm not going to be able to make it. I hardly dare make the effort. Something's holding me back. There's no one to lean on. You know, I can understand why he wants to hang on to me. I have some of those feelings myself.
Counsellor. You know what it feels like to want to lean on some one.
Mrs Murphy. I really do. Some one you can trust. Like a child.
Counsellor. Like a child.
Mrs Murphy. It just hit me. I'm like a child looking for some one to rely on. That's really it. I'm a child myself.
Counsellor. Two children here. You and Clive.
Mrs Murphy. (Switches to Clive.) I don't want to get rid of him. But I should be doing so many things with him that I'm not. I'm failing him as a mother, and I feel somebody else would be better for him. And hearing what I'm supposed to do in the class I feel worse. I'm just frustrated. . . .
Counsellor. There's a gap between what you *know* and what you *can*.
Mrs Murphy. That's right.

Then she suggests an external solution ('What if I got a change of scene? Left this place?') But she concludes, 'You can't escape: that's no solution.' Finally she makes helping herself and helping her son complementary.

Mrs Murphy. But Clive is still the biggest worry. If I can do something for him, I'll be all right.

Counsellor. Becoming able to help Clive seems to be associated with finding yourself as a person.

THE PROBLEM IN ME

Mrs Green, Mrs Wills and Mrs Murphy are all 'bad parents', using the criteria of ability to accept their child, and be available to understand and meet his current needs. All felt inadequate to meet the demands of the handicap. Mrs Green and Mrs Murphy had had an exceptional series of external misfortunes and stresses in addition, and it would be easy to blame the externals, and use them for rationalisation that 'events justify my feeling as I do'. Merely to offer sympathy would cut off the possibility of looking for insight. Both parents have found information powerless to help them with their children. Both during face-to-face talks with a listener who hears uncritically whatever they want to say, speak of their own need for help, and see in the child's unsatisfactory behaviour a reflection of their own attitudes.

But what does it all amount to, admitting a need for help, seeing that the 'need for change may lie in me'? What's the point of it? Where do we go from there?

One thing becomes clear early. There is a diminishing tendency to blame others, even though a person has not 'solved' all his problems or answered all his questions.

What next? Let's look for some possible sequels to Mrs Green who wept during all her first interview and revealed (for the first time she said) that she did not accept her son's deafness, and who also revealed that it was difficult to please her in anything, but that she was angry nonetheless if she didn't get her wants immediately gratified.

In classes of students and professional people, medical and educational, where we are attempting to increase sensitivity to parents as people, as the most effective route to help both the parents and the children, a tutor may present Mrs Green's first interview and ask the class how they would feel coming back to a second interview, if they were Mrs Green. Some say that there could be a feeling of relief that it had been possible to talk, admit an attitude that was 'bad' and be met with understanding, and it would be possible to look forward to the second interview, anticipating another positive experience. But a greater proportion of each class indicates they'd feel some unwillingness to talk the next time, they may have regrets about breaking down and opening up, and they may clam up to avoid a painful experience.

Either reaction is possible—relief or regret. It is not an easy or necessarily painless process to be self-honest. If there is unwillingness to talk, then the counsellor recognises resistance to exposing painful feelings when a person may not be sure of their reception. And receiving silence with understanding is as important as receiving speech with understanding.

Mrs Green, having talked freely in the first interview, is silent and restless when she comes for the second.

Mrs Green sits down holding her handbag on her lap. She shifts position frequently, puts the handbag on the floor and crosses her legs, uncrosses her legs, looks down, looks out of the window, coughs, blows her nose. There is a pause of ten minutes. (The record reveals the silent minutes. The counsellor did not watch his clock.) The counsellor sits quietly.

> *Mrs Green.* I feel like a fool sitting here with nothing to say. I'm not a good talker. (Pause of three minutes.) I said all that last time. And I don't know.
>
> *Counsellor.* (Accepting uncritically and reflecting Mrs Green's doubt about the benefit of talking.) It felt worse?
>
> *Mrs Green.* Yes. (Pause.) No. (Pause.) No, not worse. But . . . (Pause of five minutes.)
>
> *Counsellor.* (Recognising even wished-for communication may be accompanied by increased rather than diminished anxiety.) It isn't easy to talk of these things.

Mrs Green does not reply immediately nor does she indicate by any gesture that she hears or agrees. A silence of five minutes follows during which time she looks at the counsellor and then out of the window and then down and seems to be thinking to herself.

> *Mrs Green.* I won't accept *anything*. (Pause of three minutes as she continues to look down. Then she looks up and into the counsellor's eyes and speaks emphatically.) *I really felt better after I'd said that about not accepting the deafness.* . . . (Pause for five minutes.) If we can get me straightened out that'll be half the battle.

During the rest of the forty minutes' meeting she reiterates ways in which she cannot 'accept anything'. Time for the next appointment is arranged.

The same evening she comes with her husband to the weekly parent meeting held in conjunction with the programme of individual interviews with mothers during their child's language therapy. She appears jumpy and restless and says nothing.

When her third interview time arrives she has an appointment with the doctor and does not come. Her husband, who has a day off, brings Tim for his therapy and comes in for a parent interview. He does not talk easily and keeps looking at the clock. The counsellor again recognises that this kind of interview can be an unfamiliar and uneasy experience, explains that the purpose is to give parents a chance to be heard in anything they might want to bring up, but the purpose is not to respond with more information or advice which is already provided in another part of the programme, but to give people a chance to answer questions in a way that has meaning for them.

Mr Green. Tim seems to be getting on all right. He wants to come. You can't get very far if you don't accept it.
Counsellor. This is reality, and if we accept this we can go on from here.
Mr Green. My wife won't accept it. She's very nervous and upset. We heard a talk in a training centre for the deaf about the facilities, and some do's and don'ts for parents. The important thing was to talk to the child so he could see your face, and have the objects there when you repeated words. But you weren't supposed to teach the child to use words immediately. But my wife gets discouraged because he doesn't talk.

Mr Green tells about his own attempts to talk to Tim, and about the rules of not forcing speech before language had been poured in. He feels that it is more difficult for a father because he isn't home much of the time when the younger children are up, that it does seem to be a strain on his wife but he hopes that the parent classes will help. He says he is just filling in and doesn't really know what to say and has no pressing problem. Then he is silent and keeps looking at the clock.

Counsellor. You feel on the spot?
Mr Green. No, you're not putting me on the spot.
Counsellor. I didn't mean we meant to, but wondered if you felt that way.
Mr Green. I always watch the clock at work.
Counsellor. You want to clock out?
Mr Green. No, no. But I have no special questions. My wife does need help.

He reiterates difficulties Mrs Green has already talked about, and says he is worried about her.

The following week Mrs Green comes for her third interview. She appears much more at ease, and talks freely about the ways in which she thinks she is making things difficult for herself.

The counsellor does not refer to the absence of the previous week. In the case of a broken appointment, where there is a contract to meet, the possibility of making another commitment to rationalise a desire to avoid coming is always a possibility, and it would be normal for the counsellor to respond to the resistance implied in absence. In this case both Mr and Mrs Green had attended the parent group and ways of resisting self-understanding, including staying away, had been discussed there.

Mrs Green. I've been doing a lot of thinking since our last meeting. I had to reach the point myself of really wanting to talk again. I was relieved not to come last week. I felt I had to straighten out some things in my mind. And for one thing I've accepted now that I should wear glasses. The headache I had two weeks ago has gone. I've taken one step with the glasses. And now maybe I can take others.

Counsellor. You think you might accept other things now.

Mrs Green. Yes, I do. The headaches I kept getting, I think it's nerves. And I'm still not accepting a lot of things. I still eat sweets for one thing. If it makes me really ill, then I'll stop.

Counsellor. (Recognising something self-punishing in this.) When you've really given yourself a bad time?

Mrs Green. I know I shouldn't, but I do it.

Counsellor. You're protesting.

Mrs Green. Nobody can really tell me anything. I've got to have things my way. I've got to follow my plan. I'll work until two in the morning finishing up what I've planned to do in the house. I can't go to bed if there is a dish left unwashed. I get mad if the kids interfere with my plan. (Mrs Green gives many examples of the way she has scolded her children for interrupting her work in the house.) It just makes me furious.

Counsellor. You feel upset by anything that disturbs the path you've determined for yourself.

Mrs Green. I can't give in. It's the same with everything. The diabetes. The children. I have to assert my way at all costs. I won't listen to anybody. I fight. I can't give.

Counsellor. Battling the way things are.

Mrs Green. And I can't stand the kids messing around in the house, when I've used all my energies getting it clean. Anything you can name that I'm not supposed to be doing, that's me. Then the other kids think they are neglected by my attentions to Tim. You can hear them saying 'Tim gets everything.' If they only knew. But I have given him a lot of things. I get him any toy he asks for when we go shopping. But, as I said, he loses interest. But the other kids are jealous. 'Why can't we have some new toys?' But I do give them money to buy things for themselves.

Then Mrs Green expresses an insight which reverses a statement that she had all she wanted as a child.

Mrs Green. But I'll tell you something. I've been thinking. I get the kids out of my hair by giving them money—after they pester me, I just do it to get rid of them. No wonder they're not satisfied. 'Mother's getting rid of me.' And I think that's what it was with my mother. I think my mother gave me things to get me out of her hair.

Counsellor. (Simple recognition in a painful area of parent rejection.) You feel you do this to be rid of your kids and you think your mother was giving things to you for the same reason.

Mrs Green does not verbally follow up this thought but sits in silence for a while and then seems to change the subject.

Mrs Green. You know I'm sorry I didn't say anything in the parent meeting. I wanted to. It was on the tip of my tongue. You were discussing everything that applied to me. But I just didn't pluck up the courage. I can't talk to strangers. I can't believe they'll be that interested. And I'm afraid of saying the wrong thing. Like telling you I didn't accept the deafness. I was sorry.

Counsellor. (Does not point out she had already said it helped but recognises opposite feeling that Mrs Green needs to express.) You were sorry.

Mrs Green. I don't talk and it just came out.

Counsellor. It surprised you.

Mrs Green. Yes. (Pause.) But it *helped*. (Continues to talk with great inflection and emphasis in contrast to depressed monotone in the first interview.) And somehow I do accept it now. It seems silly that I didn't before. It's there. (Speaking with much inflection but in a relaxed manner. Pause.) Maybe I can teach him now. He wouldn't accept *anything* from me before.

Counsellor. You didn't accept the deafness and he said no to what you offered.

Mrs Green. I wasn't accepting *him* and it hurt my feelings when he rejected me. (Silence. Looks at counsellor. Appears relaxed and thoughtful.) It's easier talking today. I thought you do want to help me and you're not just prying.

Counsellor. You see me as less of a stranger.

Mrs Green. Yes, I see it. I get so much advice all round. People are always telling me what to do. And there's an aunt who makes me really mad. She wants to know why I come here. If I don't talk in the group you know I'm thinking. Like that man who just sat and said nothing and then when he did talk he took the whole hour and after that he seemed to have more confidence. Confidence. That's me. That's what I want.

BREAKING THE BARRIERS

Stated problems involve a way of seeing the external world which derives from each individual experience. We can think of 'this way of seeing' embodied in the stated problem as a 'perceptual content'. At all times this perceptual content has a two-directional value—outwards to the conscious external world, and inwards to the personal unconscious world. Defences against looking inward make a barrier against 'seeing the problems in me'. As breaks in defences become safe in an unthreatening climate, it is possible to admit the internal problem, the real culprit.

In the first three interviews then, we can see possibilities emerging.

First, there is catharsis: a person expresses feelings and looks at negative attitudes (I don't accept the deafness), and finds uncritical reception.

Second, there is affirmation of 'let me look to change myself' rather than blaming and seeking to change other people and things.

Third, reversal of expressed external problems occurs (But my work is really light) as it appears safe to reveal internal emotional difficulties.

Fourth, negative attitudes tend to dissolve when they are permitted and not denied (I do accept it now—it's there).

Fifth, with increased discrimination in recognising the real problem, the possibility of working with it emerges, rather than spending energy fighting it and blaming it.

A NEW EXPERIENCE

There are still many questions to be answered, and people do not solve all their difficulties in one, two, or three interviews. But a shift away from the stalemate in the direction of changing attitudes, is apparent in the context of the kind of listening given to these mothers.

Those who have come to medical and educational settings for help with their children, both physically normal and handicapped, not expecting a 'listening consultation' but rather a fact-finding or advice-giving interview, have expressed their personal reactions to their unexpected experience. The reactions point to the climate of the relationship as more important than any of the specifics. People react to the intangibles. 'You just knew some one was interested in you.' 'I don't now what it was but I felt I could let down and open up.' 'There was a wonderful sense of acceptance.'

Great emotional upheaval might be experienced at the time (as Mrs Green found) but relief afterwards, and the beginning of insight.

Parents may feel that trying to handle a handicapped child or other demands in their lives has brought them to the edge of breakdown.

> 'When I came for help I had very little contact with people. . . . In the first consultation the counsellor saw I was at breaking point . . . represented strength. For the first time I felt understood. My son was an impossible load. He never slept more than two or three hours. I'd become helpless. I could do nothing but either sob or beat him. After one hour of consultation I felt happy. When he started his crashing around I could relax. I was on guard all the time before. And I never physically relaxed even when alone.'

'Feeling understood means burdens and tensions seem to diminish' is not an unusual initial experience.

A mother who described herself as a rejected child, was one of those who was going to prove she was a better mother than *her* mother had been to her, wept in the initial interview when she brought her cleft palate daughter for evaluation for speech therapy. She told of her difficulty in functioning either at work or socially. She heard, 'Here we trust parents can work out their own solutions; in our experience, talking helps.' This mother commented, 'With the feelings of

THE TWO DIRECTIONAL VALUE OF STATED PROBLEMS

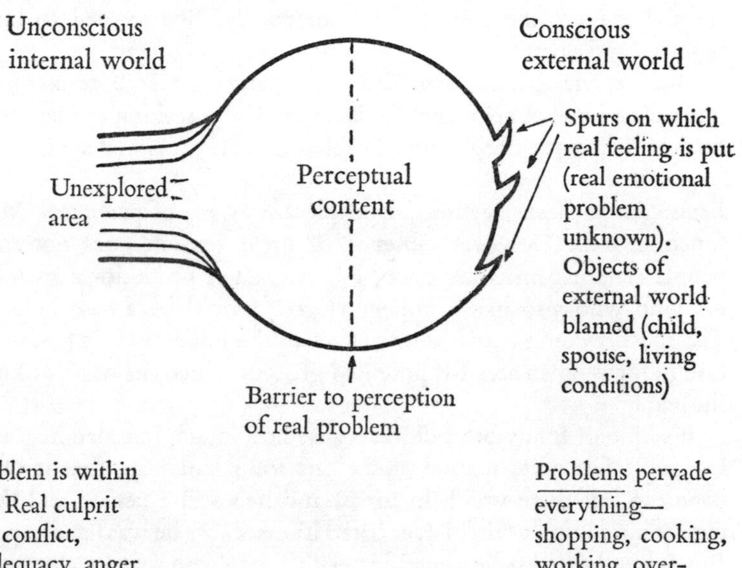

Problem is within me. Real culprit my conflict, inadequacy, anger projected on to spouse, child, living conditions

Problems pervade everything—shopping, cooking, working, overwhelming problem of the child—'too many demands'

Breaks in barrier and growing connections with internal meanings with shifts in perception of external

The more the drive to external detail, the more the direction of looking is turned from the real culprit.

loathing and hatred towards myself. I doubted whether I was capable of accepting and using methods which trusted me to resolve my conflicts. But I did talk. And it helped. It seemed to unblock me to some extent immediately. The first interview motivated me to move into long-term therapy. It was rough but I didn't look back. I was going downhill. That first interview was the turning point. I could not believe that I was being listened to as a person of worth in my own right. I trusted (the counsellor) immediately. She seemed to know my need and to care.'

The interview, then, can give an experience which results in an immediate sense of help. Second, it can motivate seeking and accepting further help with deep seated problems.

Focusing a problem. But not all people are aware of problems. Many function well. However, absence of great tension does not mean people cannot gain from 'being listened to'. A professional man and his wife who also had a college degree would be a case in point. The mother commented on the effect of the initial listening consultation in focusing an area for potential growth which she did not know she had.

'It's kind of funny but I didn't realise how much I needed help until I came. I felt quite natural about our son's handicap, that it was a handicap but there was help for it, and he's still a person and that's part of him. I don't think I ever hated him because he was handicapped. But I found that I have a terrific personal problem that I really wasn't aware of until I came—this terrific dependence that I feel towards my mother, which I think probably is the basic feeling that it was necessary, at all costs, to have her approval. I never have felt it intellectually, but it's evident in a lot of ways. That initial interview was the first time that I put my finger on this thing, that what I'm after is my mother's approval. I said, "I don't have any problems. I'm just worried about my mother." How was I going to break the news to my mother about this handicapped child? How would she take it without being too upset? And I saw in that first interview that I was talking about *myself* and my dependence on my mother. How was I going to make it right with her—for myself? And I didn't even realise I was dependent on her. I thought I'd broken away from home and was functioning independently in my own home. We both (self and husband) all of a sudden came to realise that the help that would mean most, was what we could get in our own growth and development.'

The following pages reveal the kinds of discoveries that later exploration uncovers as parents talk and the counsellor listens. The mother whose words we just heard, found later a triangle in her family she had not been aware of—she was competing with her mother for her father, and was constantly left with a feeling of wanting to make it 'right with her mother', because she was taking her mother's husband.

It would have taken two minutes to point all these problems out but it would not help—the kind of information which explains a person to himself psychologically we have found to be worse than useless. But here we open the door to discovery on the level of experience and re-experience of the self. And on this level of experience, change can take place.

A changing picture. Much information about a child's medical, educational and family background that can fill an initial interview with a parent, can be obtained in writing ahead of a scheduled meeting. In time so released for more unstructured communication, a parent can experience a shift in perception. Unpressured talk in the presence of some one a person feels to be understanding can help not only to focus a problem, but to change an approach to it even in one interview. Mothers have found they have been so busy fulfilling the technical aspects of child care that the child as an individual person needing his mother as an understanding friend, gets lost in the technicalities. A parent has a chance in these interviews to 'see for himself' without being told.

A child who, for whatever reason, presents problems to a parent, by the same token, presents pressures. The mere fact of being heard takes the pressures off. When people feel less pressured, they behave differently and where they find a new slant in seeing an old problem, the difference can be lasting.

Others notice. In hospital and clinic harassed and seemingly un-co-operative mothers and children both seem to become calmer, more able to listen and respond, when mothers have had a chance even in one interview to talk and be freely heard in their immediate concerns. A husband remarked, 'My wife seems so much more at peace.' Her friends said of the change in her son, 'Whatever happened to Jimmy? He seemed to be like an unmanageable wild man who wouldn't be controlled. Now he talks to you like a rational being and even sits quietly.' The mother herself said, 'I dare not take my son to anyone's house, his behaviour was so cranky and I was so much on edge. After the interview other people noticed a change in *his* behaviour. But my husband noticed the change in me. I'd cried and said I hated the child who brought me so much trouble. It was such a relief to have someone accept the way you feel. Just to be accepted in these churning feelings diminished the turmoil. And you don't seem to be quite the awful person you thought you were.'

Counsellor's verbal response. A few people mentioned the counsellor's verbal response as important in their shift of perception. 'What I said was restated with just enough change that I saw it differently and the light dawned.'

A challenge. All of these shifts in experience of self and in ways of seeing a specific problem take place when people can respond to and use the relationship offered them. But not all do this. Mr Green 'filled in'. Others reject the idea of talking at all. 'I don't want this brain washing,' said one mother.

What we are witnessing, of course, in all these interviews is an application of psychotherapy. The counsellor is, in fact, a therapist whose practical ends are achieved indirectly as the by-product of a relationship. One of the biggest challenges is to present psychotherapy so that people will find that threat and anxiety about it are outweighed by promise of gain, so that they will want to use the opportunity for growth.

A parent education class is one such place to meet the challenge.

4 *Opening Doors—Parent Education and Psychotherapy*

We are all more simply human than otherwise.

Harry Stack Sullivan

In making available the opportunities for self-understanding, and the kind of attitude-change leading to improved human relationships and reduced tension, we work on the assumption that all persons can benefit who can use the opportunity. We don't divide into sheep and goats. Such opportunities have been available to students in classes in communication, or professional groups of educational or medical specialists, and they have been available to all parents. We do not wait for breakdown or for the occurrence of intolerable stress. The philosophy is preventive, and for parents, offers opportunities for growth, from which the child will benefit. Many of the people in these pages are parents of pre-school children, but some have already been confronted by teenage problems, some become parents during attendance in groups. Some come with a problem of one child organically handicapped, or with functional or developmental difficulty such as speech, reading or learning problems and they find an opportunity for help for themselves. But the people who come may be young students, pregnant mothers, middle-aged business men. In all cases we begin wherever people *are* and move from there. In work with parents, or potential parents, the possibility lies not only of an individual's own growth but of breaking what seems to be a vicious cycle which hands down destructive attitudes and emotional conflicts, from generation to generation.

IMPLIED VALUES

Much is implied, as well as stated, of the social values on which our work is based. At all times, we have tended not to stress manipulation of the external environment, but becoming more able to handle it. We would not normally, therefore, aim to get rid of 'unsatisfactory parents' and put the child in care, but aim to help the parents become satisfactory. Our philosophy has been family-centred, but not just to keep the family together externally. The goals have been rather to find the ways of relating which really accept the child, and to find ways of reaching a mature and enduring love between husband and wife, discovering what both of these really mean for people in short and long range. Therefore, we would not aim to encourage a man or a woman to eliminate his or her partner by separation or divorce, because the partner appeared unsatisfactory, any more than we would encourage the elimination of a child who was born blind or deaf. We would be aware of the dynamism of projection and rationalisation, and all the other distorting defences that can lead to the blaming of a partner, or a child, or an environment. We are not blind to the possibilities of deprived and frustrating environments, nor are we negating a philosophy which offers reasonable opportunities for all people to train for and to use their maximum potential. In programmes for the handicapped, for example, we would wish, as suggested already, for resources which made every possible use of medical science and rehabilitation, making available physical resources and teaching machines, as well as trained persons. Our philosophy of education for all people would aim to meet the needs of each human being, and we would support team work which worked through community groups to improve employment and work conditions, and to ensure that no one, through no fault of his own, should be deprived of the means of survival.

But in the work described here, let us reiterate that we are concerned with helping people to become the kind of persons who can use the opportunities already given—and assimilate the information they have received and need, using the principles they may already believe in. Integrity, loyalty, being able to follow through on a commitment are all part of an implied value system. Respect for the individual and his uniqueness, go hand in hand with responsible choice, not in an opposite direction. We are concerned that short range goals and ways of reaching them would not impair long range goals: pressures on children leaving them with a feeling of inadequacy would be an impairment, as would various manipulations of people. For example, confidence tricks using others for short range gains tend to impair long range human relationships.

A major goal in helping parents is to lessen the gap between intellectual knowledge of what should be done, and the ability to carry it out. Put another way, we are concerned with resolving the discrepancy between verbal acceptance and unconscious attitudinal denial.

People first—parent reaction to knowledge. In the parent education class or group, we offer a philosophy of prevention. The goals of a 'good parent' and the means of reaching the goals, are part of the class content and discussion. But we give no information without giving parents an opportunity to react in the way they feel. In this way, parents have an opportunity to experience the uncritical reception of them, and their point of view, which we are telling them a child needs.

One group of five mothers and two fathers meet for one and a half hours each week. They have brought their children for help with speech and language problems, and part of the course is the parent class. The children are retarded in language development or organically handicapped. All parents experience anxiety in relation to their children's achievement, especially in speech. The class purpose is part informative and part therapeutic. At the first meeting the therapist outlines the programme and points out that the main purpose of the parents' class is to give them an opportunity to bring up questions that may be troubling them. 'What you have to say is more important than anything I have to say. I'll give you some information, slip in the facts from time to time. But the facts will have more meaning if they arise from what you wish to say. We have found that advice is not very helpful in giving parents the help they want. So you may freely bring up whatever you choose in discussion, but my function will not be to give answers so much as to listen to give you a chance to work out some solutions for yourselves.'

In the first class meeting the therapist outlines normal speech development in children. After pointing out with examples that there is variability in children's development as a whole, and that the normal age for acquiring spoken language—speech sounds and vocabulary—has a wide range, the therapist continues, 'The way we accept our children's best efforts will influence their *wish* to communicate with others. And it may influence their *ability* to communicate.' The parents then hear a passage from Samuel Butler's *The Way of All Flesh*. Ernest kept saying 'tum' instead of 'come' and his father wanted him to be like everybody else and say 'come'.

'I do say tum,' said Ernest, meaning that he had said 'come'. . . .

'No, Ernest, you don't,' his father said, 'you say nothing of the kind you say "tum" not "come". Now say "come" after me as I do.'

'Tum,' said Ernest at once, 'is that better?'

'Now, Ernest, you are not taking pains; you are not trying as you ought to do. It is high time you learned to say "come"; why Joey can say "come", can't you, Joey?'

'Yeth, I can,' replied Joey and he said something which was not far off 'come'.

His father gave Ernest one more opportunity to say 'come'.

He looked very angry, and a shade came over Ernest's face, like that which comes over the face of a puppy, when it is being scolded without understanding why. The child saw well enough what was coming now, was frightened, and of course, said 'tum' once more.

The outcome of the episode was that his father took him from the room to beat him.

One of the mothers in the parent group volunteers: 'You really get the feeling of the child there, and see it differently.' Others echo what she says. But one of the fathers has another viewpoint.

> *Father*. It's all right to point out how a child feels, when he's asked to do something he absolutely can't. But I have some feelings for that father. I know how I feel when my son won't say what I want him to. I can't stand it when I try to get him to speak more clearly and he doesn't do it. It makes me furious. That's the way I feel.
>
> *Therapist*. You feel frustrated, too, when *your* best efforts don't get anywhere.
>
> *Mother*. (Her first statement has focused on the child, that you get the child's point of view from the passage about Ernest. She now expresses some feelings of her own.) I don't so much feel angry, I feel guilty when he doesn't talk right. I feel it's my fault. And I think other people will criticise me.
>
> *Therapist*. You feel responsible.

First, then, parent feelings have priority over information about the child, even though a lecture may be a starting point for group reactions.

Second, the therapist's response begins to set the acceptant climate of the class.

Third, listening to one person's honest reaction, and observing its reception, leads others in a group to become more able to admit their own.

LIVING THE DEFINITIONS

In parent education classes, we do convey a philosophy of child care, whether the focus is on child development in general or on language and communication, or on the parent-child relationship as such. But the philosophy of child care is, in a wider sense, a philosophy of people-care.

On the route to our goals words like freedom, choice, responsibility, acceptance, understanding, permissiveness, reality and limitations recur. At this point, we should look a little more closely at some issues which are connected with these terms. There are pitfalls, and the terms may be misleading if we do not review what they imply for our work, and differentiate our technical definitions from alternative and even popular meanings. The way we use terms, and how we define them, contribute to the group climate which makes it possible for people to embark on self-discovery and disclosure.

We are offering parents a relationship which parallels the relationship of a good parent accepting and meeting the needs of his children in a way that will foster growth to the enjoyment of emotional maturity. Use of specific terms helps to structure the context of reduced threat and of availability to listen to people without condemnation.

What about definitions in practice then?

Permissiveness and limitations. The relationship we offer is a permissive one and, as we define it, this means permitting a person to be *where* he is and *what* he is—whatever his feelings may be, or whatever his condition. It means no censorship of verbal expression of feeling, within the boundaries of the therapy relationship; it is limited, therefore, in time and in place. It does not mean saying what you want to anybody at any time, nor does it mean acting out what you want.

> 'If you feel like killing your mother-in-law and your sister-in-law come and talk about it. Don't do it. You may be reacting to your mother in your attitudes to your mother-in-law and sister-in-law. If we can talk about it and look at it and not deny the troublesome negative feeling, it seems to have so much less power over us.'

But we are bounded by reality, the social context of our culture, and the necessity for discrimination and channelling for our wants and needs. Feelings are, they exist; they are not good or bad in themselves. Feelings are facts. Denial (I never get mad) can lead to more trouble (I'm indifferent to people) through indirect expressions, in more destructive ways than recognising the fact. Through re-definition parents learn the meaning of permissiveness:

> 'For our children permissiveness does not mean no guidance, however. The concept of limitations is as important as permissiveness, and a necessary part of it. We fail children if we do not give them the solid ground of limits to stand on, and if we don't help them constrain their frightening feelings of omnipotence. "If it's in my mind, it happened" is part of the magical thinking of the child. But feelings can be most terrifying to a child, if they are completely denied expression and not submitted to a moderating reality. Give him an opportunity to channel his feelings—a toy to beat (not the younger children) a corner of the yard to mess and make mud (not the living room). And he doesn't need you to go to pieces, too, if he gets angry. If we have enough freedom in us to stay with him whatever his feelings, he'll accept the limit we impose, the restraint.'

Freedom, choice, responsibility. Freedom implies the freedom from the internal stress which hampers choice and the follow-through to realistic goals—freedom from obstacles in communication, freedom from fear. Unconscious emotional conflict, the unfinished business of denied needs, implies fighting the self, a drain on energy. And the unconscious conflict with the self impairs the exercise of free choice. It blocks the spontaneity in relating, associated with a sense of confidence and self-worth derived from needs met. Impulsive (without thinking) and compulsive (keep cleaning the house) behaviour seem to substitute for the ability to evaluate and choose. Choice implies responsibility, owning the choice and following-through and as we use responsibility here, we imply more than responsibility for behaviour. We imply the possibility of taking the responsibility for our attitudes, and being willing to choose the self-exploration leading to emancipation from irrational fears, hostilities and compulsions.

Acceptance. Uncritical reception of each person in his uniqueness, is what we mean by acceptance. It implies neither approval nor disapproval. The dynamic aspect of acceptance, which has the greatest potential for change, relates to acceptance of needs in the area of unfinished business, acceptance of a person's needs to see as he does. Thus he can begin to look at his need with diminished threat. Uncritical reception does not mean approving him as is. The problem is that he does not accept aspects of himself—they are 'bad', he is unworthy. Then the challenge is to go back and admit, accept the 'unacceptable' child needs in the adult. But we cannot force the steps by which he does it, or the original trouble of by-passing the need is perpetrated. He has to grow at his own pace, in his own time, as does the child.

Understanding. With permissiveness and acceptance, go understanding. And in these pages, understanding is not intellectual dissection and analysis, but simply 'feeling with' (empathy), seeing with another person's eyes, knowing how his world looks to him.

> 'If we can see with the eyes of a child we can teach him.'
>
> 'But we are saying, "Come here and let us see with *your* eyes." "I'm not free enough of my own needs to be able to give and give and give," you tell us. We want to listen to you. We're not even going to tell you to love your child, but let us accept you until you become able to love your child. We can become more sensitive to children's needs, learn to read their behaviour, become more alert to their emotional language. But first we have to become more sensitive to our own.'

FEARFUL LABELS—RE-DEFINITIONS

In setting a climate, then, positive aspects of the parent class may be spoken as well as made use of in practice. But there are other terms which tend to trigger feelings of fear or shame. Re-definition can help to reduce the sense of threat associated with these labels, and open a door to talking about them. As they tend to be an immediate concern in the parent, rejection and selfishness are two such words, similarly all the manifestations of hate—the hostile anti-social attitudes.

Rejection. Rejection of children is, for parents, condemning in its association and therefore to be denied, for, 'or course, a parent loves his child.' But it becomes more possible to look at rejecting feelings for a child if we see them in a new light. Parents listen to re-definitions.

> 'A parent who can't handle the situation is a parent who rejects. He wants to get rid of these devastating feelings of inadequacy.

Anyone who seems to produce in us feelings of impotence and frustration, is some one we would wish not to have around. A father who says his child is a monster, tells us his needs have not been met, not that he's bad. But what of the mother who can't let her child go? Is *she* starved of affection? Smother love maybe over-compensation for not wanting in the first place. We have to make up for it, protect him, tie him to ourselves. But it is a mistake to think we are completely accepting or completely rejecting. It's possible to hate and love the same person.'

Selfishness. 'He's selfish' is automatically understood as a derogatory label. But again, a re-definition helps to open the door to its meaning for each person's life.

'Selfishness means you haven't found yourself yet. You're lost and you're terribly concerned to find your way. Somehow you haven't managed to feel anything was yours. A child who won't give, like the jealous child, may be very unsure that he has gained the acceptance of his parents. He tries to hang on to the toy or the bag of candy. He seems to be saying, "I don't want to lose this thing that gives me a sense of me-ness". And without a sense of *me* it's very difficult to have a sense of *you*. We can give to others only if we have received. When your basket's full, then you can give. If we chide our children for not giving, what of *our* capacity to give? Is our basket full enough to give to them? We need to be able to receive first, before we can give. Are we able to receive?'

Hostility. 'He's just a stinker' may dismiss the hostile child with a label. We don't like him. He gets in our way and challenges our composure. But need we feel so threatened if we are able to read his meanings?

'A hostile child is a frightened child. He needs acceptance but fears rejection. He'll hit first. It's his defence against being hit. How many of us get a chip on our shoulders, when we feel we can't trust anybody? They're all out to get you. It's *who* you know, not *what* you know. The child needs trust. What of *our* capacity to trust?'

'Anger is part of life, and suppressed feelings may do more harm than temper outbursts. The compliant child perhaps daren't be himself. When children's behaviour is dominated by wanting to be accepted, this may not be healthy, this may be a strain.'

'If a child has a tantrum he is frightened as well as upset. We can slap him or throw cold water on him and he'll stop because he's frightened even more, but that may drive his temper inside for life. Tantrums are normal at two as a child meets with frustration from us in doing all he wants. But are they fewer at three? How many people do you know who have brought unresolved temper tantrums into adult life?'

In parent classes, when we re-define socially stigmatic attitudes parents may laugh. In response to a question like 'Who brought unresolved temper tantrums into adult life?' a husband and wife may look at each other and smile. Some say 'me'.

'A child's tantrum may be frightening for a parent too. But if a parent goes to pieces that can be terrifying for a child. And if you're frantic already, it's bad to have someone walk out on you. If you don't understand, you might say, "I'll wait. I don't quite know what's making you frantic, but I'm here." A child needs support. As you are able to give it he learns inner controls. And that's a help in adolescence.'

Psychology. Another source of fear is psychology itself. Here again, a function of the therapist-leader, in structuring the group environment for emotional growth, is to reduce the threat, the stigma, popularly associated with psychotherapy. The frankly preventive approach is clear:

'We don't wait for you to break down, and a breakdown isn't the only reason for psychotherapy. If you don't get along with your neighbour, come and talk about it, and look at the feelings. Maybe you are rebelling against your father in your attitude toward your neighbour.'

'We are firmly taught that the first five years are most important, and the relationship with the parent then determines later attitudes. But, fortunately for us, there are ways of undoing the damage that might have been done in our first five years. You have seen trees that grow in the shadow, that root under rocks. How stunted and twisted they are. But if the sun gets to them, they begin to grow straight. You can have a childhood that seems to twist and stunt your growing, but you don't have to stay knotted up in that. Whatever your hidden angers and desperations, you can change if you let in the light.'

'It could be us.' In the classes psychological jargon is reduced to nothing.

Parents hear information in everyday words through stories of everyday events. They are not struggling with technical vocabulary about whether their emotional attitudes are 'congruent' with the lecturer's information; about their and other people's complexes. Definitions and re-definitions are in terms of their experience.

'There is never no-reason for the way we behave. If we blow our top because a glass of milk was knocked over, it's more than a glass of milk that caused our emotional explosion.'

'A child doesn't understand "too far". Point to the corner, make a mark on the pavement. But if he doesn't feel we're with him, he wont't accept the mark.'

'It's normal for children to love the wet and the mud. One little girl in a clean white dress found a mud puddle while her mother was talking to a friend. She bent down and put her hands in the puddle. Then she knelt down to get her elbows in it. Then suddenly, Wham! A big adult was swatting her and pulling her away. "Naughty, naughty. Dirty little girl." How much better to say: "Lovely mud puddle, but let Mother get you another dress to play in and we can make a puddle in the garden." Our sudden intrusion into a little girl's absorbed joy, can do more than stop her playing with the mud puddle.'

'A child needs to experiment with materials, to enjoy through his senses if he's going to be free to learn and create later.'

'There's nothing more constricting than a fear of dirt.'

'Dirt, if we can't bear to touch it, literally gets into everything. Ordinary observation and experiment in the social sciences, tell us of ways in which touch is the primary communication, the first way of receiving messages from the world and the first way to self-knowledge. Tactile experience is the most basic part of sensory experience. We have seen the effects of sensory deprivation on Harlow's monkeys. Reared in isolation, deprived of primary communication by touch, monkeys grow up unable to defend themselves or to relate to a mate. The licking of animals is the primary communication of touch. Kittens cannot urinate or defecate unless the mother licks the anus or urethra first. In bodily touch with his mother, the human baby experiences a kind of emotional touch in which he comes to know his earliest anxiety and his earliest sense of well-being.'

'Through touch, the baby communicates with himself. He begins to learn his body-image and his separateness from other objects, through touch. The way we learned to feel about sex, stems from the way we learned to feel about touch. And such feelings are pervasive. Don't touch! If it is a taboo given with disgust and threat of rejection, it later becomes "Don't mention, or mention only in furtive ways. Sex is dirty, like elimination." If we are going to teach our children about sex, the genitals have names—a man has a penis, a woman a vagina. But labels alone won't teach a healthy attitude. Nothing is more powerful in teaching our children about sex, than our attitudes and the way we live.'

'A child needs a deep dependent relationship with the human beings who initiate him into the social world. It is the foundation for a basic security, necessary for him to be willing to master his environment and meet its demands. And a sound dependency derives from a comfortable tactile experience, in which a child feels accepted and at home. A child who is always whining, and won't leave you alone, hasn't found what he's looking for. Maybe he needs your arms around him, really feeling you're with him. Security in touch for the baby, becomes later security in the symbolic touch of speech. Later, if he wants to talk to you, if you really listen to him, he'll know it. It isn't time-consuming then. He'll leave you alone. He'll be content to go and play.'

'Silly' problems. People may hesitate to talk of feelings which bother them, because they are conscious of fear of stigma, that their problems are negligible. 'I don't like moths', 'I can't sleep on a ground floor', 'I can't stand the colour pink', 'I freeze on the telephone', 'Why am I a slave to my house? I just keep cleaning it, even when everyone says it doesn't need it. And I could kill my boy when he doesn't hang up his jacket.'

One of the group members said that before she came to the parents class, she could not talk to anyone about the things that worried her, except her husband, 'even though they seemed silly to him'. The therapist commented.:

'It may seem silly to other people, because the thing that worries you is not the real cause of worry, but the place where you put the real cause of worry. You feel like breaking down when a little moth flies in the room. Now that's silly, you say. But the moth is only the place where you've put all the feelings which you dare not look at, about the thing you are really worrying about. We'll talk about moths or the colour pink for as long as you can and need, but it will stop being a recurrent problem when you get down to the real thing.'

'Not only do manifestations of hostility come in for social disapproval but tender feelings also. Dependency for example.

'We need to deny feelings if we don't trust them. If you have no experience of your dependency being accepted, it's hard to trust it. People with the deepest dependency needs, deny them most. They're afraid of being cast out if their needs were known.'

The therapist leader's verbal recognition, with examples from other people's lives of universal problems, opens a door and tends to encourage the feeling, 'I'm not alone. Maybe I dare to reveal this.' Such spoken recognition helps to reduce threat in the group.

REDUCING FEELINGS OF DIFFERENCE

Members of the parent classes have expressed relief about the lack of jargon. They have said they felt encouraged to bring up their problem as the therapist's lecture made them aware of their difficulties in a different way, and made them feel that others in the world had similar difficulties and it didn't seem so bad.

Let's return to Mrs Green, and hear both some changes and some recurrent problems. Repetition is normal until a problem is worked through. She has been absent from an appointment with an ear infection. In the previous interview she spoke of her house-pride. 'Dirt' is a continuing problem. The parent class seems to stimulate talking about it.

Mrs Green. I can't stand a speck of dirt. If the kids bring in a speck of dirt I'm wild.

Therapist. Then what I said about the mud puddle reached you?

Mrs Green. Yes.

Houses versus humans. Today, she begins by talking about tangibles—the difficulty of ear infection and her son's progress. She seems more relaxed in expressing negative feelings. At the same time, she has found that she and the children enjoy each other—a seeming paradox typical of increased inner freedom manifest in less fear of negative feelings.

Mrs Green. Ever since going over the mountains I seem to have picked up an ear infection. I can't wear my glasses because they press on my ear. Perhaps it'll be all right if I forget it. I nearly didn't come but didn't want to sit at home complaining. It's my meanness coming out. I'm full of it.

Therapist. You feel full of meanness?

Mrs Green. Yes. But I didn't want to deprive Tim. He talks more, uses his voice more. He cups his hands and makes a noise, and the kids come and he smiles as though he really has done something. He used to poke me and say nothing. Now he makes noises. And he wants a kiss.

Therapist. He's freer.

Mrs Green. And I can accept it.

Therapist. You're freer too.

Mrs Green. Yes. And he feels it. (Pause.) You know I left two or three clothes un-ironed last night. (Laughs.) And it felt all right. They could be done today.

Therapist. Is this a progress report?

Mrs Green. Yes. (Pause.) But I still have to do all the dishes and the floor every night. (Lights a cigarette and misses the waste paper box with the matches).

Therapist. (Responding to the action in context of talk about keeping dirt down. Smiling.) A mess? (Referring to fallen matches.)

Mrs Green. (Laughs.) But I do things with the kids now, go out and play with them. I thought they wouldn't want me.

Therapist. You thought you'd be rejected.

Mrs Green. Yes. But they like it. And we have fun. And they talked all night about the fun they had with Mum in the park. It wasn't just Tim I wasn't giving attention to. It was all of them. But it seemed harder with him.

Therapist. It wasn't because he was deaf. But the deafness seemed to intensify the difficulties.

Mrs Green. Now he's always asking for a kiss if he's done something.

Therapist. He wants approval.

Mrs Green. Yes, and he'll come up to me now.

Therapist. There's a different quality in the relationship?

Mrs Green. Yes. Before I wouldn't accept his deafness. No wonder he wouldn't learn.

Therapist. That is, it's hard to learn when you feel rejected and unlovable.

Mrs Green. And the children will help me in the house if we do it together. If I say, 'Would you like to dust?' they want to. But if I say, 'Do this,' it's 'no'.

Therapist. When people are driven they resist.

Mrs Green. I don't drive them as much. (Pause. Then shows readiness to read the meaning of her children's behaviour, of other people's feelings.) I think they resent me because I don't want them to make a mess. And they do it just to get me mad. And I want my husband to put on clean shoes to walk through the living room. Sometimes he'll walk through it anyway. But he has to, of course. But I want things my way. I don't seem able to give. I have to get my way and get what I want, and I can't allow that other people might want this too. I always had everything I wanted and was sorry after my father died that I'd asked so much of them, instead of helping them. My brother's the same. He has to have what he wants. He can't give up. And if I know I'm not supposed to have it, I want it all the more. (Getting wants met remains a problem and has to be talked about again.)

Therapist. You fight this denial.

Mrs Green. And my children are the same. I can't expect them to be different if I'm not. I'm growing up with them. Tim's mean the way I am. He has a temper. I hope when he grows up he won't be like I am. I can see now that he can be all right. (Pause.) This wanting everything! But I'm never satisfied.

Therapist. (Using image which ties with a literal craving to eat.) That hungry feeling.

Mrs Green. I had all I wanted, but . . .

Therapist. Getting what you want doesn't seem to be getting what you need?

Mrs Green. I'm wanting something but don't know what I want. I feel I've got to have chocolates. And ice cream. I never pass the grocery store without getting any. When I heard I had diabetes I could give up and die. Then my friend said, 'What about your children?' That set me thinking.

Therapist. You were needed. That set you thinking. Wanted and needed.

Mrs Green. My husband won't go out. He wants to watch television. One time I wouldn't go out either. I've borne a grudge for weeks just 'cause he wouldn't go to a movie. About nothing.

Therapist. Nothing in the situation seemed to justify that much reaction but you felt that way.

Mrs Green. Now I've been to movies with the two older boys and enjoyed it, and they enjoyed it.

Therapist. There was satisfaction there.

Mrs Green. Yes. (Pause.)

Therapist. They enjoyed what you gave them and you enjoyed that fact.

Mrs Green. Yes. (Pause.) I've told you about my floor the way I keep it clean. My neighbour said you could eat off it. One day she came and the children had a mess on the floor. I was embarrassed. (Mrs Green smokes cigarette, flicks ash and it misses tray and falls on the tile floor. Laughs.) Then I admitted my floor could be messy.

Therapist. You admitted it was possible to accept something less than perfect. Something different from your plan for it.

Mrs Green. They said, 'How do you keep the house the way you do with five children?' I said, 'If you want to stay up till two you can do it.' Any mess I can't stand. It's a nervous strain. When my husband isn't there and I give the kids their meals, I just put them on the table and leave the room. I can't stand the noise and dirt.

Therapist. All these things going out of control.

Mrs Green. There was nothing but my house. It wouldn't matter about me. I'd clean house all day and not even comb my hair. If anyone walked across the floor sometimes I couldn't stand it. If people just move.

Therapist. If people just move.

Mrs Green. But they disturb things.

Therapist. The human element.

Mrs Green. My husband is easy going. He just cleans up the mess.

Admitting negative feelings seems to release positive ones as well. For Mrs Green there seems to be an increase in positive feelings and relationships. She begins by using the past tense about the overwhelming priority of keeping her house clean and suggests a possibility that 'the disturbance' of people could be allowed. It is easier to impose a preconceived order on a house than on a human being. The imposed external order Mrs Green's insecurities drove her to was extreme and an impossible goal for people. Increase in inner confidence as feelings appear allowable means less need for a compensatory extreme imposition of external order. She is working on the problem, and also on the question of what it is she really wants, since whatever she gets brings her no satisfaction.

There is some unresolved guilt in relation to her parents. But she seems to see possibilities of moving closer to people, and reducing feeling of difference.

MY PARENTS IN ME

Self-examination means for some parents, an early realisation of the ways in which they may be like their parents, in feelings that hamper appropriate action. Recognition points to the possibility of freedom from the toils of past reactions.

Fighting disorder. Mrs Wills, like Mrs Green, has difficulty when anything interferes with her plan, but she also recognises that her plans are an effort to fight disorganisation.

Mrs Wills. I'm always rushed off my feet. Everything is such an effort. I never get done what I have to do, and this last thing of helping Jim with his speech—I just don't know how to fit it into my schedule. (Parents are following suggestions of child's teacher to help make a speech scrap book with him.)

Therapist. The last thing you wanted was this extra to make another rod for your back? (Slips in a fact explaining the teacher's purpose.) The idea is to gather pictures informally, as you or he come across them in a paper or a magazine.

Mrs Wills. I can't or don't get things done that way. I can't be deflected from my plan and what I'm trying to do, anyway.

Therapist. You point out the futility of advice here.

Mrs Wills. When Jim was little, his foot was turned in and the doctor said I had to do exercises with him. So I had to make a schedule that at these times I'd do it, or I never would have and his foot might have been turned still. Maybe I make too much of things. I make a mountain out of a molehill. I noticed my mother did that. Once I was hit for something I hadn't done. There are five of us and we'd all get it when Mother was mad. She'd have a switch and the first four got it the hardest and then the youngest got off more lightly.

Therapist. You could see your mother's reaction was disproportionate to the child's behaviour—it did not deserve this response.

Mrs Wills. Maybe I make mountains out of molehills. Maybe I have something of my mother in me.

Therapist. Maybe, you say, you're making it rough on yourself, the way she did.

Mrs Wills. I have tried not to punish the children for little things the way she did. I've tried.

Therapist. I'd like to slip in one of the facts just here. When we're trying we haven't found it. When we've become that way, it isn't trying then. But you know what it is when a parent takes his anger out on children, and you're trying not to do that.

Mrs Wills. I noticed my mother couldn't stand it if I brought a friend home without warning.

Therapist. She couldn't stand this interruption of her schedule either.

Mrs Wills. She was really very upset.

Therapist. She had her needs and preoccupations, too, which got in the way of accepting this thing.

Mrs Wills. (Laughing and recognising her mother may have needed help.) Maybe she should have had a Doctor X. (Therapist's name.) I know how crushed we used to be, the way she was if we brought a friend home unexpectedly. And I have made an effort to be different. My children can have their friends around. I make sure of that.

Therapist. That is, you know, what it meant to you when your mother couldn't accept your friend, and you make a conscious effort not to do what she did.

Mrs Wills. Yes. (Pause.) But I'm selfish. I can't stand unexpected extras. I don't have people dropping in nor do I drop in on them.

Therapist. Sudden interruptions throw you, too.

Mrs Wills. I think I'm actually a scatter-brain. It's an effort to keep my mind on anything for long. I'm so easily distracted. Everything just falls apart. I can't keep a hold on it.

Therapist. That is, you have to fight this disorganisation, this going out of control.

Mrs Wills. Yes. It means that I take a long time to do a little. It takes me so long when it seems to take other people such a short time. Maybe I'd have more time if I didn't have the kids. It's the kids that take the time. (Pause.) Yet I remember when I was in an apartment and had no children. I don't remember what I did, but I didn't have any time.

Therapist. It's something more than time that is the issue here.

Mrs Wills. I'm selfish. Yet I shouldn't be. So I try to do things for others.

Therapist. You don't like this 'selfishness'. You remember our definition? Selfishness means you haven't found yourself yet. You're protecting yourself, aren't you, from being jangled and hurt? If we're going to get at this thing that bothers you, we need to start where you are, not fight it, not deny it. You're protesting against this concern with self.

Mrs Wills. I have tried to do things. I took on the chairmanship of the local women's auxiliary—twice. And now I've decided to make a sweater. And I can't knit. I want to help others. But I don't know how to get it done. I've got too much to do now. But there's still too much effort for too little result. Like my mother. (Long pause.) I like talking to you.

Therapist. Are you saying there seems to be a quality in this talk. that meets what you're looking for?

Mrs Wills nods yes.

'*Women's work.*' In the next parent group meeting, Mr Wills speaks. He is reacting to his father in his handling of his son.

Mr Wills. The burden falls on a wife in bringing up children. Now especially with a handicapped child, men could help. But they don't. I'm not inclined to work with Jim's speech. Mr Lorrie said it first. I want to hand over to the expert what I can't do. And I can't do this work with Jim's speech. I can play ball with him, but I can't do this. I'm sorry. I don't have that ability.

At the end of the meeting he suggests a change in viewpoint.

Mr Wills. After all this apologising I think I can do better. It's the way *I feel* about it. My father thought only women bring up children. It's not a matter of ability. I think I can help if I feel different.

Therapist. (Reinforcing facts in the parent education class.) It's not just a matter of ability. Whatever our abilities, the way we *feel* is at the heart of successful functioning and good relationships. You remember mentally retarded Lizzie, who earned her living helping at a hot dog stand? She had learned to be comfortable with herself and everyone loved her. And you remember John who was born a genius, but was so tied up in himself, he wasn't functioning even as well as Lizzie?

Mr Wills. It's not a matter of intelligence, I know that. What I want to do, is to be able to reach a point of being able to work with Jim, without being jangled.

Therapist. That is, you assert again that the way you feel gets in the way. It's not what you *can* do.

Finding an inner ear. In another group, the father who said he was furious when he tried to get his son to speak more clearly, and his son didn't do it, brings up some feelings about obedience in a later meeting.

Mr Wallace. I had to do exactly what I was told when I was a kid —to the letter. My folks used to take me to church and I'd have to sit still for an hour and a half if necessary, or I'd know why. One day I didn't sit still. It was hot and my shoes were hurting me. I fidgeted around. And when we got home I tell you I *couldn't* sit down from that leather belt of my father's they laid to my backside. 'Now you've got something not to sit still for' my father said. 'From now on you just sit still, you'll do as you're told, and that's all there is to it.' They didn't see the kid's point of view that you're talking about here.

Therapist. That wasn't in your experience, having a child's point of view heard.

Mr Wallace. No, I just learned to conform and not question. Not show anything on the outside. Anything you might say in explanation they used to call backchat. And they wouldn't tolerate any backchat. You felt completely powerless, I can tell you. I was so miserable sometimes, I just didn't know if I could make it. Especially that church bit. I can't stand to sit still for any length of time now. And I've noticed something else. If anyone crosses me I'd just like to crack his jaw. It doesn't seem to take much, and I'm ready to hit.

Therapist. You'd like to strike out.

Mr. Wallace. You bet I would. But you know you can't. It's the same deal of sitting in church. Whatever you feel, no attention's paid to you. You're just helpless. But you go on seething inside, and then you panic in case some of it shows.

Therapist. That is there's some rebellion as well as helplessness, and at the same time, fear that you might reveal your feelings. And then you'd 'know why'? Do you see how all these feelings have got into the question of obedience, children obeying parents? And you've described how helpless you feel and how furious you feel when Lennie doesn't say what you ask him 'to the letter'. Literally 'the letter'.

Mr Wallace. It's the same deal, isn't it? It brings up all the old turmoil. But it doesn't have too much to do with Lennie, does it? I'll buy that. It doesn't make too much sense to push him around because I'd have liked to push my folks around—because I was pushed around. And I suppose I do ask too much of myself. I'm doing it to myself now. I suppose I could relax a bit about my own standards. And if I can't get Lennie to say what I want right then, that doesn't turn me into a total flop.

Therapist. You haven't failed as a person because you haven't succeeded in one thing, you're saying. And if we measure ourselves in terms of the wrong goal, then we'll always feel we've failed. And there's one more thing. The more impossible the goals, the higher the aspirations that we're not likely realistically to meet, the more we're probably thinking of ourselves as right down there. The lower our opinion of ourselves, the higher the goals we can never reach. One of the things we're trying to do is to lessen that gap. From both ends. First, feeling more adequate in ourselves as people. Second, accepting goals we can realistically reach, not wanting everything to happen all at once, whatever the more distant goal. If we don't feel adequate we'll even make goals we'll fail in, to keep feeling inadequate. We're 'bad' you see, in our own minds we don't deserve better. And one of the strongest forces in personality is to stay the way we are. It's the only way we know how to protect outselves.

Now in this parent group, Mrs Wallace is the mother who said at an earlier meeting she felt guilty, rather than furious, when her son didn't follow her direction; she felt it was her fault. It looks as if she, too, has some feelings about not being listened to as a child—husband and wife revealed they had this experience in common. And now in different ways they are having difficulty listening to their son—and to each other.

Mrs Wallace. I was thinking as you were talking. I always used to feel it was my fault if my folks wouldn't listen to me. It was always 'Keep still and leave me alone'. And I was thinking of two things. Len hates to be interrupted and that's really his feeling, not mine. But I get mixed up in it. I hate it when he reads the paper and won't talk to me. I wonder, 'What have I done?' A second thing, I had a few problems catching on at school—maths, and a little bit with reading. And I remember that I always wanted someone to take time to teach me. I had a teacher who was good that way, and I remember how quickly I improved. And now with Lennie I've shut him up so much. I can't be bothered with all his questions. All the why's. I just say, 'I don't know leave me alone'. I'm doing just what my mother did to me. And I don't know where he's got the feeling he ought to be punished. But if he's done anything we've told him not to do, he just goes and puts himself in the corner. 'I'm bad, Mommie,' he says. He uses that phrase too often. He must be getting those guilty feelings. And you know I think he does things sometimes out of line, just to get me to notice him. I know I always used to feel left out with my mother and father. I never felt as if *anyone* listened to me. And I'm sure that's why I feel so bad when I can't talk to Len. When people don't listen it is a problem for me. And I'm doing the same to Lennie. I begin to really put myself in his shoes now. It looks as if he's got his father making impossible demands on him and getting mad, and me just pushing him aside when he wants to talk, and then getting upset and guilty when he can't talk plain.

Therapist. You seem to be saying it's not surprising that he has a talking problem, when you and his dad seem to have listening problems?

Mrs. Wallace. That's about it.

Mr Wallace smiles and nods affirmatively.

Mr Wallace. But we're learning to have ears to hear.

The following week, Mrs Wallace says she has taken some time out to listen to Lennie and to explain the answers to some of his questions, and Mr Wallace says he still gets furious if anyone frustrates him but he doesn't think he is taking it out on Lennie so much—in fact he tries to understand what Lennie is saying, without riding him about talking differently.

An active silence. Mr Cullen did not talk at all in his parent education class but he talked to a research psychologist who was interested in the benefits, if any, of the group for silent members. He told what his experience had meant to him. He was a college administrator. Both he and his wife had read widely, including books on child development, and they had taken courses in child development and felt knowledgeable in the area.

Mr Cullen. We'd thought we'd gain in techniques and skills and ways of handling the child. We didn't know what 'parent education' was. Despite reading, we knew nothing of the psychological side and thought of parent-education as aids and helps. And I think my first reaction to the class was negative, as I was expecting gimmicks. Especially when it was child development. I was negative, as I felt very sophisticated in the area. Do I have to sit through all this again? But it was not long before we discovered that it was not lecturing in the formal sense of the word, but a dynamic situation. About halfway through the class, I began to gain insight into things I hadn't thought of before. For one thing I would see the way my life had been regimented by my parents. An hour for this, half an hour for that. There was one man I really tuned in to. And when he brought up anything, it was me all the way. I can remember times when I went home from that class and didn't sleep a wink, thinking through and tying things up. I was regimenting my older girl exactly as I had been regimented, and I could see too that I was neglecting her for the handicapped child. I'd treated her like a machine, and left her to take care of herself. Then she started making a scene every morning before school. Or she developed symptoms—a running nose, stomach ache and so on. We both started giving her more attention. From the whining nagging little kid, she became a wonderful little girl, The bickering with her sister lessened. And there were physiological changes through psychological media —her whole physical appearance and growth structure changed. When people are loved, isn't it wonderful?

Allowing my mother to be where she is. Mr Cullen began with insight into the way he was repeating his parents' regimentation with his daughter, and ended by focusing on an improved relationship with his daughter. Mr Parker used to want to change his mother and responds to another group member.

Mrs Hilton. I don't want to be told 'Once you're all straightened out, everything's going to be O.K.'

Therapist. You feel attacked.

Mrs Hilton. Yes.

Therapist. You want to be left where you are for a minute.

Mrs Hilton. I'll scream if I'm told it's my fault again. I want what I call mutual co-operation.

Therapist. You want the essence of understanding and acceptance as you are, so you're not alone.

Mrs Hilton. (She said in a previous meeting she was still wanting her mother's approval.) I got to thinking if only they would be different.

A group member. No that's not it. You can't change others. That's not where to start.

Mr Parker. (To Mrs Hilton.) Up to yesterday I felt as you did. Yesterday I had a consultation and many things became clear. I could see I could never satisfy my mother and I never will. I can now accept it. If you can only see this. You don't have to change other people. I gave up trying to get my mother to get help.

THE CHILDREN

As the experience of being heard in a parent class seems to lead to an increased sense of self-acceptance, parents' demands for themselves become less insistent and less restricted, and they are able, like Mrs Green to be more available to their children.

Parents are people before they are parents and bring to their parenthood what they are. Children, whether physically normal or handicapped, all share in attitudes which are part of the parents' way of relating to their world, and all share in changes which result from changes in parents' attitudes. A handicap may confront parents with enough need in a child for them to be challenged to look at their *own* needs. But the stress of the handicap, painful as it may be, is not the cause of the deep disturbance parents may feel. They become aware of difficulties in their relationships, which had existed long before the handicapped child was born, as Mr Cullen became aware of difficulties with his physically normal eldest daughter. In other instances, no stress of sufficient urgency had forced parents into an examination of their relationships with their physically normal child, unless he developed functional behaviour or communication disorders and needed clinical help. However, a number of the students who shared the classes, parents or potential parents, came to believe in a frankly preventive philosophy—we don't wait for a handicapped child, we don't wait for a marriage to 'fail', we don't wait for breakdown, we don't wait for situations of intolerable stress.

All children have strengths and limitations and their own individual needs, and challenge parents to meet their individual differences with understanding. A parent's changed experience of himself leads to his changed reaction to children.

Mrs Hilton, a college graduate, comments on the new meaning which the parent-education course brought to her previous knowledge.

Mrs Hilton. Since coming in here I've been looking back on things I've read and learned in the past, and I've suddenly had the feeling 'Oh, so that's what it meant.'

Therapist. It has opened the door to past intellectual observations

Mrs Hilton. And there have been some changes since I realised I was looking for my mother's acceptance in everything I was doing. I've been staying with a friend for two weeks. She is a good friend and has been for a number of years, but it hasn't been until the last two weeks that I have accepted myself to the point that I don't, care whether she thinks I'm good or bad. I don't think before I speak 'What shall I say?'

Therapist. You can risk letting her know your real self, and not be afraid of rejection.

Mrs Hilton. It doesn't matter to me. And I don't stop to think before I say anything, 'What will she think about how I am, when I say that?'

Therapist. You're not living on guard so much, are you?

Mrs Hilton. Because before, not just with her, with anyone, I thought through in my mind what I was going to say. 'Do I dare this or not?' I had to say I liked the programme, whatever it might be, because I might be beaten down. But I thought it all through before I dared. . . .

Therapist. Reveal. Reveal your real feelings about things.

Mrs Hilton. I always wondered what they were going to think about me when I said it.

Therapist. What they thought, was more important than what you *were*.

Mrs Hilton. I had to agree with their opinions. It was a lot easier to go along with a person. I did it to a point of mimicking them. My husband would say, 'You sound like that person.'

Then she speaks of a resultant change in her relationship with her son.

Mrs Hilton. I feel so different. I used to punish my son because he embarrassed someone else. But I'm not doing that any more.

Therapist. You're finding out now something of what acceptance is.

Nothing but the punch. Mrs Hilton's feelings are spilling over to her son.

Mrs Hilton. You used the word acceptance the first day I came in and I said 'What does that mean?' What is it to be accepted by someone? You know, it isn't going to be a miraculous overnight cure, but when I feel that way—comfortable and acceptant of myself—it's much easier. As you said, your problems dissolve. The other day David punched me in the stomach and I leaned over. It almost brought the tears to my eyes; and I controlled myself and recognised the fact that he was showing me something. I didn't crab about the pain and I accepted that he was showing me, and then I explained, 'We don't punch Mother or anyone.' He was showing me how fighters go—mmm—punch. It was a new thing. For the first time in my life I didn't cause a scene.

Therapist. The first time you didn't cause a scene.

Mrs Hilton. I was pleased. It felt good.

Therapist. It's rather fun to conduct yourself maturely isn't it?

Mrs Hilton. It was real nice. Because I thought he was trying to show me and that was what he did. In that particular moment he was demonstrating.

Therapist. You didn't feel attacked.

Mrs Hilton. But a while ago I'd have felt nothing but the punch.

Therapist. The kind of people that we are, and the kind of feelings that we have, apply in *all* our relationships.

The who and how of authority. Probably for parents, one of the most urgent questions brought to a class is a variant on, 'How can I get my child to obey me?' 'How can I set the limits I'm supposed to set?' Ready made answers to such questions would be particularly futile, since discipline comes directly from the kind of person a parent is. Lectures as well as any reading he has previously done have given him all the facts.

Questions, as we have seen, ostensibly seeking for more facts, may cover a search for a new quality in the parent-child relationship. Who the parent is, and his way of relating, will determine the kind of authority figure he is and what kind of controls the child internalises. These inner controls will become manifest in adolescence. Who the parent is will determine his child's accompanying attitudes towards authority, and the kind of authority figure a child, in his turn, becomes. A group leader's acknowledgment of questions about obedience, then, responds to the way the parent sees, here and now, to the present core of perceptions from which the real question springs. (See Figure 1, page 53.) A group meeting may be characterised by attempts of group members to answer questions by direct advice. In the process, they learn for themselves the limitations of advice.

Mrs Roberts speaks for those parents who do not know how to control a child, and discover that the reason is that they are not really clear about what they want to control. Her feelings about control itself, seem to be ambivalent. Her child is handicapped by hearing loss.

Mrs Roberts. Rickie keeps going on the street. He won't stay on the sidewalk. He seems to get through and over everything. And I don't seem to have any confidence about stopping him. I just don't know what to do. How do I go about setting limits? Where do you begin?

Therapist. Mrs Roberts has told us two things: first she says she can't trust herself, and second, she wonders what she ought to be doing about it. But she really doesn't know what direction she's going.

Mrs Roberts. That's right.

Therapist. She isn't clear in her own mind.

Mrs Roberts. I know I don't want to upset the neighbours.

Therapist. That's important to you.

Class members contribute. 'You're worrying too much,' 'Neighbours are very understanding,' 'You do have to watch a child, it's normal for him to go out of bounds if you don't keep an eye on him.'

Mrs Roberts. Rickie doesn't seem to be any different from other children—my brother's for example. They all seem to do the same things.

Therapist. It's not because he's handicapped.

Mrs Roberts. No.

Therapist. He's a child in spite of his handicap.

A class member again contributes, 'Is she afraid she'll warp her child's personality by setting some limits?'

Therapist. (Listening to the speaker.) That means something to you?

Mrs Roberts. I'm just not sure. I'm concerned about the effect on him of whatever stand I take.

Therapist. You *are* worrying about what you are doing to your child.

The parents offer more suggestions: 'We have to teach them control to the point where the control becomes theirs. And it's the manner in which the control is taught.' 'Show them, make it definite. If we want to cross the road, we stand on the sidewalks and we look,' 'I explain exactly where he can go and where he may not,' 'When I felt it was very important, then he learned.'

Therapist. (Responding to the cue of the last remark.) That is you were very sure in your mind what you wanted, weren't you?
A group member. With a harness, he knows.
Therapist. When you were clear, you could operate on this.
Mrs Roberts. I have a harness, but I'm fighting the use of it.
Therapist. You're saying again, 'I'm fighting against control of my child. Somewhere I am not clear about it.'

Not confirming dependency. Members of the group continue to ask questions and make suggestions about controlling children: 'I just go out and stand on the sidewalk and show him how to keep off the street.' 'Do feelings about controlling the child have anything to do with being able to do so?' 'We want to know how we can manage them, not only down the street, but on the playground when they want to ride someone else's bicycle. And when we are not there to oversee.' 'How do you go about answering these questions?'

Therapist. (Restating.) 'How can I reach a decision about what I want to do?' 'How do I become adequate to answer this?' We're trying to give you a chance to become the kind of person who'll answer the questions yourself. I know it won't help Mrs Roberts to hold her in that position of dependency, though I do recognise, on one level, she's asking for it.
Mrs Roberts. I've found out you don't answer questions. (Laughter in the group.)
Therapist. I'll stay with you until you can work it out yourself.
Mrs Roberts. I think I'll think about it.

Others voice problems about control and the therapist responds to the underlying feeling, the individual perception in each person's statement.

Mrs Phillips. How do you get that control and stop a child getting control?
Therapist. You're concerned with that very problem aren't you? We want to keep control.

Mrs Phillips. How can I get to be the sort of person who can keep control? My son gets me so mad that I give him a sock, to get it out of me.

Therapist. That's an honest statement. When *he* gets control *I* get upset about it.

Mrs Phillips. Then it's worse.

Therapist. It's a threatening situation then.

Mrs Phillips. I don't know where you go from there. Probably the main thing that's wrong with it is that I don't feel confident in the way I'm handling it.

Therapist. In other words, you don't feel safe in the control that you've assumed, prior to its breaking down.

Mrs James. Lots of times I've been on the verge; I don't feel at all in control. I feel, who's going to win? And I'm hanging on by the hair of my teeth, and I just manage somehow to hang on longer than she does, keep control. If I don't lose my temper, if I can just outdo her one second. And sometimes she can last longer than I can. But most of the time I don't feel in control, I'm just hanging on, suppressing violence long enough.

Therapist. It's not the deep quiet kind.

Mrs James. Sometimes I feel easy about it and it comes.

Therapist. When you're at ease, you don't have to exert control, do you?

Mrs James. No, I can manage without having to.

Therapist. Then you really are in control, aren't you?

Mrs Franks. I can't control mine at all. (Laughter.) I've been told that by my husband.

Therapist. You're saying, evidently my control is nowhere near what Mrs James' is. Evidently you can't even hang on.

Mrs Franks. I make up my mind to get the children to do exactly as I wish, but it breaks down somehow. How do I get control?

Therapist. I think you've said it when you say 'I make up my mind, I determine.' The '*good resolution*' doesn't do it, because we haven't come to terms with what it was in us that led to breakdown before the resolution. And we may set up goals that always cause our efforts to break down.

'Accept the fact.' In a later meeting Mrs James told of the beginning of a new found experience.

Mrs James. I told my husband, 'Accept the fact that Jimmie wants to stay up, but it's the time for bed'. And he said, 'I know you want to stay up, Jimmie, but it's late, time for you to sleep.' I don't know what he did, but Jimmie stayed in bed. It does work. It sure does work. We were eating dinner and Joan had a fit; she was crying about something. I wanted to see if Jim could accept it, like I've been trying to do.

Therapist. 'I have learned that what I have to do is accept.'

Mrs James. He said, 'Joan, I know that you want to play with your colours, but it's time for eating and so come on.' And so Joan came O.K. And I told my cousin, 'Accept the fact that they want to do it and they seem to be all right.' So instead of, 'Mummie, I want to go in the bathing pool' and 'No, you can't, so shut up', it's 'Bennie, I know you'd like to go in the bathing pool, but you have your bath now.'

Therapist. One of the first things you do when you begin to feel your way into this thing, is to reinforce your conviction by trying to make everybody else do the same.

In their shoes. But acceptance of children is more than a verbal device.

Mrs Phillips halfway through the course says she is finding a new kind of way to discipline her son, which is not 'punishing him to get my mad out'.

Mrs Phillips. I've been putting myself in Ronnie's place. Yesterday he went away, I mean away, clear down some place. I had to go and take the car and go and look for him. We were frantic. We finally found out that he was down by some oil well under the hill. So we were frantic about it. We said he should stay in the house for the rest of the day. Well, he came up to me, so I put my arm around him and said, 'I know you wanted to go over to that oil well, but you know that you're not supposed to go out of calling distance.' He said, 'I know where I'm supposed to go, but I wanted to go with Jack.' And from then on things were better. He didn't feel too good about staying in the house all day, I know he didn't.

Therapist. 'I know where I'm supposed to go.' So do *you* as parents, but you don't always do it, do you?

Mrs Phillips. But I think because I said that to him he was able to accept the . . . the

Therapist. The prohibition, the restriction.

Mrs Phillips. The restriction of staying in the house. We didn't have a scene and this crying, screaming, yelling, 'You're horrible people.'

Therapist. The whole mood was different.

Mrs Phillips. Yes it was.

Instead of scolding her for being the way she was. Mrs Wills, like her husband, found the demands and interruptions of her children jangling. One day, in the last week but one of the course, she speaks of some changes here.

> *Mrs Wills.* Things are much better. Can I keep the clues, or shall I slip back to my old nervous self when this is over? Problems disappear when you are able to enter into the child's world. I'm handling Jim's (five-year-old deaf child) interruptions at meal time much better. If you really listen to him and let him know you've understood, he stops. Before it was 'Keep still, Jim, keep quiet. Your mother's talking.' Now we show him he has his turn, we listen to him, and then he's able to wait without interrupting. And Carol (three-year-old physically normal) who has been so demanding, and really whimpering constantly, I think she has felt neglected because of our attention to Jim. Instead of scolding her for being the way she was, we loved her. And she stopped.

HOSTILE PARENTS

Used to relying on authority and 'getting the facts' from an external source, parents may express impatience for an answer. 'The method' of trusting them to work out their own answers makes little sense to them. They have heard, 'The hostile child needs understanding, and not attack, he is looking for acceptance of his needs, but fears rejection.' They have heard, 'Make a child secure emotionally, and he will learn.' The leader's response to hostility of parents exemplifies the concepts: 'I don't want to hurry you beyond your capacity to learn', and 'Hostility needs understanding'.

'Why don't you tell us the answer?' Mr Metcalf speaks for those who are annoyed by what he sees as the authority's 'refusal to answer questions'. He himself is an educator and asks many questions. He does not see why the therapist does not answer Mrs Roberts' question about how to stop her child going on the street. This is the fifth class meeting.

Mr Metcalf. This is a simple problem, how to keep children from running in the street. But everyone may have a different solution, and no one knows which is right. An answer may be urgent. Are you going to let us work it out and risk losing the child? We need an assurance that we are going to arrive at a good solution to this. Is it possible that many of us will arrive at a worse one? Is it better to have people work it out for themselves, at the expense of going the wrong way?

Therapist. (Uncritically receiving the way Mr Metcalf sees it and responding dispassionately to his perception.) I think you've said two things there. And one is that this is a simple problem. And then you begin to doubt that maybe I shouldn't let you take a trial and error approach.

Mr Metcalf. We all might arrive at a different solution to this.

Therapist. I think what you're saying is this: 'Can we take the risk of trusting your answer?' You're challenging me. Do I trust parents?

Mr Metcalf. In this age, highways have many dangers.

Therapist. (Recognising reality.) Some of us live on highways.

Mr Metcalf. I don't trust myself.

Therapist. I think what you're saying now is, 'I don't trust my solutions.'

Mr Metcalf. But an answer may be necessary, and I question the method in these circumstances.

Therapist. You would sooner have an authority give you an answer than risk trusting your own.

A group member. (Stating the purpose of the class as she sees it.) But we do have other problems. I mean a handicapped child, and other problems to handle, and this business of keeping a child on the sidewalk is just one of them. And, as you were saying, answering one of them won't give the answers for all time.

Mr Metcalf. I'm asking the question: When decisions are arrived at in this manner, are they valid decisions?

Therapist. Do I mean what I say? Do I trust you? We're all here as people who are of sound mind. If any of us were not, we'd be taken in care and our children protected until we came out of it and could work on it ourselves again. But as a person of sound mind, I think you can deal with the problem and I think you can deal with it yourself.

A group member. (Admitting 'You have to learn to trust your decision.') You can be frightened of your own decision, but still be willing to risk it. The swing sets, for instance, we stood out there and gasped when we first got them. And there hasn't yet been an accident on our swings. But the first day I was ready to take the whole thing down. I couldn't stand to be frightened that may times. But I had already decided that for the other values involved, they must have the equipment.

Mr Metcalf. At what level of problem, what class of problem, does it become necessary to step in? Shall I let my boy play with nitric acid? The next thing, shall I let him play with knives?

Therapist. (Affirming necessity for parent responsibility, as well as affirming the purpose of the class.) I wouldn't have them too sharp though. (Laughter.) I am concerned that your children survive.

Therapist. (Continuing.) I'm concerned with the attitudes of parents rather than with the problem of going on the street. I'm concerned that Mrs Roberts should grow. This question is using the street as an excuse to cover something deeper. And that is why it is so much more precious to work on a deeper level, than to answer a simple problem, because I won't be there tomorrow to answer your problem. My concern is that you are going to help a child grow up because it's safe psychologically to do so.

In the tenth meeting Mr Metcalf speaks again. He's been looking for answers from authority by reading.

Mr Metcalf. I've been reading about therapy, and I can see the therapist here on every page, but I still don't know what it's all about.

In the eleventh meeting he is still trying to reconcile this new approach with familiar academic intellectualised methods.

Mr Metcalf. Class discussion doesn't point to any dichotomy between intellect and emotion. And it looks as though if you resolve emotional conflict you can free the intellect for maximum use.

In the thirteenth meeting he is no longer questioning the method, but he tends to pose questions in the abstract, rather than directly to express the way he feels.

Mr Metcalf. I'm concerned about people having the image match reality in terms of goals, and not strive for something unrealistically high. Shall a person change his image or shall he be satisfied with a reduced reality?

Therapist. You're saying, 'When I begin to look at it, there's something rather painful in this high goal.' You're affirming in your own experience what we know—we think of goals as unattainably high when we think of ourselves as very low. And put in another way you're asking, 'What am I going to do to change myself as a person, so that I don't think of myself as that way?' I am concerned how you feel about yourselves.

In the sixteenth meeting he says he has a little more idea of what the goal of the class is.

Mr Metcalf. I'm still using words and looking at myself academically. But I want a *frame of mind* where I don't have to use words. It's a *frame of mind* we're after, to go the whole way.

In subsequent meetings he expresses feelings from his present 'frame of mind'. In the eighteenth meeting, for example, which is the next to the last, he expresses some angers.

Mr Metcalf. My son was sick at the weekend and we wanted a doctor. When we phoned we were told that the doctor did not make house calls. We explained our situation and the doctor came. But I'm disgusted at the price he charged. There's nothing you can do. You're powerless. I feel completely let down and cheated by this authority I had to rely on.

Therapist. Taken when you're helpless.

Mr Metcalf. Yes. And I have some other irritations, too, that I'd like to express. I resent my mother's criticism, and then when I find my wife joins my mother to criticise me, it really makes me mad.

In the final meeting of the class he says that he and his wife have had the first real talk of their lives and found for the first time a sense of real understanding. (They attend the class together.)

Six months later he wrote:

'Originally I felt pretty cool toward this idea. I considered it as overemphasising little insignificant problems. I though it emotionalism. I still admit to not having made complete use of it, mainly I believe because of (1) ignorance of what it was and is all about, and (2) the reluctance to break down the curtain of resistance built up over the years.'

'I am not quite able to let my hair down *completely*, but farther than I thought. Still have a few (ha) problems not solved, even though I've expressed them. I think the method is *terrific*, if handled by a trained person who really believes and lives it.'

'P.S. Should Mrs Roberts put a halter on her boy?? Puleez!!! Ha.'

His wife wrote:

'Suddenly it seemed as though the course would end with me in a turmoil. However, after a wonderful discussion with my husband —and, by the way, I did not think his understanding was possible to acquire here—I already felt much better and can see that this system has definite merits. I might add that it would not have been easy for me to come this far (and I know I've only begun), had my husband not been in class with me throughout.'

Anger in the open. In all the therapeutic work, the therapist can expect to meet open hostility, but it may take a little time for a person to feel free enough, or secure enough to express hostility openly. Mrs Green, we remember, never felt satisfied no matter what she had, and we would expect these feelings to come up in the class, too. She seemed to find positive gains early, but 'the hostile child' in her needed expression. In the sixth meeting she is able to be openly angry at the therapist.

Mrs Green. I've had my fill of indefinite answers. I can't get anything from a bit of paper, and I can't help in something I don't know beans or pea-knuckles about.

In fact she has been currently observing, week by week, a teacher of the deaf with another deaf child. The next day she says she thinks she can learn. In the next group meeting, she speaks of progress in a sense of freedom.

Mrs Green. For the first time in my life I spent one and a half hours with Tim—when he asked. And other people leave their dishes. Why not me?

At the end of the course she talked to a teacher of the deaf whose work she had observed, and the teacher said she was a different person from the first occasion, when she seemed extremely disturbed and un-co-operative. 'It was a pleasure to talk to her', said the teacher.

Mrs Kelly has discovered feelings of resentment to all her three children. 'I envy them their play and clamp down on their enjoyment because I wasn't allowed to play as a child.' But she is angry one day because she finds the process of self-examination is disrupting.

> *Mrs Kelly*. (Looks at the therapist. Pause.) I hate you. (Pause.) You've taken away my alibis. I can't even get mad at the kids. But I'm going through one hell of an irritation with my husband. Why can't you leave well alone?
>
> *Therapist*. You're finding this taking yourself out of the cupboard upsetting, and it seems to be my fault.
>
> *Mrs Kelly*. It's better to blow up at you than to take it out on them at home.

At the last meeting (interview) she spoke of a changed climate at home. 'I'm not picking on my husband or the children the way I used to. My goals are more realistic and so I feel more successful.'

> *Mrs Kelly*. You have given four children a new mother. That is more true than you can ever know. And I'm happy to admit I want to play with them now, and I don't feel guilty about it. Thank you.

There are times when increased freedom to express hostile feeling comes as a surprise. But when the feeling is out in the open, it seems less of a problem, less of a threat, and positive relationships follow a reduction of the feeling of being on guard, of 'nervousness'. Mrs Wills came to a parent meeting towards the end of the course, and said they had got some feelings in the open, in their house.

> *Mrs Wills*. We got mad the other day and it wasn't the tense atmosphere we've had at such times before. I thought my husband should do more, and he talked again about women's work. So I got mad. Yes. I said, 'I hate you'. So he said, 'I hate you, too'. It was hard to take. But we did. We hated each other at that moment. And I banged my first door. I was never allowed to show any strong feeling to my mother. It was all such a relief afterwards. We seem so much more relaxed. I don't need to bang a door now. It doesn't seem important.
>
> *Therapist*. That is, now you're not on guard as much against these frightening angry feelings, they don't seem to present as great a problem.

Mr Wills. I might even get to work with Jim's speech now I've blown up a bit with my wife. It's less jangling to have somebody to talk to honestly.

LEARNING TO LISTEN

In the parent education class, people are learning to listen to other people with increasing sensitivity to their meanings. Impatience like Mr Metcalf's with 'little problems' or 'irrelevant problems', give way to awareness of the importance to individual people of their particular way of seeing the ordinary things in their environment, their particular personal synonyms.

As we have seen, when an individual person brings up questions which are important to him, others find similar questions and attitudes in themselves, they find they are not alone, and begin to work on their own solutions and respond more accurately to the underlying feelings of other people. There are times, however, when a need in one member does not have this kind of general application in the group. Then hostility of the group can become a learning experience in listening. The group is not able, for example, to hear Mrs Brown when she expresses her unpopular view.

Mrs Brown. (Appears tense and anxious.) I've been speaking to someone who says it's possible to control the negative emotions. You just stand back and take what life gives you without the negative emotions upsetting you. It's a beautiful thought, I think. Of course it takes time. He's hated and been angry. But you don't let the person know. You cover it up. And you do that long enough and after a while you don't feel that way.

A number of people gasp audibly. Remarks follow quickly. 'Is he married?' 'Does he have a mother-in-law, by any chance?' 'I have a strong feeling that he is handling his feelings by denying them.' 'We don't know what our problems are.' 'I didn't know I had these feelings.' 'I just don't believe this man is doing what he says.'

Mrs Brown. He frankly admitted he used to hate and all these things. The next time he wouldn't be so acute. He wouldn't be quite as angry the next time.

Therapist. Can you see what's happening here? You're all so concerned with disagreeing with a viewpoint, with the man who says he's got rid of his negative feelings, that you're not hearing Mrs

Brown. You're listening to the subject, not to her need. Let's accept her where she is. He's giving her an opportunity of considering control. She's mulling it over. And that's what she wants to do. Some of the rest of you don't. But let's let her have her way. (To Mrs Brown.) The possibility of repressing hate and so forth is very important to you.

Some members still want to object to the man. 'I think that he sounds as if he's being very noble and godly' (one mother speaks vehemently and ironically). 'He's certainly setting himself up as above the rest of human beings,' 'I simply don't believe him.'

Therapist. (Pointing to the possibility of listening to inner meanings, whatever the external subject.) Let's listen to her, to what she's saying to us. You see you're not hearing her. She's saying, 'I'd like to get rid of the turmoil that strong feelings make.' She's considering the possibility of repressing the negative emotions as a way to handling feelings. She needs the opportunity to think about and evaluate this possibility.

So, again the class reiterates the most important necessity for growth: We start where people are.

At the other extreme, every person in one parent group feels he is with Mrs Carter, when she expresses the feelings produced in her by the discovery that her child was handicapped. (They said later they tuned in to her tumultuous feelings, to her not wanting to talk to people, and wives recognised feelings of resentment, because a husband leaves it 'all to me'.)

Mrs Carter. I can't stand my child screaming. He's got me right under his finger when he screams.

Therapist. He's learned that he can control you that way.

Mrs Carter. Well I nearly lost my mind when I learned he was deaf. I wouldn't talk to anyone. And I'd look at Tony and think 'I've never been as awful as this. Just ugly.' My husband showed nothing, but I just fell apart. I wanted him to say Momma and he could only make those awful screams. I kept crying. I couldn't help myself. Then I visited a school for the deaf, and something inside me came out, and I stopped crying. The doctor told me to go, and he told me to come to this course. I'd never seen any deaf children. I'd thought *dumb* and deaf. But the children were playing and saying words. One little girl was very attractive and she kept calling me and saying 'Ball'. I wanted the teacher to explain they were deaf, and how they learned.

Therapist. You needed help.

Mrs Carter. I couldn't teach him. People would say, 'Why don't you?' I can't. (Cries).

Therapist. (Simply accepting.) You can only do what you can do.

Mrs Carter. Yes. My husband won't help. He says I want to be babied. He won't listen that I've had a hard day.

Therapist. You have felt that you have had neither understanding nor help.

Mrs Carter. You can't leave everything to one.

Therapist. You have felt very much alone.

BACK TO THE SAME PLACE

The parents who came for help with their children explored, and made discoveries for themselves. A mother speaks for many when she says her most stirring experiences in her group were

> When I found that many of my feelings were not unique to me—*I was not alone*.
>
> When I believed that here was a person who accepted me right where I was—*without regard to good or bad*.
>
> When I found that the rest of my unhappiness was the search for acceptance—*and what to do about it*.

But their situation had not changed. They went back to the home and neighbourhood and the work they had left.

What did they feel about their experience together when they went their ways?

5 *New Eyes for Old Scenes*

They have happened to deposit a grain of strength in my mind.

E. M. Forster

The purpose of the parents' meetings was to offer a learning situation which could make a difference in people's lives. What seemed to be the long term values? Over a period of time the same kinds of pattern tended to emerge.

The experience of the class had meant bringing feelings into the open. Expressing feelings and listening to others' expressions of feeling decreased the individual's sense of isolation and made him aware of the similarities between his problems and those of the other group members. This process of participation tends to reduce tension in people quickly; student and work groups or groups with residential problems have resolved acute relationship difficulties this way. Apart from the immediate decrease of acute stress, the parent education groups also help to change attitudes in a lasting way.

NOT A QUESTION OF BLAME

An uncritical reception of all a group participants said (including statements which were negative to the methods of the class) seemed to make it possible for parents to change their own initial perception of themselves and others.

First, they tended to blame others less. Six months to a year later parents wrote of continuing differences in the way they handled their children: 'I don't take my anger out on the children as much', 'I can channel my feelings elsewhere and not blow up when dealing with the children's expression of feeling', 'I can correct the children more easily without anger'. Secondly it was not a question of blaming themselves either but of taking responsibility in an expanded way that seemed to be freeing rather than restricting. 'If I have been angry I don't feel so guilty and I don't feel as bad afterwards. I seem more able to sit down afterwards and evaluate the position objectively if there's been anger or upset.'

The question 'What is it if a situation upsets me?' became a frequent route to problem solving and improving interpersonal relations. Mrs Johnson said she had twenty-four hours of mental torture during the course before she realised how much she hated herself and others. Talking about her hatred of herself was an important stage in feeling better about others. She wrote in the second half of the following year that she never used to read feelings into her behaviour.

> 'Now (not all of the time but most of the time) when I am behaving badly I can soon find at its root a feeling of bitterness or hate.'
>
> 'When I am behaving in a mature manner, I find that it isn't because the situation is pleasant but because, somehow, at that moment I have a feeling of confidence or self-importance, acceptance which gives me peace of mind.'

She spoke of many other changes in her way of life. Her relationship to her children was part of a bigger change, not only of liking others but being able to accept affection.

> 'My relationship to everything has changed.'
>
> 'I did not really like people but now I find I truly am *interested* in them and I feel now that quite a few people like me. I can now make the first friendly overture towards other persons.'
>
> 'I have recently resumed a career which I left six years ago. During those years I believed I *hated* social work. I now have confidence in my ability to be a good social worker and, so far, have found it surprisingly easy to do and I have enjoyed the work.'

She had used housework as a self-punishment, restricting and depriving herself and her children:

> 'Lately I have left house and housework to (a) take my children and the neighbour's children skating, (b) play some special games with the children, (c) go and visit my neighbours.'

This mother's marriage had broken up before the parent group started and there was no possibility of reconstructing the husband-wife relationship. However she felt she was adjusting to the necessity of her situation and was 'making a home and carrying the responsibilities of bringing up two children with greatly reduced tension'. Also she had 'found many resources and satisfactions outside the home' from which she had been barred before by isolation and her hostility to herself and others.

First, then, parents were aware of a lessening of the blaming mechanism both of others and themselves. Secondly they were increasingly aware of the sources of their anger, and thirdly they acquired a greater ability to see the other person's point of view. This provided new and continuing dimensions in the parent-child relationship. One mother had always thought that her own education in the traditional sense would give her the capacity to train her child so that he 'would be socially acceptable'. She later wrote that she could now see that her new ability to put herself into his shoes and be with him was helping him to feel normal and accepted.

AVAILABILITY AND LIMITS

Both during and after the classes parents found they were able to put themselves in their children's shoes and understand their children's needs; they were also able to set realistic limits for the children.

Something to worry about. Mrs Kay was startled by the idea that a parent's availability to and acceptance of a child will decrease his demanding behaviour. Her daughter was slow in developing what the books said were the 'normal responses'. The mother spoke of her experience of expressing her feelings in the class and finding the therapist did not deny her right to feel as she did.

> 'I was worried to death and kept going to the book and seeing many of the baby's responses were abnormal. Then in the class I talked about my worries. I was sure my child was mentally retarded. But everyone said to me "You're looking for something to worry about." But the therapist said, "Well you have something to worry about." And that was the first person who accepted my feelings. Then my husband accepted them.
>
> 'Then I began to relax and I could see some other meanings in Jane's behaviour and not just abnormal responses. The baby rocked a lot and I would learn to understand for the first time why she was rocking in pain. She needed security in her surroundings. Then I became able to hold her when she screamed to be held. I'd heard in the class, "If the child is secure enough he'll get down from your knee". Then I felt more comfortable and the baby seemed to relax too. Then she volunteered to get down. The words in the class stayed with me. "When you are really comfortable and enjoying every minute, she'll get down." The next thing was

that she was less fearful of other people and instead of screaming when anyone came to the house, she'd play games with them.'

'You must share.' 'He has to be selfish before he can be generous' 'hit home' for Mrs Nichols.

'Our older children were six and seven when we first came to the class, and to this day they have difficulties in sharing because when we were beginning to bring them up, we demanded "Why you just share. I don't care what you feel like, you must share." And now with our younger children we've reached the point where we feel you have to have and hang on to before you can give, and they are ahead of the older children. The only thing I keep hoping and desiring is that we can give those two older ones enough so that they can get there too.'

Temper tantrums also meant a great deal to Mrs Nichols. She was a college graduate and had 'done the courses in psychology and child development'.

'I'm able to take a view of my children's behaviour which, although I knew intellectually from college, I certainly have never felt until I got on the level of feelings myself. I'm able to accept the fact that my daughter says she hates me, and know that she means that she doesn't like what I'm doing. I let her say it without being angry. I'm able to let my youngster have a tantrum because I could not accept it when he was two. Although I know he's really beyond it chronologically, he still has to be there emotionally. I don't think that I would have reached that point without the class.'

A fear. For Mrs Fitzgerald children's fears seemed easier to handle after the class. She wrote six months later:

'We have had one major round with a fear since the class—normally we have few problems in this line. This current one I believe we handled much better than we would have done before the class. The toilet started to act up and made a horrible noise which scared Teddie. Unfortunately he had just gone to the toilet and had climbed into the bath tub for his bath when it happened. He was extremely frightened and he shot out of the bathroom and kept talking about the toilet being broken. I didn't think much of it until I heard him talking to himself about the broken toilet—over a period of days we saw the reaction. Teddie would not sit on the toilet and would not take a bath and while talking about the broken toilet imitated the noise. We decided that we had to let Teddie know that *we* knew how he felt and we started out with Teddie and his father taking the toilet apart and repairing it. When the opportunity arose we talked about the noise the toilet had made and agreed with Teddie that he didn't like it. Needless to say toilet training broke down and we had an accident a day for about a month. We never commented on it, but slowly lured Teddie to the other bathroom and gave him a sponge bath. Eventually he could laugh about the funny noises that the toilet made and *on his own* went back to using the bathroom. I think this more than anything else made me recognise the need of recognising one's child's feelings and making him realise that we understood.'

Less time. 'A wonderful sense of warmth and acceptance' were Mrs Hallam's words about an initial interview. Later, of her parent education class she said:

'For the first time in my life I was in contact with something that made sense—and I felt understood. This it seems to me is what made it possible for me to relax enough to use the knowledge in the class. In one meeting the therapist spoke of delinquent boys who, in a therapeutic situation were allowed to regress and behave like babies and were accepted in their infantile behaviour. This made such sense that I decided to be twenty-four hours available to the handicapped child. He relaxed in my arms ten times in two weeks. Before this he wouldn't be touched. When the next baby was born I was able to give him acceptance from the beginning and he was a different baby from the other two, and *he required much less time*. Before the class I wanted my children to grow up and be off my hands. Now I can allow them their childishness and enjoy it. I don't have to push them into a false appearance of independence. Before, I could not accept their limitations which are normal and natural. I can watch them grow into maturity rather than watch them grow to an outside appearance of maturity.

Limits. Parents repeatedly write that limits become easier and the child more manageable as they find they are more able to see with the child's eyes. 'I set fewer but effective limits since I got to be more secure in myself and stopped insisting on perfectionist standards in which I was always the loser.' 'Children respond to trust and a discipline the parent is sure of.' 'Setting limits was an expression I did not know before the course, but learning to set them has given me confidence and better co-operation from my children.'

Parents could find information frightening at first but they felt that talking in the group was a valuable resource and they could ask for an individual interview if the group meetings did not include regularly scheduled ones.

> 'I was frightened out of my wits when I heard that children feel what you feel. The class had touched me on a level of feeling when I meant to hide my feelings. I sought an interview immediately.' 'In the class I heard you could both hate and love someone and I had never accepted an idea like that. But that's the way I felt about Allen. I love him because he's my baby and he needs my help. But I hate him because he takes all our money, and too much attention. I can't stand his being deaf and I don't know how to help him. In an interview I said how I felt and the therapist said I was trying to be the perfect mother and that I did hate him.' I cried. It was such a relief, just to admit it. I have learned that it wasn't just Allen that put me in a desperate situation—Allen was the precipitating factor. The therapist accepts your viewpoints, doesn't tell you what's wrong, lets you participate and express an idea, agreement or disagreement. The handicapped child likes to cook and I wanted him out of the way. I was told to "Give him something to play with, a bit of dough, for example." But when I gave him a bit of dough he wanted to stir the bowl. I gave him some money to go and buy something and finished my cooking while he was gone. The therapist didn't tell me I'd done wrong, but I came to see that the child would accept limits if I was clear in my mind and if I found a good half-way point. Now I let him stir or pour if I'm in a hurry and he's content. If I have the time and the patience I let him do as much as he can. He's now reached the point where he can make biscuits.'

NEIGHBOURS AND OTHERS

Parents wrote to say they had experienced changes in the quality of their relationships with neighbours as well as with their family. There seemed less readiness to take offence as parents had less need for reassurance of their acceptance through others. 'There is more comfort in neighbourhood relations, less hurt feelings.' 'What is it *in me* that I react so strongly?' again applies if there is difficulty.

'One woman bothered me in the past and for the most part I have avoided her but this is not always possible, so I decided to work out my feelings and try to understand why she seemed to bring out the worst in me. She seemed able to throw me completely off balance. I didn't dislike her as a person, but disliked the feeling of inadequacy she made me have. Slowly I discovered that I had reached a point where it was no longer important to have her acceptance. I had confidence in myself and she no longer threatened my security.'

One of the fathers wrote that life at work was easier as well as at home: 'Understanding that strong feelings exist in all of us has made the handling of problems much easier at work.' He was a high school administrator.

When others attack. When other people show anger parents report less defensiveness, less need to react angrily and a greater ability to see the other person's point of view. 'Everyone is nicer—even when they aren't, they don't make me as angry with them. I can begin to understand how they might feel.'

The husband-wife relationship benefited.

'He decided that it was a shame he'd married so young. He didn't like having the responsibilities forced upon him (We're expecting another baby on the fourth of July). I have lots of faults and he hated me. I was really angry at the insults, but after he went to work I had a chance to think and put my new self to work finding the right way to look at a problem. He was very surprised at the fact that although I was sorry the honeymoon was over, I was glad to know what he was feeling. He didn't leave. Nobody had to apologise for all the nasty things said. It's wonderful that I can love him and he loves me without always trying to have everything sweetness and light. *He has grown up since I attended the class.*'

Goals and roles. Newly acquired attitudes means accepting that much in relation to human beings could not be resolved quickly. But goals in fact become more attainable because more realistic.

'I find now that I set goals that I can achieve more easily and they in turn are stepping stones towards others. It is much easier to climb the ladder step by step.'

Parents became more able to wait for the realisation of long term goals:

'A greater determination is needed for long term objectives. The classes helped to provide the basis, the confidence and the patience to achieve them.'

A realistic acceptance of the role of housewife could mean more enjoyment outside the home too:

'I'm more content to be a housewife. I've not had any spells of depression for months and I think I am more ready to do the things outside the home which I had been frightened of.'

Mrs Bevan who dealt with her husband's anger in a new way also wrote:

'My sister teases me because she's noticed that I don't complain any more. I'm not concerned enough to join in my friend's complaints that children and housework are terribly boring. I've even been asked for advice. It's never been taken and I'm glad to be able to understand why.'

Teachers. All our work in changing feelings is concerned with attitudes of and attitudes towards authority. Even where childhood rivalries with brothers and sisters *seem* focal, we find the real source of the conflicts lies with parents. Parents learn this by understanding their own children's behaviour and by gaining insight into their own reactions. Mrs Abbot, for example, made a specific discovery about a learning block.

'I discovered how I felt about teachers. In the past seven or eight years I've attended many classes of one type or another and I've always been unhappy with my inability to learn. The real reason escaped me or I wasn't aware of it. I was afraid of teachers and instruction, and this all stemmed from my feelings of fear and hostility towards my father.'

THE HOW OF TRUSTING

The method of the parent education class ('working out our own solutions rather than telling us answers') did not necessarily make immediate sense as we saw with Mr Metcalf's opposition and struggles to understand it. A shift from content oriented classes (information-giving) to process oriented (opportunities for emotional growth) may not make sense until the members' own change in perception makes them realise the validity of this method of dealing with people and of integrating information with their life and experience.

The method meant a radical departure from the educational procedures with which people were familiar. For some this meant an immediate reaction of relief because of the permissive climate of the class. For others it meant immediate frustration—they were impatient for solutions and they disliked an approach which threw the responsibility on them.

In all the parent groups over a period of years about half the parents like the method from the beginning. Those who do not see the value of working out their own solutions consider it a waste of time. They are sceptical of their ability to find their own answers, and angry because the therapist does not answer questions; some participants are bewildered at being put in the position of finding their own solutions.

Later, as they begin to gain from the class, reactions change. 'There is greater freedom in bringing up problems and anticipation of help in hearing others.' 'I hesitate still about speaking but get more out of it than if my questions were answered directly.' 'It leaves us free to work at the level we're at. We can operate better without pressure.' Not all can state clearly whether they liked the method of trusting them rather than answering questions. About thirty per cent say they would have liked more answers and more lectures even when they feel the discussion was profitable. About seventy per cent state a positive liking for the method. They feel it provides a technique they can use at home: 'By understanding my feelings and others' feelings I can cope with everyday problems more easily.' Gains most frequently named are 'Greater understanding of self and children', 'Accepting the handicapped child', 'Enjoying the children more', 'Greater tolerance of people', 'Greater liking of people', 'More relaxed', 'Greater understanding between husband and wife'. Some who still wish they had had more direction and more lectures say they are really expressing impatience with their own slowness and are not really convinced that answers from anybody else can give them what they need.

Numbers in the parent groups from which our records are taken vary from twelve to more than thirty. Whatever the size of the group parents speak of a developing feeling of trust as each person feels he is known to the therapist through initial or other interviews; then in a gradually developing common frame of reference, group members gradually know each other. The number of scheduled meetings varies from twelve to twenty for a shorter course of intensive work in a summer class to more than twenty in a nine-month course between autumn and spring.

Those who seem to benefit least are amongst those who can only attend a small proportion of the meetings. Such are some of the fathers who may have been able to attend only two or three meetings. They do not have the time to reach the understanding of the class that Mr Metcalf or Mr Cullen did. Two fathers who had not yet made sense of the group meetings wrote of their reactions. Both had an above average education and were accustomed to ordered and objective solutions to problems. One wrote:

> 'My experience with the class was not too favourable—especially the help given to parents. It was negative to that given by X Hospital. The procedures solved nothing. During my visit to the class of parents I found no evidence of any objective purpose. Observations were made with the background of classroom teacher, secondary critic, teacher, school principal, and superintendent of public schools.'

The second father who expressed negative reactions to the class had a strong background in academic psychology. He was knowledgeable about the dynamics of parent-child relationships and personality development. He had difficulty getting beyond the intellectual approach and felt he was beyond the class.

> 'From the purely psychological angle, I probably had less to gain than most of the others, for several reasons. To begin with, I had been exposed rather thoroughly to psychological problems at university through my degree work in psychology and pre-medical work. As a result I think that the processes of self-analysis and behaviour analysis of both the normal and abnormal child were more familiar to me than many in the class. I admit that I was partly amused by some phases of the lectures I attended. Some of this was because of the shock to the mother that perhaps it was she, not the child, who needed help.'

He saw the method as an invitation to unchecked confusion.

> 'I must confess I was amused by the "method" of not answering questions, of letting the mother express and work out her own

confusion. I recall a chemistry professor who said that self-education of this sort is excellent but often costly. He compared it to disregarding information in books and obtaining information by direct experience.'

'As a scientist engaged in highly technical research, I would frown on any method which ignored information gained by years of experimentation by my predecessors.'

'The role of teachers in education is to aid and help and not merely allow confusion to run riot. A very vivid experience I had at college points this out. A student in one of the psychology classes came from a family where father and mother were in conflict. Under the pressure of the course the student concluded that he was not completely normal and subsequently committed suicide. How much better had the educator attempted to solve the problem rationally rather than drive him to the extreme mentioned.'

'To return to the subject—Trust? Or answer questions? A little of both, depending on the individual problem, but let the group instruction serve only to introduce the general problem and method of analysis.'

But his interest in the class was aroused:

'To conclude, however, I'd like to say if the opportunity presented itself, I would gladly attend as many of such classes as I could. Whether I agree with all that is said or not, it was definitely stimulating, and when this is present in any form of teaching, we must consider the class worthwhile.'

A student in the class who also had a higher degree in the social sciences had heard this father's comments and commented on them.

'Although this man was knowledgeable and well educated by every traditional standard—and in psychology too, his emphasis on "rational" handling of emotional problems in the disturbed parent or student shows that his courses in abnormal psychology had not taught him that severe emotional stress cannot be resolved by reason. He had not been able to see for all his knowledge that the therapeutic approach in the parent class had just the aim he asked for—to help students integrate psychological knowledge and to resolve tensions so that problems *could* be dealt with rationally. He saw the mother's devastation from an external and diagnostic frame of reference. He had not learned the difference between the intellectual knowledge of personality dynamics and the emotional empathy with a human being's shock and anxiety; the patient sensitive route away from patterns of self-hate and guilt if a mother is to be able to love her child for himself without the burdens of her anxieties weighing down his growth. Of course she knew in her mind, intellectually, she was failing. The therapist did present the problem and method of analysis and then exemplified wonderfully and consistently what it was in practice.

'As for myself, attitudes have been completely different since the class. First of all there was a climate of acceptance in which you didn't have to put on a show. There was always an implied invitation to be yourself. I have found it impossible to judge or condemn others because I don't like their attitudes which they need and which they acquired from experience. That doesn't mean I don't ever get angry but I take it out on others less. I am impressed by the amount of "scapegoating" that takes place amongst educated people who give lip service to principles of respect for the individual. The class made me infinitely more compassionate. I can see the fear and hurt in the hostile child or adult now and not react with hostility. This is about the only meaning of turning the other cheek that makes any sense. It's a very mature idea and so is the idea of forgiveness—which you can't help if you understand. There was something else in the class too which I shall never forget. *I* knew all the answers. I'd read the books, I had the degrees and I wanted to jump in with the answers and tell all those parents exactly what they were saying, what they meant unconsciously. This sort of interpretation seemed to me to save time.'

'The therapist said "Let them work it out themselves", and I began to realise that with all my education *I knew nothing*. I had to learn to listen to people and feel their meanings, not tell them my superior answers, which were not answers at all for them. I achieved some insight into my own needs for control—the insecurity that made me want to hold the rein. The dominating husband or wife is a very frightened person because he or she is sure of rejection. I felt liked in the class and understood so I'm not so defensive or afraid. I can even allow other people their way without having to be in control all the time myself.'

'I could see that the students in the class resisted the kind of learning that was offered much more than the parents did and I wondered if it was because there is for many in the academic setting a false investment in the intellect. By false I mean that the intellect is used for purposes of status instead of as an instrument that can be a blessing to mankind.'

'They didn't seem able to see that freeing energy from needless emotional conflict could free the intellect for constructive use. This class was a means of reducing alienation and distance between people. But it meant regressing, "becoming as a little child" in order to develop true maturity. I could see the students' own insecurities and fears in their resistance.'

OLD AND NEW WAYS TO EDUCATE PARENTS

Parents stressed the failure of the information course compared with the group where they found help for themselves and where the information, therefore, became directly relevant to their lives. After a three months' class a mother of a mentally retarded girl wrote from home:

'I had an information course, but I needed emotional help to make use of that information.

'I worry less now about the eventual outcome of Anita's problem and it seems to have helped me to be a little more sincerely demonstrative in my affection for her. I am less impatient with all the children and less apt to lose my temper.'

One mother recalled her feelings in another class which was information oriented.

'If you had any question in the other class, the lecturer just tossed off an answer. He was authority on a pedestal. You might be bursting inside, but no attention was paid to *you*. In our class you felt that anything you might say, no matter how small, was worth listening to and you were important.'

Another mother wrote of a subsequent class which she called *Lost Opportunities*.

'The lecturer gave a talk on the developing independence of the child, his need for autonomy and individual accomplishment, as well as his need for dependence and guidance, Then the class was thrown open for discussion. I made some notes of questions. The first came from one of the women, "Is a child's hate really a concealed need for the parent?" '

Some of the group had read the books and a woman commented that we hate *them* (the children) and teach them to hate. A man added that hate concealed fear. Then another woman said that she tried to make her son not need her. Nobody responded to this but a father asked 'What place do friends have in a child's growth and independence?' This question was related to the content of the lecture and the lecturer said 'Let's discuss this'. A discussion moved on to the question of parents as guiding agents. 'Where do we set limits?' asked a father. However, the mother who had said that she tried to make her son not need her seemed to be pre-occupied with her problem and asked why did one need to conceal the need to love? The lecturer, keeping to the content, asked her to leave this until the problem of limits had been settled. The rest of the discussion reinforced the idea that parents' own feelings kept them from setting limits which children need. The mother's personal problem was never discussed and other topics arose in succeeding weeks. The class seemed such a waste—one lost opportunity after another to listen to people. During the intermission parents expressed a mounting sense of guilt and inadequacy.

Our class situation would have provided a means of expression to every one of those questions of the parents. The concept that the way we felt got in the way of setting limits would have been only a beginning. The questions about trust and delinquency which the lecturer ignored seemed to me to be very much part of the question. I wanted to tell her that knowing the child should be more independent is all very well but *trying* to make him be so doesn't bring it about. As long as you're *trying* you haven't the knowhow. You must become that kind of person. The mother's later question, about the need to conceal the need for love made me want to respond to *her* and her obvious anxiety in this area. I remembered my own surprise when I discovered that my dislike of my father concealed a deep need for his love—and it was fear of rejection that made me hide my affection. Many of us in our group found if we needed our children's love and feared rejection, how impossible it was to set limits.

SILENT LANGUAGE

Large numbers of the parents who were members of the parent education groups from which our records are taken, were there because they had a handicapped child and sought professional help; this entailed medical and educational co-operation. Disorders included organic handicaps such as deafness, cerebral palsy, cleft palate, mental retardation, or the inability to learn language because of brain injury. Others came because their physically normal children had developed speech and other learning or behaviour problems. There were also many parents in the classes (from which these reports are taken) who came as students taking professional or elective courses in communication, and child development. In addition they also acquired some self-knowledge.

The central problem of living is one of communication and our central thesis is that communication involves the whole person—not just his spoken words but his 'silent language'. One of the most important dimensions in the work with parents is giving them an opportunity to understand their own 'silent language' and to increase their ability to convey to their children the unspoken confidence and security in relationships which make for adequacy, self-worth and belonging.

The improvement in relationships seemed to come in three steps: First 'I change the way I see myself and others', secondly 'As a result, my behaviour changes', and third 'Other people, including my children, react differently'.

The classes meant, for those who chose to make use of it, the beginning of psychotherapy. From the beginning there was further help available for the very disturbed who needed more than a parents' class could give them, even with an occasional individual interview. Everyone who urgently needed help after the class was able to get it. With the method of listening and accepting people where they are as long as they need to be there, the danger does not appear to exist of pushing any person past the stage he can handle, though deep emotions are touched as people voice their difficulties and face self-understanding for the first time. But many of the parents, although they were functioning normally at work and at home, wanted to go further in changing their attitudes and evaluating their experience in order to understand and improve yet more their relationships with their children and others. So they chose psychotherapy, a journey into self. The kind of experience this choice can entail is the subject of the next chapter.

6 *Self-Chosen Journey Into Self*

and blest are those
Whose blood and judgment are so well commingled
That they are not a pipe for Fortune's finger
To sound what stop she please.

Shakespeare

As we move from a class which provides both information from a lecturer and the opportunity for people to talk to a situation in which people have decided to search for understanding, we encounter both familiar and unfamiliar experiences.

Originally parents came to an authority for advice on how to bring up children. Then they found a relationship for themselves in which there was a deep concern for them as persons. They have now concluded that the best thing they can do for their children is to grow and mature themselves. The means of accomplishing this can be a therapy group, individual interviews or a combination of group and interviews.

The most familiar experience for parents who join a group is the lack of criticism that characterises its emotional climate. However the lack of structure without lectures comes as an unfamiliar surprise for some. For one father such a group was an abrupt transition.

Although parents choose therapy, their understanding what their choice really entails grows with their own exploration of themselves. The discussion of topics in a parent education class may have been of greater help than they consciously realised. Complete responsibility now rests with people to bring up whatever problem in their current lives they want to talk about. Only time can reveal what this means to each individual. The father who said the first night was a shock continued to attend because he asserted, 'I enjoyed it and I got something off my chest.' For him, the cathartic aspect of the class was of greatest help. He could vent his feelings of hostility. Other group members, accepted relatively early that the only relevant questions in therapy spring from experience and individual perception and they develop profound sensitivities to their own and other people's personal symbols; catharsis is followed by insight and personality change.

The first meeting of a parent group indicates patterns and themes likely to emerge and the potential levels of understanding. The group is open, that is one in which some old members leave and new ones enter every year; it meets as a year-long class and husbands and wives attend together.

Least familiar to new members is the use of fantasy and dream symbols to explore experience. Carol, an old member who attends with her husband, speaks first. (The use of first names reflects increased intimacy.)

A PRISONER ON PAROLE

Carol is troubled by a recurrent fantasy.

> *Carol.* I'd like to begin. . . . (Pause.) There's something bothering me. I find myself daydreaming about being a prisoner on parole. I don't know why.

As we listen to responses of parents in the group, different levels of understanding immediately become apparent. Some of the new members especially may respond literally; they may also pass judgment, offer reassurance and advice; intellectual discussion may take the place of self-exploration. Others usually old members, deeper in their own self-explorations may respond to the personal meanings of the symbol.

> *Father.* (New member. Literal and reassuring.) You are not that sort of person, Carol. (Then passing judgment.) Criminals do not deserve pity. They're inherently vicious.
>
> *Mother.* (Old member. Responds to the need in the prisoner symbol which has meaning for her.) My thoughts about prisoners is that they cannot be responsible for themselves and that going to prison is a way of being cared for.
>
> *Mother.* (Old member.) I feel the same way about it.
>
> Then some members object to the remark calling prisoners inherently vicious. 'People aren't born vicious. They become so because of their experience.' 'Prisoners may be unhappy people in need of help if they can accept it.'

At that point an intellectual discussion on heredity and environment follows until a father intervenes.

Father. In all this discussion we've left Carol's problem. What else does she have to say about it?
Carol. It isn't only that I keep thinking of myself as a prisoner on parole. I also daydream that I'm a dope addict trying to break the habit. (Pause.) The only thing I can feel about it is that I'm trying to break out of something and away from something.
Therapist. Break out of something and away from something.
Father. She is an easy-going person and fears she may be pushed into something wrong.

Here we must remember that whoever is speaking reveals his own attitudes which may not necessarily be relevant to the person he is talking about. Now the therapist responds to the father with a question, focusing his personal perception and at the same time suggesting he may be projecting his meaning on to someone else.

Therapist. Are you speaking for *yourself* or her?
Father. I feel that way about myself, so I imagined Carol felt like that.
First mother. (Recognising a common recurring wish to relinquish responsibility and the acompanying feeling of guilt.) Carol daydreams to get away from her present responsibilities and so punishes herself for it by going behind bars.
Second mother. What is dope-taking but a form of escape? Has Carol got more responsibility than she wants, and does she want to get away from it?
Third mother. (Slowly.) Break away from, and out of.
Carol. (Responding with her own dawning association to her fantasy.) It's clear to me now that 'break out' is to 'break out' of my family which is difficult and painful.

Like Lennie who, his mother told us in an early parent group, put himself in the corner when he had done 'anything he'd been told not to' and said, 'I'm bad, Mommie', Carol has wrestled with impulses which frightened her and filled her with a feeling she was 'bad and should be punished'. Her problem was to free herself emotionally from a sexual triangle in her family. Her childhood conflict about her emotional involvement with her father was painful and hard to resolve. She wanted to be close to her father but found herself in competition with her mother for his attention. But she also needed her mother and resented her for conflicting reasons for coldness to herself (Carol), for intimacy with her father and for her lack of pride in herself as a woman. (Her mother has in fact died but child needs for a mother's caring and remorse for bitterness against her persisted.) Meanwhile her father is a recurrent theme as she works on her conflicting feelings for both parents. Her father has now attached himself to her as a source of emotional satisfaction. She realises his needs and has used them as a reason for trying to be everything to him. But her crucial question is: 'Am I going to be able to renounce my father as a boy-friend, and deal with my guilt for my inadequacy in giving him emotional satisfaction?'

The therapist responds.

Therapist. You feel you ought to be in prison.

Carol. (To the group.) Don't worry about me. I've got something.

For the rest of the meeting and the next few meetings she said little. Six meetings later, Carol again opens the hour.

Carol. What happened to me tonight was such a shock. My father came in tonight and told me he was going to get married. (Pause.) So, of course, I'm delighted! I just hope nothing happens to prevent it. (Laughs.) Coming down tonight I was thinking that maybe it is the fact that I wasn't giving him everything he wanted —which wasn't possible anyway—has helped to push him toward this much more natural solution.

Therapist. He looked elsewhere for his emotional satisfaction.

Carol. Yes. Because I can remember being quite nasty to him when we went out for dinner together and he said to the waitress, 'Well you know I'm not her father, I'm her boy-friend'. And I told him afterwards, 'You know you embarrass me very much when you do that. You are my father and not my boy-friend.' And maybe that helped. Could have. (Laughs.) (Pause.) I'm in a state of shock. (Laughs.)

Therapist. The shock is on the side of exhilaration rather than depression.

Much social conversation is disguise. There are certain things we talk about and certain things we normally don't discuss at a formal dinner table. We do not openly express every conscious thought that crosses our mind; we censor our thoughts. But there is an unconscious as well as a conscious censorship and therapy is concerned with getting behind the unconscious censorship as well as the conscious one. Fantasy and dreams are in a sense analogous to a person's social conversation with himself. He reveals in symbols the things he cannot talk about—not because he consciously censors them but because they are unconsciously unacceptable and provoke anxiety.

Carol has suffered from deep depression arising from her childhood feelings of unworthiness and inadequacy in handling the conflicting relationships in her family. Certainly in her own mind she was sure she would be cast out if she revealed her feelings. When she came to her first parent class she was careless of her own appearance and that of her three daughters—one way of isolating herself and of identifying with her mother as a woman who had felt unworthy. Now her appearance has changed and she has lost weight as well as the emotional hunger which provokes over-eating, has more pride in her appearance and in the appearance of her three daughters. But her daydream of being a prisoner on parole, or a dope addict trying to break the habit revealed remaining difficulties. She wasn't clear of her emotional involvement with her father which was like a narcotic, so difficult was it for her to leave him to live his own life. Experiencing the meaning of her own symbolism helped to free her. She had found in therapy—parent groups and individual interviews—a dependency she could trust; self-revelation could bring a sense of both self-worth and belonging. So now she can leave her childhood mother (whose image has continued to exist in her adult mind) and her father to live their own lives; and in the present she can allow her father to marry again and move into a more satisfying life of her own.

A PARENT GROUP—PROVOKE, PROTECT, PROVIDE

The education classes in which parents first experienced a therapeutic approach could be large or small; therapy groups could also be large or small. Size seems to be less important than the therapist's consistent attitude and a continuing uncritical and unthreatening atmosphere.

As each parent feels he is known to the therapist—in Carol's group everyone had at least an initial interview—and each has been in a parent education class with the same therapist, a feeling of intimacy arises which characterises the class even at the beginning. The sense of intimacy grows with continuing meetings. Varied educational and social backgrounds seem irrelevant compared with reduction of psychological distance in finding experiences in common. In Carol's group about thirty per cent of the average attendance had finished college. Occupations included housewife, factory worker, office worker, salesman, business manager, store keeper, teacher, lawyer, surgeon. Slightly fewer husbands than wives attended the group.

Traditional therapy groups derived from psychoanalysis have been small—six to eight participants—and they have been structured so that members are similar enough in personality to stimulate interaction. Similar educational and social status is also regarded as helpful. The focus in the traditional analytic group has been on interaction, and emotional growth arises from talking and working through those projections from early family relationships called *transference phenomena*. In other words, members transfer on to the therapist and other group members rivalries, hostilities and affections derived from their childhood and family. In analytic therapy the group is thus a new family (new parent, brothers and sisters) in which members gradually learn to discriminate present reality from projections transferred from the past.

Every person of course does bring his frame of reference his transference, to every situation in life, but the heterogeneous parent groups we are sharing do not *focus* on the strong emotional transference interactions which are the focus of analytic therapy. The assumption is that we can listen to the present perceptions of the *individual person*—whether he is alone, or in a group of two or eighty two—and our experience shows that he can gain in emotional growth from both listening and actively participating. As we have seen, the parent classes from the beginning provided an opportunity for emotional release and group support which helped to reduce anxiety (as all group therapy does). Similarly, from the beginning, parents learn to deal with present realities like waiting one's turn and becoming able to ask to speak. One of the therapist's functions is to represent reality as the *setter of limits* as well as to be the completely accepting listener. Limits include the reality aspects of the group, and limits on acting out in real life the anti-social impulses that may be talked about in therapy.

Provoke, protect, provide. In general, the parent therapy group seems to have three functions. It *provokes* thought as people listen. Second, it *protects* those who are not ready to speak; there is no coercion to participate actively as there frequently is in the small analytic group focusing on interaction. Third, the group *provides* an opportunity to express and to work directly on personal problems. All three functions of the group are important for the uncritical reception of people and all are a stimulus to self-understanding. For Jim who speaks next in the same meeting where Carol told of her day dream, the thought provoking function of the group has been of value in making him want to continue coming.

AN ANGRY MAN

Jim brings up a current problem at work. The problem—resentment—is familiar. But the way the group responds to him is less familiar from the point of view of those who are new to the group.

Statement of a problem. Jim simply states his problem briefly.

Jim. I've been angry for two weeks. I'm so tied up in anger that I haven't been able to do any positive work. I'm trying to get my four bosses to agree. It isn't really my problem to get them together. They're not smart enough to get my version. (Smiles ironically at this. He is known for his ironical statements and smile.)

A Father. Perhaps Jim is angry with himself because he can't sell them the idea.

Jim. If I were smart I could sell it to them.

Jim says nothing else for the rest of the meeting. He simply listens.

First he hears how others see the problem. 'Discord among the bosses would add to the burden of responsibility.' 'It reminds me of discord among parents disturbing a child. Parents should realise how they hurt a child.' Then Ralph points out a reality from the boss's point of view.

Ralph. Employees forget that for every single problem that they have, the management has the problem of the entire business.

Gerald. Well, I get mad when they won't accept me. (A reasonable analysis doesn't alter what he feels.)

Jacqueline. (Jim's wife.) I feel that Jim's problem with these four men will be solved. But I am more concerned that he should be helped with his anger. I'm sure he doesn't need to have this much anger every time this comes up.

Therapist. (Taking a cue from the group to affirm the group's purpose.) Do you hear what she's saying? Let's help him so that if this comes up again, this won't happen.

Ralph. (To Jim.) Is it absolutely necessary for you to do this, or do you need self-confidence?

Other members ask questions. 'Are you trying to run the show?' 'Perhaps you want to have control?'

Ralph. I have the feeling that if you can drag it out of me you'll probably get the right answer. A year ago I was in exactly the same position, only it was with my partner.

A year ago I'd have wanted to change him. Then Ralph speaks at length about his past business difficulties. The central point he tries to make is that his difficulties were really a product of his attitudes but he used to see them as his partner's responsibility. Ralph himself has been so afraid of making a mistake that he avoided taking responsibility for decisions in the firm.

Ralph. But I'm over that now and I say to hell with it. If it turns out wrong, it turns out wrong. It doesn't bother me.

Therapist. (Focusing increased discrimination of response.) You haven't failed as a person if it turns out wrong.

Ralph. That's right. But the point I want to make is that up to a year ago I would have wanted to change my partner. I've come to the realistic understanding that if he makes mistakes, they are made in good faith. I mean he tries to do the right thing and if I'd been in his place I might have made the same mistakes.

Therapist. Yet a year ago you'd have thought he was awful. You'd have thought you couldn't put up with such a dangerous man. And now listen to what you say about him. (Laughter in the group.)

Ralph then gives an example of what he feels is his increased reality in handling a real mistake by his partner. An important account close to his partner has been in town . . .

Ralph. He went off at three o'clock in the afternoon and they walked in at three-thirty. Well, a year ago I would have been so rattled up that I'd still be wound up. But it didn't bother me. I did what I could to take care of them and that was that. Now it bothered the fellow who was working for us. We drove home and he was like I was a year ago. The people who came in, I mean, their feelings were very definitely hurt. They only come once a year. I was bothered in the sense that he should have been there, and he was a damn fool not to be there, but that was all there was to it.

Therapist. It was too bad but you didn't get ulcers over it.

A mother comments on the shared experience of change.

A mother. You can't change the other person, but you can change yourself.
Ralph. That's right. You're different. But they look at you differently too. They have more respect for you.
A mother. But you feel different.
Therapist. What she's saying is that when you did change, you felt in him a respect for you as a person.

Ralph has recognised that he had literally been stepping all over himself and that his attitudes had invited others, including his partner, to step on him. His statement ends the meeting and Jim's listening.

A sequel. The next week Jim speaks first. He, too, has discovered that an 'unmanageable' situation at work became 'manageable' when his attitude changed.

Jim. Would you like a report on last week?
Other members murmur assent. 'Yes.' 'What happened?'
Jim. The second day after the class I went in and sat down with the boss at nine o'clock. We kicked it around a little bit and he got on the telephone. The other parties were scattered about a hundred miles. At nine-twenty we reached agreement. At ten o'clock things were rolling. I can't believe it. Everyone else must have changed. (Ironically.) (Great laughter from everybody follows this remark. Long pause.)
Carol. What really happened. Do you feel you relaxed enough so it got over, or what?
Jim. I feel that very definitely. When they looked at me when I was talking, they must have been seeing some antagonism in me, rather than the problem itself.
A mother. Does he really understand this? The bottom of what happened?
Jim. It will probably happen again. Not so bad I hope. Funny the technical part in the problem didn't change at all. These four people had to rely on my judgment. Up to that point they didn't trust me. Then they had to trust me. That's what it amounts to.

'Same job, same people'. Jim is a man of few words in the class but in an individual interview he tries to put his experience about the group into words.

'I didn't say anything for a long time.'

'It's more helpful to talk about a particular problem.'

'It seems a short time between seeing a problem and coming up with an answer.'

'The thing that's hard is to know you have a problem. The typical remark is, "I don't have any problems". Did you notice the first meetings the new parents didn't know they were working on their own problems?'

'I'm awful busy and it's hard to take time to come. But I really get quite a lift out of being there. I don't quite understand how it operates, but listening to others hits home.'

'In an information class I just sit and sleep. In this class I'm stimulated, it hits home, and every once in a while you get an insight that seems to change the picture quite a bit. It's hard to be objective and honest. I need to keep coming back. The things I've been helped with most are problems at home and people I'd fight with. There are many things like that. I used to get frustrated and angry, but it's like you just take youself out of the picture. "Well, why, how silly I am." And you can change, definitely change inside. Get insight. It's definitely true you bring in yourself.'

When he found he could both accept and control not only his own children but groups of other children on holiday the experience filled him with a profound sense of achievement. It was as though he made a literal discovery of his own adequacy and ability to relate to others.

'I was camping with the Junior High School boys. I slept with ten of them and they were raising the roof. Our counsellor had tried to shut them up. It took me a few minutes and before the class I couldn't have done it. I discovered something I could do I didn't realise. It was a real powerful elated feeling. I was able to accept the fact that they wanted to be rowdy and, when they were, not just let it go.'

'Then there's this "always right and always wrong" talk. I have to laugh because I was always right—even when I was wrong—I couldn't accept, because I was so right! It's self-respect. I think I've noticed a change in attitude about having my own way. It had to be my way down to the last detail. Now I'm easier to work with because I'm able to look at other people's suggestions and compromise. We used to have a jealousy between departments, bickering about who should do what work and it used to bother me. Just in the last few weeks I could have felt this department is trying to do me out of my job. It has been a bit of an effort to be helpful and constructive instead, trying to help them out. But I have managed and I think it's led to a friendlier atmosphere.'

'I was talking to a friend of mine and he said to me something which surprised me. "I envy you. You have such a good time at your work." A couple of years ago it must have been just as obvious how I stewed and fretted. Same job, same people.'

'I used to have tantrums at home—"for no reason at all". (Smiles ironically.) I used to go off and not speak to anyone for a day on end—I don't know how often, but more than occasionally . . . I can see why I get angry maybe beyond the reaction called for when a glass of milk gets knocked over. But it's not so often now.'

'The changes couldn't all have been in me!' (Jim smiles ironically as he says this.)

He uses an insurance term for the way his employers see him—as a 'better risk'. But he sees deeper aspects of personal change.

'I make more money so the front office sees it . . .'

'It's funny, but until I sat down and talked about it, I never admitted to myself that I needed to dig deeper, to learn more.'

Parents heard in an earlier class, 'The hostile child—or the child in the adult—is a frightened child. He wants acceptance but fears rejection.' Jim can't pin down 'how it operates', why he's not as mad as often, why he doesn't offend people, why it's possible in all kinds of situations to sit down and discuss realistic problems without getting angry. But he knows, like Ralph, 'something happened in the class'. But he does see the therapist as a friend he deeply trusts and this makes a profound difference.

'I didn't know till I started talking (referring to present interview) I've never had a friend I could take my problems to.'

'THE PERFECT SON'

For Jim the parent group provoked thought; for Ralph it meant an extreme of protection. He too tries to say in an interview what the class meant to him. He describes how he came with his wife Jill and said nothing for two years; he shut himself off from even silent participation by sleeping frequently. But there was no pressure on him either to come or to participate if he did come. He was completely accepted.

For many members in the group admitting problems was difficult. But, for Ralph, admitting that he had positive *qualities* was difficult. It was not only that he was afraid of making a mistake. He felt he had nothing of his own. He was an indulged child.

An indulged child. Superficially, an indulged child may seem fortunate and accepted. His needs have been anticipated and he has not had to work for anything he has. Everything he could want is provided. He is the centre of attention and constant reassurance from attentive adults tells him he has nothing to worry about. For example, a girl may be showered with compliments for the accident of being born with good looks and she may learn to concentrate on appearance; cosmetics and a constantly changing supply of clothes continue to bring reassurance —and escape from herself. She has abilities but never seems to use them; she is forgetful and constantly relies on others to take care of her; she cannot bear to be alone. A boy may be adored by his parents, but, given a free hand and opportunities for achievement, he fails; he won't study, he won't use his initiative; it is as though he cannot suddenly move from everything being given to him to making an effort for anything. Such a boy and girl have never had an opportunity to find their true measure. Inwardly they doubt and fear the omnipotence they seem to command. Self-knowledge is frightening since it means stripping away the accidental indulgences on which they have come to rely and acknowledging the small child within who still needs to depend and still needs love; it means making an effort and taking responsibility for oneself. It means anxiety in self-discovery instead of reassurance to keep defences going.

Ralph was crippled in this way. He was short of nothing materially, but he had not found his true measure.

'Before I went to the class I wasn't mature. But that didn't bother me. I had no problems. You know the fellows who have no problems. (Smiling.) But I had an inferiority complex—the one problem I knew about—because I didn't go to college. I didn't want to when I was at school. I was given a free hand and didn't study.

> I thought I couldn't get into college. I could talk to my folks but I was always right, I couldn't risk trying anything because I couldn't risk failure. And I never thought I earned anything. It was just there. I was made a leader in the Boy Scouts, but I used to put it on to other things but me. I thought I was in a good troop. It was not me. I always felt they picked the troop, not me for a leader.'
>
> 'I'm one of those guys, I know what happened, but didn't know how. The first incident happened. I couldn't skate. But the kids were going, so I arranged with a few friends to go ice skating and went along with the kids. And in the middle of the afternoon I was ice skating. I can't tell you how it happened. Something had happened in the therapy. Just before the ice skating, I started talking. I'd never have gone out like that before, I'd have been too afraid of making a fool of myself.'

Then he reveals a continuing need to be dependent on someone he could trust and to relate to people in his own right.

> 'You don't have to be perfect and can still be comfortable. Once in a while when the kids get a good scolding, there's no guilt now, but good feeling after the scolding in the whole family. And sometimes I get good and mad and it's my fault (he owns the responsibility) and not theirs. But apparently there's a good enough foundation that there's good feeling.'
>
> 'I think one of the big things in therapy is the way it's presented to us. Many people are ashamed of therapy. But our kids know. And Marie had one or two sessions. The way I feel is that everyone should go into therapy. It's a difficult topic to discuss socially though.'

The completely acceptant, non-coercive climate in the group made it possible for him to continue coming for two years before he spoke, hearing what he could when he didn't escape hearing by sleeping, and it made it possible for him to begin to move into himself. Talking in the group had not proved a mistake and he dared to venture in other ways—learning to skate, taking the initiative in business.

But he is still wrestling with original dissatisfaction with 'living the way my parents wanted me to live'; like Ann Crane and Nora Kalman who protested they did not want their parents' gift of education if receiving it was not accompanied by acceptance of themselves as people. Financial success and a good standard of living are 'just what my parents wanted for me', and so Ralph equates them in his personal synonym with spurious love, with his own (for him) spurious status of perfection as a ready-made adult before he found his own sense of reality through achievements by his own efforts. So all his success seems to fall short of what he really wants since he still feels less than his parents' "idea" of him and inwardly he still protests against it. In the ninth meeting he mulls over an old problem.

The pedestal. A cloak of omnipotent rightness is terrifying for a child who hasn't learned his own real powers and limits.

> *Ralph.* I'm living the way my parents thought I should live. They thought I could do no wrong. I didn't feel it was me who was picked but that I was the victim of circumstances.
> *Therapist.* You could always put it on to something outside.
> *Elizabeth.* He's afraid to accept his own ability.
> *Therapist.* It's too dangerous to face.
> *Ida.* You're pushed up to a pedestal.
> *Therapist.* It's not a safe place to be.

Various members comment: 'He is defeatist and self-punishing . . .' 'He doesn't really want responsibility'. There seems to be a suggestion now that he is looking for responsibility to *prove* he's 'all right'—a swing in the opposite direction from avoiding it. Other remarks follow. 'His expectations are too high.' 'He should come down to earth.'

> *Ralph.* I always used to think that when I turned my back that nobody was there. Was the rest of the world there for me to see?'
> *Therapist.* You were its centre to your parents.

Peter, new in the group, expresses some hostility. He is widely read and uses terms he has studied. He projects his own conflict and search for an authority to give him what he needs.

> *Peter.* I'll be blunt. Why don't you seek the psychiatrist's door? Are you using the group as a narcotic to disperse anxiety?
> *Ralph.* I've solved many problems and can do many more things. You don't know what progress it was to open my mouth.

Towards the end of the next, the tenth, meeting, he speaks again.

> *Ralph.* (To the therapist.) After class last week you said you'd like to know what I dreamt. It doesn't make too much sense, but I worked on it and the conclusion that I came to is that I'm

not too anxious to work too hard for anything as far as finance is concerned, though the dream had nothing to do with finance. But this is what came out of it. And I'm wondering why. I had a dream in which I was in the limelight without working for it.

Therapist. Back in your childhood.

Ralph. I dreamt that Rin Tin Tin was there with his trainer. And there was a fellow from one of the studios going from block to block performing. I'm the one that walked him back to his owner and I made him do a couple of tricks along the way. Everybody thought that I owned Rin Tin Tin and I remember somewhere in the dream that this took years and years of training. And also that the training had to start all over again. This was Rin Tin Tin the twelfth. And I realised in my dream that this man had been training all these Rin Tin Tins all these years and here I came along just happened to be there and the people in the street thought I was the one who taught him.

Therapist. Ralph's come down from his pedestal, hasn't he? Come to the bottom to make a place for himself.

Ralph. And there's one thing I'd like to say to Peter. Because this is what would have been the answer. You can accomplish things here and not realise you're progressing. When Peter spoke to me at the end of last time, it didn't really bother me. When we were going home, Jill said to me, 'You've come a long way.' And I said, 'Why?' And she said, 'Well, a year ago you would have practically walked over and hit Peter in the face.' Do you remember if Jack made a remark, I would fly off the handle. And I took it from Peter and it didn't bother me at all. But a year ago I'd have some remark for him and I've had to sit on my hands.

Therapist. And you didn't realise it.

Ralph. No, I didn't, not till Jill mentioned it. She wanted to know if I didn't get a little hostile. And I really didn't.

Therapist. You weren't aware of it in this way. You had no defences or resentment.

Ralph's dream is rehearsal. He is living out his parent's gratuitous investment of himself with perfection before he achieved anything by his own effort. At the same time his dream is recognition of his true status: he sees he did not come into sound ownership of the 'man's dog' and is handing back the 'false man'. But he seems to imply he wants to be provided with what he needs in a dependent way as a child. So he says he does not want to work too hard for anything 'as far as finance is concerned'.

Shortly after this the group work motivated him to go into concurrent private therapy and things moved faster, he said. But he had to be ready to make his own decision about how far he could go in his exploration into himself.

DANGEROUS THOUGHTS

Why should a child feel that recognising his own ability is too dangerous? Why should a man or a woman not use ability, not finish tasks or commitments begun?

We have seen in general that his fear of looking at his own need for and anger against his significant adults may block his learning and performance in many ways. 'I can't win', 'I'll be rejected, so why finish anything just to find out what I know already—that I'm no good.'

'The thought is the deed'. But where a child has not had a chance to find a safe channel for his feelings, has not tested them against reality, his fantasy may seem his reality and thoughts become facts. The personal equation of ability may then be frightening. Ability to kill in thought those who frustrate—parents, brothers and sisters—can make any recognition of ability hard to accept. Frank envied his young brother. His jealousy made him want to get rid of him and in fantasy he killed him. One day his brother was killed crossing the street and Frank carried a burden of guilt into his adult life. 'My wish killed my brother.' But he was never able to talk of his feelings. 'I could never express my feelings of resentment and rebellion against my mother's domination, my anger against my brother, my guilt for his death.' He expressed his real feelings in the therapy group and came to understand them in a new light. He found a sense of masculine adequacy and was able to separate his fantasy of childhood jealousy from actual responsibility for his brother's death. Fantasy in the child's magical thinking is omnipotent: the thought is the deed, so thoughts are dangerous.

'Vastly uncivilised feelings'. Looking at uncontrolled and untested primitive feelings is deeply disturbing to Peter who discovers that on an unconscious level he seems to be wanting to kill his child for not meeting his expectations.

Peter. I'm afraid of my feelings. I can't solve the problem of dependency needs. As I understand it, people want to return to their parents because they have not been weaned from their basic dependency needs on them.

Therapist. We cannot assert our independence because we are still feeling dependent.

Peter. But why this basic conflict? I have tapped some vastly uncivilised feelings in me. Do you struggle for dependency? Parents are authority. If you had no father or mother would you be faced with all these feelings?

Therapist. I don't know if it fits you, Peter, but you said, 'I find myself still counting on that dependency because I need the stability of feeling that limits can be set by my mother or whoever represents the parents to me because I would be too afraid of the basic impulses that come up in me unless I could feel somebody would stop me in them. I've just got to have a feeling that somebody will set a limit on these things that I'm afraid of in myself.'

Peter. I'm glad you said this. Is it me, or is it universal? I just read a book (mild laughter from class—Peter is known for trying to get his personal answers from the authorities in books) which talks of the need for authority limits to reduce the threat of frightening feelings.

Therapist. (Continuing to point out reality as well as to respond to Peter.) It would be so frightening that one of our infantile needs is to have a parent who can be depended upon to see that we don't go too far. It saves us from being too afraid of them when we can depend on someone who can contain us and stop us. As one man said to me who's been in individual therapy, 'My mother and father never gave me any disciplining.' He feels the need for someone to help him contain these violent anti-social feelings.

Winston. (To Peter.) It sounds to me like what you need is an authority to tell you exactly what is right. But you won't trust your own feelings unless you've read that feeling in a book—if you've read that in a book and then you can feel it in yourself, then that's the answer. But if you can think it yourself and have never read it before, you'd do better. Do you see what I mean? Just trust your feelings and let them come out.

Therapist. And he's just suggested, not said it, that the reason he may not trust his own feelings is that he's afraid they're not acceptable.

Peter has achieved a great deal scholastically and athletically, but he says that, although he has always been in the limelight, he is not comfortable about it; he feels guilty. He is just beginning to look at his aggression, to recognise consequent guilt and self-punishing feelings expressed in feelings of unworthiness ('I don't deserve this'). He is tapping some 'vastly uncivilised feelings' in himself. His own thoughts are too dangerous to trust—authority in a book is his safeguard; the intellectual concept has been safer so far than allowing his direct experience to tell its story.

Don't speak the thought. The omnipotence of untried fantasy was also terrifying to Jean. She moved from an education class into her own private therapy.

When parents first come expecting advice it is a normal reaction to want to avoid the pain of self-exposure. More surprising to people who choose of their own free will the route of self-knowledge through therapy is their own continuing resistance. Consciously wanting to change to more adequate ways of relating to others does not change the fear that honesty may bring more rejection.

Jean had exceptional difficulty in talking at all when she actually chose therapy, a setting where honesty is the only means to growth. In her education group her difficulty was not as apparent. These members had an opportunity to talk as freely as they wished to help them understand their own communication better. They also had an opportunity to write as freely as they wished in a notebook to the therapist. Writing therapy for any who wanted to use it provided a form of individual interview and Jean was one who was able to use this means of communication. She spoke little in class, but listening stimulated personal examination. In one class topic after another she found herself and admitting negative feelings seemed to release more positive feelings towards herself. The therapist wrote brief responses in her notebook.

First she found an intellectual acceptance of the concepts discussed in class. The principles appealed to her although she did not express personal feeling.

> *Jean.* Discussing permissiveness in class helped to clarify the permissive situation. I feel very definitely that all children would profit from the opportunity to make their own decisions and to do what they would like, with realistic limitations wherever possible.

Second, she discovered some uneasiness about possible disclosure of the self she wanted to hide.

Jean. Now I am beginning to feel uncomfortable about this writing. I realise how much can be got from it.

Third, some positive attitudes made themselves felt.

Jean. The person who tears everyone down is saying, 'I don't really like myself.' After thinking about this for a while I couldn't help thinking, 'That's me.' But lately I've been getting to the point where I'm beginning to like myself, even though it has taken a long time.

Fourth, freedom in communication began to be enjoyable.

Jean. I have come to realise actually that it is fun to write like this. I don't feel so uncovered any more—you can think what you please, as you will anyway. Are you by any chance giving us a chance to make up for the play therapy experiences that we missed? I probably need it more than anyone.

Therapist. You can see deprivations and would like your needs met.

Jean. Just as an observation in which you might be interested. As I am sitting here writing these comments I can't help but grin. It's nice to know that I can write anything I please. I'm having fun with my newly found freedom.

Therapist. It doesn't feel so bad, does it?

Jean. It's funny to think that I know the basic rules of the therapeutic procedure, that I can see exactly what you are seeing in my writing and yet I simply don't care. Now I know that it is probably a basic desire to be understood. It seems foolish to say so, but thank you.

Then doubts alternate with confidence. Writing seemed safer than talking.

Jean. I have an inferiority complex. Why? Many reasons. I think it all probably boils down to a feeling of insecurity. I could talk to you but I still feel better writing and am not in your presence to determine the reaction which you aren't supposed to show.

Therapist. You feel it may be negative? That the attitude would differ from appearance?

Jean. In writing this I can furnish myself with reactions which I think you should have. But I really like this free expression.

Shortly after this she marvelled at her changing reactions.

Jean. My feelings towards the whole class experience have changed so much that I simply don't want to write the previous ones down.

Towards the end of the class she hinted at deeper emotion.

Jean. What a tremendous impact your words 'your own past unresolved deprivations' has on me even now. I can't even remember the context.

At this time Jean asked for an interview. She revealed that she lost both her parents by the age of thirteen but they had been divorced before then. She said that her father was a heavy drinker and she was afraid of him; that she could talk to her mother but was socially pushed. She stated problems and needs in a staccato series of statements and questions with pauses.

Jean. I have to have everything too organised. (Pause.) I try to be prepared for what I'm to say or do. I'm on guard all the time because I may make a mistake. (Pause.) Can I ever be spontaneous? (Pause.) I want to belong and I feel if I really express myself I'll be the loser. I can't stand to lose, even at cards. (Pause.) My trouble is I don't trust myself. I don't even attempt many things because I can't stand to lose. I don't know why I attempt anything.

Therapist. You seem to be saying, 'Why try at all?'

Jean. Why do I keep trying? It must be an urge for survival. I find it difficult to ask for anything. I always feel I'll have to pay it back and I don't know if I can. I feel guilty when I ask for anything—am I worth it? And I can't stand to have people borrow from me. But I don't want to be taken for granted the way my brother takes me for granted. He assumes I'll just take care of his kids any time he and his wife want to go out. I want to be asked. I don't just want them to be dumped on me.

After the first interview she wrote some more, at length, about her feelings of resentment to everybody. She mentioned her brother especially.

Jean. I'm always either arguing with my brother or belittling him behind his back. I know I mis-spelled belittling, or at least I think I did, but I don't even care to look it up. How different from the perfectionist I usually am even my writing is.

Therapist. Is this a progress report?

Jean. 'Anything that doesn't go quite right can throw you.' That's me. The stupidest little thing can throw me into a fit of temper. And 'difficult to please' fits me perfectly. I always think that I can do something better than anyone else and don't hesitate to say so. But since my discussion with you I have improved in this respect. And for some reason I even feel that I can ask people to do things for me.

But following the class, individual therapy each week proved a frightening ordeal. In face-to-face interviews she kept her eyes down and did not look at the therapist. Each time she sat in silence for long periods before she could say the thought that was troubling her. Angry thoughts against her parents were especially frightening since they had literally died in what was for her final desertion. Relatives had told her that the children had caused trouble between her mother and father and she felt to blame for her father's first desertion, and for her mother's unhappiness. She felt she survived only by holding feelings in. In the sixth meeting she tried to explain why.

Jean. I want to be protected. I have always felt this way. I'm afraid to go out on my own. I'm afraid people won't like me, or that something's going to happen to me. I was always the last to go to sleep. I was afraid people would say things about me and would get rid of me.

Therapist. You were so much on guard against being rejected.

Jean. I was afraid to go to sleep for fear of what might happen. And I had a nightmare the other night. I don't remember it very well. But it was raining and I went in a swimming pool with a woman friend and then we couldn't get out. I was terrified but mad at her for doing such a stupid thing. I was afraid of what would happen to me but even more of what would happen to her. I thought how awful if I got out and her husband came, how he would feel. I'd wish I hadn't got out in those circumstances. And if the dream is all my thoughts I just can't see why I'd want her to drown. And if she represents my mother why would I want to attack my mother? (She talked on another occasion about this nightmare, focusing then on homosexual meanings and her confusion about sexual identity.)

In the eighth meeting she sat in silence for several minutes before speaking.

Jean. I've been trying to find courage to say this. I've been bothered by a dream I had at thirteen. I've struggled against talking about it. I think it was just after my mother died, the night after she died and my father had come for the funeral. There were a lot of relatives in the house and my sister and I were in the same bedroom. We were making a noise and my father came and told us to be quiet. He was naked and this frightened me, as well as that he was very angry. And the next night I had a dream that the man next door attacked me sexually. I feel the man was really my father, but it was too terrifying to dream my father attacked me sexually. The night he came to tell us to be quiet he was holding his penis. And it's so terrifying because I can see in the dream that I must have wanted him to attack me like that. I was afraid of him but I did want to be with him and I felt my mother deprived me of him in the divorce. And then after my mother's funeral he left again and I didn't see him and he died. And at the funeral he was crying and I tried to comfort him by holding his hand and I didn't cry myself. I felt I had to have the courage not to cry. I had to be strong.

For Jean thoughts were dangerous and she fought speaking them at every step. 'I want to talk, but I just can't' Speaking the thought makes it so different from thinking it. '*Then you are found out.*'

But the initial experience of feeling understood when she communicated freely in her first class seemed to give her both strength and desire to continue, though her resistance when she chose therapy amazed her, she said.

Discoveries, plateaux and regressions.

Learning is never a constantly ascending curve—up and up and more and more. There are plateaux and people even slip back and have to re-learn.

Emotional learning and developing insight also, have their plateau and regressions. Repetition of old problems is necessary until new solutions emerge. But emotional learning is never linear—the journey of a straight line. For the individual person it is a complex process of reorganisation. One insight may effect many aspects of relationships: 'making a mistake does not mean I have failed as a person' leads to daring to venture in many ways with greater enjoyment and a greater sense of freedom; 'I don't have to have my own way down to the last detail' means reduced frustration, less anger, more accomplishments, improved relationships at work and at home. Growth takes place unobtrusively, gradually, in a climate of uncritical reception, so that without knowing what has happened a person discovers abilities he did not know he possessed. He may also discover strength in recognising his limitations, not wanting goals that demonstrate inadequacy, as Elizabeth found.

Ralph had difficulty accepting his positive qualities, but Elizabeth has difficulty accepting her husband Dan's qualities. She is a wife who criticises all his efforts to help. She is new in her group after a year of a parent education class.

'I couldn't accept one thing he did for the children'. During the second meeting discussion turns on the way our parents' expectations create our self-image, so that we become in our own eyes people who do the right thing or do the wrong thing. Thus we may think of ourselves and others in derogatory ways as a result of parents' expectations. Later, if some one tries to make a better person out of us we resist it.

Therapist. If some one is trying to *improve* on you, it is an implied criticism isn't it? But if you are a child and people expect you to do the wrong thing, it isn't only because they expect it that you do it. By then you have a picture of *yourself* as a person who does the wrong thing.

Elizabeth. As you were talking, I was just thinking back on things that really happen there. Similar to that. Dan would do something and it would annoy me so much. He would do the same thing over and over again to the child. It annoyed me. Actually I have found (talking slowly as if trying to understand what really happened)—and I don't think it's just him, it's me. I can't explain. But all of a sudden he seems to be doing the right thing with the children. He was doing the wrong thing for seven or six years—he did the wrong thing every time, every single time (laughing) and it annoyed me and he knew it annoyed me. But now all of a sudden he seems to be doing the right thing. I don't have the feeling that it's him. Well, he's not doing the wrong thing but I'm sure it's not him.

Therapist. You're seeing something different in it now than you did before.

But Elizabeth still struggles to explain an intangible quality, a sense of discovery, that has made a difference in the same situation. Growth is not streamlined and neither is the speech associated with it.

Elizabeth. I would grab the child and say, 'No, that's the wrong thing.' And it would irritate me. But I don't think it was the thing he did. Do I make myself clear? He's all of a sudden handling the children right, *better than I can*.

Dan. What she means is that I'm not doing anything different from what I did before, but she's seeing it in a different light, I think.

Therapist. (Restating more specifically.) You can see that what he was doing was more useful than you thought it was.

Elizabeth. That's it.

Therapist. Now it isn't so questionable what he's doing with the child.

Elizabeth. It isn't questionable at all. It came over me in the last two weeks. I don't know. Now I look up to him.

She is becoming more acceptant of her limitations and therefore can accept Dan's qualities since they no longer threaten her with a sense of inadequacy or failure. Paradoxically, recognition of Dan's strengths reflect her own increasing inner strength.

Therapist. You said he was handling things better than you did.

Elizabeth. Yes.

Therapist. Therefore you're not hunting for situations where you can attack him because you've accepted that fact.

Elizabeth. What makes you always feel you're right? I thought he simply could not handle this situation. And I realise that it really wasn't him and that he could.

Therapist. You did not realise that it was because you could not risk someone else helping you.

So great was her fear of her inadequacy being exposed that accepting help would mean she was no good. So she had to attack the would-be helper, her husband.

Elizabeth. I kept on even though I knew I wasn't handling it right.

Therapist. You knew in your heart that you weren't handling it right and, therefore, you needed to defend yourself all the more.

Elizabeth. But isn't it funny happening like that all of a sudden? (Pause.) Well, it is funny. (Smiling.)

Therapist. What you're saying is, 'Isn't it funny that we grow and change emotionally?' You accept the fact that you're not quite so hot at handling these situations.

Elizabeth. Well, I knew I wasn't really. (Laughter in the group.)

Therapist. You knew it but you didn't want to expose it. You were so afraid someone might handle them better.
Elizabeth. Everything is much easier. It's wonderful.
Therapist. It was there all along but you didn't realise it, did you?
Elizabeth. It's such a wonderful lift, the weight of the burden gone. He always wanted to take over situations and whenever he did, I was right in there pitching a battle.
Therapist. You couldn't accept it, could you?
Elizabeth. I couldn't accept one thing he did for the children. And I'd say, 'It's the way you're handling it.' (Laughter.)
Therapist. You'd justify taking it away from him by finding it wrong.

'He was going to be your A'. Elizabeth is moving to a more accepting relationship with her son as well as with her husband. But she is concerned because there are periods when she seems to make no progress and even to slip back into her old feelings: she is worried by plateaux and regressions in learning.

Elizabeth. If I go along with my son, accept that he's high strung, everything's wonderful.

But she does not feel sufficiently secure in her self-acceptance and so she is vulnerable to outside events. She is seeking to find a more stable centre of evaluation in herself.

Elizabeth. Then something will come along and I'll slide back. I feel guilty now. Something happens at school and why do I slide back? This guilt . . .
Therapist. You're threatened when something happens at school.
Elizabeth. He does something at school and I attack him. Why do I attack him? (Pause.) I feel responsible. What can I do to stop from sliding back? I'm doing well, I know I'm doing well. But, if he's sat on a bench at school.
Therapist. He's punished or rejected.
Elizabeth. (With much inflection.) His rejection means that I'm not doing a good job.

Along with sliding back she is concerned with unevenness in herself. She is still asking why in the sixth meeting of the group.

Elizabeth. Why can't I accept unevenness in myself? Some days I can't do well. Some days I can.

Other members in the group say they have similar experiences.

Elizabeth. I don't think I'm just talking about being uneven. I'm talking about becoming comfortable with it, accepting it.

Therapist. You want to accept yourself as you are.

Then she listens as others talk of ways in which their relationships with their parents influence their present reactions. In response she reveals some negative feelings about her father.

Elizabeth. I was very fortunate that I had a very understanding mother. My father was away on business. I used to dread him coming home. I loved my father but he was always right. My father ruled my mother. It was the same with everyone.

She gives many instances of his dominating behaviour.

Elizabeth. Imagine what it would have been like if he had been around all the time.

Jacqueline. I'd like to suggest to Elizabeth that he *was* around all the time.

Therapist. He doesn't have to be there physically.

Elizabeth. I'm afraid of him.

Therapist. Listen to what you've said. You've said you love your father and you've said in other sentences that you're glad he wasn't around. And the first of the evening you were afraid of inconsistencies in your own feelings. (Pause.) You don't feel comfortable in the presence of ups and downs, you said. And now you say how up and down you felt about your father.

Elizabeth. I know he never tolerated inconsistencies.

Then again she listens as others speak of their relationships to their fathers. Ellen didn't think her father knew her name till she was fifteen, but she tried to get close to him by going down to his workshop and working side by side with him and never saying a word.

Mona competed with her brothers for her father.

Mona. I helped him make chicken coops. He'd hunt alone, they'd go fishing with him, so I made the chicken coops.

Therapist. Can you see how hard you tried to reach your father.

Winston. We're all fathers, too.

Mona. And yet I know he had very little to give.

Winston. We have to work so that we don't pass these things on.

Then Elizabeth begins talking again.

Elizabeth. I'd like to say that that is exactly why I'm here. I'd like to add a few things about my father. I think my feeling about my father has something to do with my relationship to my son.

Therapist. (To the group.) You hear what she says. (To Elizabeth.) Feelings towards fathers have something to do with feelings of mothers to sons.

Elizabeth. It's funny, I thought he was wonderful until I got married and then he didn't look wonderful at all. And when I was a child I had the same feelings. I didn't have it as a teenager. But as a child I didn't want him to come home. I was always in his way. But as a teenager I was the pet. And he'd always tell me if I even thought I was going to get a bad mark, '*You're going to get an A*. There's no question.' Both my mother and father always built me up all through high school. So I got this feeling I can do anything. And I think that's what I started with my son. He is going to be perfect. Only I didn't know about children. I can remember thinking. 'You have to be perfect and I'm going to make you perfect.'

Therapist. You were going to prove it.

Eliazbeth. Yes, I was going to prove something.

Therapist. He was going to be your A.

Elizabeth. He's going to be nothing if I don't get rid of this. Well, now I don't want him to be my A. I just want him to be himself. But I'll say, there's just no comparison. Two years ago I couldn't stand him. Every time he got near me I just cringed. I mean, that was a terrible thing. I wouldn't admit it two years ago to anybody. But now I don't have these feelings. I have a real warmth when I think of him. But it comes back.

Therapist. The old rejection comes in at times.

Just as she'd placed her husband in the wrong, Elizabeth saw her son as the source of trouble and not her feelings about him.

Elizabeth. But I used to feel he was completely obnoxious, I'm feeling better about it and as a result he feels better. It has come so much further, I feel that warmth. I feel I want it to come the whole way.

In the sixth meeting, she found on the level of feelings and not of theory, that her dislike of her son really reflected a dislike of herself. He mirrored her own characteristics and she 'just didn't like him'.

Elizabeth. I see it. My child is very highly strung and nervous and I am that way. And I don't like it when he shouts, I don't like it when he gets all excited, because that's the way I get and that's why he's doing it, and I know that now. (The therapist smiles and nods and says nothing, accepting her statement in silence.) I finally found out. It's been long enough. And for the first time I got his report and I didn't, I didn't, it's not what I said to him, I didn't *feel* ashamed.

Therapist. It isn't in what you say.

Elizabeth. The last time I spoke very nicely.

Therapist. It was false.

Elizaebth. And inside I felt, 'Darn it, why can't he do better?' This time I felt he can't do any better. He was doing his best. And I didn't feel badly. I was amazed.

Therapist. You were amazed to find yourself *not* discouraged at something less than good or perfect.

In the seventh class meeting she again talks of her father.

Elizabeth. I want to get rid of the feeling of not wanting him to come. I can't wait for my mother to come. A friend asked me if my father was coming and I said, 'My father isn't, thank God.' It just came out. But I want to get rid of the feeling.

Therapist. (Reaffirming a route to emotional change.) The best way to get rid of a feeling is to look at it. To invite it, not deny it. You want to get rid of it, you don't like it. You want to eliminate it.

Elizabeth. Yes. (Pause) I don't want to change him. He'll always be that way.

Therapist. Intellectually, at least, you accept the way he is.

Elizabeth. But I can't accomplish anything when he's around.

Therapist. You'd like to have his presence not be disturbing.

Elizabeth. Why do I want my father to approve of me? Why should it make that much difference? I want his approval.

Therapist. Why are you still seeking his approval?

Six weeks later in an interview she said her feelings for both her son and her father were more accepting.

Elizabeth. My son was *my* report card and he had to show I was succeeding. I couldn't accept him because he wasn't as I wanted him to be. I wouldn't mind if my father came now. I've had so much help from the group. You pick up little things from them and dig out things in yourself. Things you have forgotten. It makes me shake. It happens all the time.

RECURRENT THEMES

As parents seek for the centre of evaluation in themselves, variations on old dilemmas recur. 'Knowing I'm doing the wrong thing', yet being unable to change means 'I'm not there yet'. The therapist's response gives clues.

Mona. I know it's the feelings in me that make me over-protect my child not what he needs. I know I'm protecting myself, yet I continue to protect my child, rushing in and saying, 'What's the matter?' before the child has time to catch his breath.

Therapist. You've got something else in there. The urgency to protect the child. You see the child as so vulnerable that he needs protection.

We hear again old questions. 'How far must you go before you know yourself?' 'Each one has different solutions.' 'Which one is right?'

Such questions become fewer in time, and group resources handle them more quickly—group members attempt answers, the therapist responds.

A mother. Where the individual is most comfortable in the situation, he's reached a solution.

A father. Accepting your feelings where they are . . . The criterion is your own comfort.

The therapist relates the 'criterion of comfort' to goals of behaviour. It does not mean 'doing your own thing' in a vacuum.

Therapist. Elizabeth illustrated it very well. She knew there was something phony in the way she was blaming Dan. She wasn't comfortable about it, but she defended it to the last ditch.

Of all recurrent themes in continuing therapy, two particularly are most prominent in individuals' lives: the first is the necessity to be right, the second is shifting the liability. A third is associated with learning to say no.

'Having to be right'—defensive dogmatism. Variations on the necessity to be right, to have one's own way, are forms of protection against

self-discovery, a kind of defensive dogmatism that may seem practically to be a synonym for personal survival. Frustrated and angry, fearful of his own acceptance, Jim had to have his way; Ralph, unable to perceive his own qualities, fearful of making a mistake, had to make sure he'd be right before he ventured at all. Elizabeth unable to face her own sense of inadequacy had to prove her husband wrong to make herself right. Jill, Ralph's wife, finds she has had to have the whole world at fault until she can look at her own self-doubts.

Jill. I'm getting to the bottom of my trouble and it hurts.

Therapist. She's been working at this a long time and it hurts. That's why it's hard to get there, because it hurts when you get there.

Jill. It's myself. I'm finding it all over the place. I say this is what's eating you. It's permeated everything, just everything. It's shaken my confidence. People who are always right and dominating. It hides their doubts from others. (Speaking quietly and with much inflection.) It's everybody, just everybody. If they don't do it the way I feel, they're wrong. And of course, now I realise how wrong I've been. (Very long pause.)

Therapist. You don't know how badly you need it. It's life or death, almost, to keep it.

Charles. I remember how I was three years ago. Three years ago I wouldn't have spoken three consecutive sentences to two people. (He now gives lectures in the Air Force.) I've changed and I know it's the class. And this business of being right. I'm with Jill a hundred per cent on that.

A discussion follows in which Ralph and Jill both say they are no longer upset by other people having to be right.

Ralph. It used to drive me crazy until I matured to the point myself where I really had a mind of my own.

Therapist. You have the centre in yourself and your assessment is in yourself.

Jill has become aware of another aspect in her defensive dogmatism.

Jill. Well you see the thing is that I'm getting to the point where I don't feel quite so right. (General laughter.) I realise that in conjunction with being right was a feeling of being different, and I never realised that until tonight. And it's a funny feeling. And it doesn't seem any more a matter of right or wrong.

Therapist. It's a matter of being different now.

Jill. Why should it upset me? It upsets me to the point it shakes me. The whole thing is out of proportion. It's just ridiculous.

Jill had been an adored little girl, the centre of adults admiring a pretty child. She felt very different inside from this image. To look at the difference was shattering.

Shifting the liability: 'Anything carries the burden'. If we are unsure inside, anything external can serve to carry the burden of proof that there is something unacceptable about us: 'My cooking is no good', 'No one will come to my party', 'If people don't respond to my effort it *proves* there's something wrong with me'. A disappointed expectation throws us. We blame ourselves.

Charles. (He was just beginning to venture by giving lectures in the Air Force.) I was expecting to give a lecture to an audience of twenty-two hundred. Only fourteen showed up. It really puts me off.

Jim, growing in his own sense of adequacy, feels he is not as easily put out by a similar experience as he would have been at one time.

Jim. I'm teaching an evening class and only five of the thirty people turned up last time. And I had an initial reaction, 'Why didn't these others show up? Maybe I'm failing as a teacher.' But I went on with the class and I really enjoyed it. I decided it didn't make any difference. The important thing was to talk to the people who were there and do a good job. I really did feel adequate.

Ellen. I have some feelings along that line. I'm afraid to give a party because I'm afraid nobody will come.

Therapist. You go out on a limb and assert your availability and you're afraid you'll be turned down.

Ellen. You don't just think, enough of yourself. If I had Charles' experience, I'd die.

Therapist. I think what Ellen is saying is, 'My own question about my worth is so deep, I question it so terribly and am so anxious about it, that if my anxiety were confirmed by only a few coming. I would die. So few would have been evidence that my own impression of myself was true, that I wasn't any good.' And, therefore, you just curled up, lest your fears should have been confirmed by only a few coming.

Elizabeth. I don't invite anyone to dinner because I'm worried about my cooking.

Carol. The way I see it, I feel uneasy when people come into the house and I am the hostess, and I wonder how things will go. When we go somewhere for a party and Andrew says, 'Ask them over,' I feel, 'What shall I do with them?'

Therapist. Can I restate that? I have a feeling of uneasiness if people come around and I have the responsibility of making things go. I feel that on me the success of things depends.

'I'm no good because this happened', or 'I may be proved no good if I try this thing and it doesn't succeed' means a pervading need for reassurance from outside things. It is a variation on the scapegoat theme with ourselves as the scapegoat. Innumerable incidents may carry the burden of 'the way I feel'—my son received a low mark; my daughter wasn't invited to Gillian's birthday party; even 'I'm this way because I live in X-town'.

Elizabeth. Dan was always trying to make me conform very formally when we lived in X-town.

Dan. You don't know X-town.

Elizabeth. X-town! It wasn't X-town. It was him. I'm not talking about X-town and I don't think Dan is. He's getting at the way he felt.

Therapist. That is ten years of living in X-town had confirmed in him the way he felt.

Elizabeth. (Slowly, as though with dawning realisation.) Yes, that's right he'd always blamed it on X-town. That's it!

Learning to say no. Being able to say no seems to be a variation on the ability to set limits, so frequently a concern of parents in bringing up their children. But taking on more and more work at the office, becoming the drudge for all the family at home, feeling run ragged by trying to meet the demands of another person's problems, may all be variations on difficulties in saying no; these are associated with unconscious fears of rejection if one does not do what others want, with unconscious aggressions that one must appease. Lorraine has these kinds of difficulties with her mother-in-law who lives with her and her husband. He is one of the few husbands who does not attend the group. She is frustrated because she feels she is not able to have a good relationship with her husband and her mother-in-law at the same time. She tends to treat the two as rivals for her affection.

Lorraine. I do have a better relationship with Carl but I'm feeling some antagonism towards him at the present. The thing is his mother reminds me a dozen times a day of what he isn't.

Therapist. When she rejects him you move in with her.

Philippa. If you reject her, then what happens to her?

Lorraine. Oh she gets quieter and quieter and more and more withdrawn. She's really a very demanding person, but she turns her demands into all sorts of little ways of asking for attention, like wanting her hair to be done. And if she doesn't get it then she retreats in a defeated kind of way. And I don't know how to handle it; I'm mixed up in it. I don't have to be mixed up in it. I don't have to be thrown this way. I'm getting to the point now where I want to understand her without getting messed up in it.

Therapist. Without being pulled into the pool. (Parents have heard in a previous class that you can be available to help your children if you aren't made to feel insecure too, if you don't jump into the pool and drown with them.)

Lorraine. She can get me this way.

Therapist. She can push you into the feeling, can't she?

Peter. (Supplying a label from the books.) 'This neurotic insatiability.' With this kind of person I always feel charity begins at home and *I* have my problems.

Therapist. (Responding to his need.) You know what it is to feel the demands of others who are asking some help with their problems. And you say, 'I have enough at home without this.

Lorraine. (Labels herself.) If I were not neurotic to a certain extent myself, I mean, it's me and I can see the point here, it would not bother me if I knew how to handle it. You wouldn't go on and on until it drains you, if you were all right inside.

Therapist. You're saying, 'There's something in me which is sensitive to it.' You're using the term neurotic. Neurotic is not knowing what you want, not knowing what the something is in you that makes you react this way, with your own needs.

Jill. It's something that vibrates in me. And I know that I have always felt that if I had to satisfy these demands, there would be no end to it. But it's *only being able to give*, that's all it is. But not feeling good in two places at once I have experienced too. But it's better, a sign of growth, if you can feel good in all areas.

Lorraine. I thought of something. When Daddy and I read together Mother rejected us. And when I'm close to Carl, I feel his mother's rejection of both of us.
Therapist. Carl wants an understanding between you and him, but because you want your own mother's acceptance so much, you do what *his* mother says.

Peter still seeks an intellectual, a theoretical answer.

Peter. If Lorraine is the dynamic factor, what, then, if her mother-in-law is static?
Therapist. What is involved in saying no to a neurotic, you ask.
Peter. How can you say no without being affected?
Lorraine. You can say no if it's friendly, with the feeling, 'I know what you want', and accepting that.
Therapist. There is a way of saying no which is very different from saying no without acceptance of the person.
Peter. I can see that a person who has the dependency needs isn't asking for her hair to be done, and so on.
Lorraine. No, no.
Therapist. She's asking for acceptance.
Jacqueline. And I want to say that the no isn't important as much as the feeling of the person and whether or not the feeling is good. And you can't make it right by saying yes, either.
Therapist. It doesn't help if you say yes without feelings to match it.

SPONTANEOUS CHANGE

Along with pervasive and subtle changes in handling problems, *suddenly* finding that 'I am different', that the same situation or relationship appears in a new light, that 'I could do something I didn't know I could do' is a recurrent experience in becoming a different person. Change is spontaneous. We have seen Jim's sense of a new found power when he could both accept and quieten the junior high school boys, Elizabeth's sudden sense of change when she found enough acceptance of her own limits to accept her husband's help with the children.

We hear sometimes that a knowledge of psychology produces self-consciousness about behaviour. But in the parent classes we learn, 'When you're trying, you haven't got it, when you are self-conscious about it, you haven't become that way. When you just are different, a change in behaviour is inevitable.' Phil has found such a change in his reaction at work. Members of the group are talking about chronic feelings of inadequacy. One man has turned down as many as five jobs because he was afraid he could not live up to the high expectations people had of him. A mother says she has to be asked and would never volunteer for anything—she has to have proof that people think she can do something, as when she was asked to serve as secretary of a parent-teacher group. Others speak of a chronic feeling of being wrong.

> *Phil.* Well, not long ago, I did a job and the boss talked to me about it and asked me why I had done that, made a mistake. And I just up and said, 'Well, I'm only human. I'm entitled to a few mistakes now and then.'
> *Therapist.* You surprised yourself.
> *Phil.* It surprised me and made me feel good about it. He said, 'Yes, I guess you are,' and turned around and walked away. (General laughter.) I felt like they did before—always in the wrong, inadequate. And it made me feel very good.
> *Therapist.* 'I up and asserted myself where I was and stood on it.'
> *Phil.* It wasn't premeditated or anything. When he said it, I just said it back to him, without thinking.
> *Therapist.* It came to you spontaneously.

The sense of surprise, of wonder when habitual reactions seem to be different comes to Denise in relationship to her mother. We know that, as parents resolve the unfinished learnings in themselves, they see their own parents differently. Changes have gradually been taking place in Denise's attitudes. Then she suddenly becomes aware of a marked difference in her feeling for her mother: it is like an unexpected discovery. She has moved beyond the intellectual knowledge that it is fruitless to look to parents for a quality of understanding they are incapable of giving, to a new feeling about it.

> *Denise.* I want to say this. I've gradually come to realise that a lot of my problems were because of the way my mother brought me up, but I have also learned I don't have to stay at that stage. She can be the same, but I feel different. She has gradually come to accept me as a person instead of as a daughter. She even said the other day that I'd make a wonderful friend. I told myself that I don't need her acceptance any more, and I have come a long way.
> *Therapist.* There probably was a time when you felt considerable resentment against her because of the way you have been brought

up until you came to realise it wasn't her fault. And now you begin to understand her, because you have got some of your resentment out, you become a person who can understand her.

Denise. Instead of battling against my resentment.

Therapist. Instead of battling against your resentment, resisting it, being bothered by it, you have come to a relationship which is an understanding one and in which you have arrived at this thing which you hoped for as a child—that is, your mother's acceptance.

Ellen. And then you don't care whether they accept you or not.

Therapist. She came to accept herself and, in accepting herself, she can accept her mother.

Denise. I was trying to explain things to her. And then I find she can't accept it. I would carry on a long conversation with her. Couldn't get anywhere.

Therapist. Aroused the old feeling.

Denise. Trying to explain myself to her.

Therapist. You were trying to get her to understand you, weren't you? And now you're discovering that not only can she not understand you, but it doesn't bother you so much that she doesn't understand you, as it did when you were smaller. You're getting some self-understanding so you don't need her understanding.

Denise. Why did it come to me so suddenly?

Therapist. That's what we call insight. That is where it seems to come over you suddenly. It just suddenly comes on you, and you have a new understanding.

Denise. I used to understand it logically, but suddenly I feel it.

Therapist. 'I feel it.'

Denise. But why so suddenly?

Therapist. 'Why so suddenly?' (Laughing.) It isn't yours until you do see it. For all our thinking about it, it isn't ours until we feel it.

PROCESS AND PROGRESS

Other parents are still struggling with their vulnerability to their own parents' limitations. There is no simple alternative for the process of finding in themselves the centre of evaluation, of finding enough security in their own sense of self-worth.

Parent's parents. Ellen is still trying and speaks in her way for others.

Ellen. I've just visited my home and I feel so emotionally fouled up I can't even think straight. I'm just not a very important person and nothing I can do is right, if it doesn't agree with what they think.

Winston. (Ellen's husband.) That's right. I spoke to her dad and he said, 'Ellen's the baby of the family and it will always be that way.'

Therapist. She doesn't carry any weight.

Winston. Her sisters are older and what they say is more important than what Ellen says.

Jill. (Emphasising that the way we continue to feel tends to determine the reactions of others.) It would seem to me if we could reach the point of being what we want, if Ellen could just go home and speak up with some confidence, they'd listen.

Therapist. If she changes.

Ellen. But I want to get to the point of not being jumpy when my mother is. Her logic doesn't impress me any more, and I used to think she was always right.

Therapist. That, at least, has thinned out; it is no longer so powerful a thing.

Ellen. But I'm trying to please, even though I see it's not logical.

Therapist. (Re-stating dilemma of trying to be someone else's image.) 'I'm trying to be acceptable to her, even though I see it doesn't make logical sense.'

Ellen. My mother goes on about things, tells me I'm ruining my whole life. And I can't stand up to it.

Therapist. You still want her acceptance so much that you still want her to find you satisfactory. You can't stand up against her statement that you're not.

Ellen. I miss home—though, at present, I don't care if I never go home again. But I know I'll want to go again. I forget what it's like.

Therapist. The pain of this will disappear and the thing that will come up will be this desire to get in right at home, accepted by your mother, and to be comfortable there, returning to the place that you want to work through.

Ellen. I know the place is really myself. It's all in myself and how I feel. It isn't home.

Therapist. You're trying to get something there that isn't there.

Philippa. If Ellen wants to be accepted so much, how much has she tried to sit down and accept her parents?

Ellen. I can accept them when I can accept myself.

Therapist. She doesn't feel acceptable you see. And let's accept that she can't. That's an impossible road that she would embark on.
Ellen. I've spent my life trying to get this acceptance. It is ridiculous
Therapist. She's spent her life trying and it's ridiculous, she says. She is aware that to become acceptable to those who can't accept is an impossibility.

'*Two horrible weeks*'. Anne, too, had found a logical answer but feelings well up which she doesn't understand and can hardly name except as generalised anger, the more frightening since she can't pin them down to a source.

Anne. I thought I had things resolved and the old feeling came up. I could recognise it. I've just had two horrible weeks.
Therapist. You thought you knew the answer.
Anne. I knew, but I still felt resentful. This time I just wanted to fight.
Therapist. You had a more open and direct feeling of wanting to fight than you've ever had.
Anne. It reveals so much of feelings of anger that I couldn't handle it. I'm looking for a cause.
Therapist. (Pointing out reality.) Are you looking for a specific cause? I think I'd like to say this. I think we make a mistake in thinking it may be one particular episode, that our mothers did so and so and so. I don't think it's that simple. One can live in a generalised atmosphere. There may be feelings in that situation, but there aren't any words for it. It's very pervasive and harder to place, because it isn't a single episode. If you have a feeling, follow your feeling on it.
Anne. I was very afraid of the feelings of anger I had and felt I must act on them.
Therapist. That is, the feeling was one that it was dangerous to have, wasn't it? 'I must not act out that feeling.' But we are trying to become free to *look* at feelings and talk about them in appropriate places, not to carry into action and into behaviour everything that crosses our mind.
Anne. The only thing that has stopped me expressing my feelings before was a fear of going out of control. (Here Anne expresses a common fear as denied feelings come into awareness.) It seemed insane.

Therapist. What you've told me is this. I have associated my wild feelings of anger with lack of control and even with insanity and have been afraid of them accordingly. I haven't been able to look at them because I got so frightened at what their extremes might mean.

Anne. (Speaking in broken almost inaudible voice.) I need help. What shall I do? I want some one to rely on.

Therapist. What you've said to me then was, 'Please give me a hand, give me directions, let me be dependent on you, I need some help right here.' 'Let me be dependent,' you said to me.

Anne. I used to think that my children could help and then I suddenly realised that they couldn't. A lot of people think they can. They can't help.

Therapist. That is, it's a mistake to look to our children for help, for understanding that we didn't get. That isn't the direction to look, is it?—to children? A lot of people do. That is, it was probably appalling to realise that, if you had been looking for understanding and help there, as we all look for it every place if we don't have it. You realised yesterday that isn't the proper place to look for it.

Anne continues to struggle in a quiet broken voice to articulate what she feels.

Anne. I told my husband how I felt and even though he laughed, I know it helped. He knew how upset I was.

Therapist. Your feelings were accepted by him.

Anne. And I'm not asking *everything* from him now, any more than I am from the children. I appreciate what he *can* give and I'm not asking him for what he cannot give. My feelings were accepted just enough.

Therapist. And you were evidently aware of the fact that his laugh was covering the deep desire to be available when he couldn't.

Anne. He is not to be blamed. I'm not blaming him. And I think he responded to my new attitude. He helped me do things he hadn't before.

Even in the middle of 'two horrible weeks' and the pain of the process of self-discovery, there was a sense of progress.

As original experience in a parent class goes deeper, self-exploration brings pleasing surprises as well as painful negotiations towards increasing freedom from hidden but inhibiting angers. While the process may be an upheaval, looking honestly at denied feelings continues to free more areas of the self from inhibiting defences. Protective walls are found to be prison walls and, in destroying them and revealing real internal needs and feelings, parents find more and more that their outside world is more inviting too. As we diminish the need for reassurance from the outside, we become less

> 'a pipe for Fortune's finger
> To sound what stop she please.'

All the experiences we have shared are part of a continuing process. With different people we have shared different stages. We have seen the way in which airing a dilemma in the class leads to emerging solutions as inner feelings change.

But there are still other frontiers of the mind. Gerard Manley Hopkins has two lines in one of his last sonnets which suggest how precipitous the terrain may be:

> 'O the mind, mind has mountains; cliffs of fall
> Frightful, sheer, no-man fathomed.'

Not all people who choose a journey into the self attempt to explore such depths. They do make discoveries which give greater ease and enjoyment to many areas of their lives. But some choose to go further to the fullest possible self-knowledge. Some of their experiences and what they mean in terms of everyday living, the way therapy may continue to be a continuing resource of help in times of exceptional stress, mark the last chapters of our journey with parents.

7 *Becoming as a Child*

I am a smiling summer sea
That sleeps while underneath from bound to bound
The sun and star shaped killers gorge and play.

Edwin Muir

Notions of depths and heights are pervasively part of everyday talk about emotions; we speak of being up or down, elated or depressed. But the depths and heights that we are concerned with now call for a reconnoitring that looks and comes to know in detail hidden personal worlds peopled with shadows not easily yielded to view. Once met and recognised for what they are, they change their forbidding aspect and we find greatly expanded inner freedoms, and deepened meaning in intimate relationships and the human world.

Dante, who made himself the Everyman of his most human epic, *The Divine Comedy*, speaks of taking 'the little vessel of his mind' into the abyss of an inferno where light is dim and which is inhabited by hardly recognisable shapes, before he climbs, meeting other shapes on the winding ways and mountain ledges of purgatory, to the eventual light. His guide is reason, embodied in Virgil who is in touch with a reality which helps Everyman to become acquainted with every aspect of his private hell literally without losing his mind. As he observes and finds compassion for the worst that man can experience, he moves into more complete knowledge of himself. Essentially for Dante-Everyman the search for the whole man was the search for the meaning of love, going beyond reason. The sudden ascent to paradise became the spontaneous finding of a new and freer self resulting from insights made possible for Everyman by Beatrice, image of inclusive love.

Accompanying parents as people into the furthest reaches of a human struggle to find self we see here, too, a search for the insights which make possible the capacity to receive and give love. In these modern epics human Odysseys of the mind, the completely available listener is the guide who too represents reality—the setter of limits as well as the giver of freedom and choice. We already have had a glimpse of the sense of disturbance, of deep upheaval that the beginnings of self-discovery can bring, as well as some of the gains that find spontaneous expression without conscious thought, when we become freer to look at ourselves without fear. In living with them the further journeys of a small group of women, we shall share their experience both of the depths of their minds, and of the changing vision that this experience brings of the everyday world of their own home, and the men, women and children of their universe. We shall hear them in groups and face-to-face talks, listening to each communication in its own right.

WHAT IS NEW?

Some very ordinary questions may occur now. Haven't we in a sense said it all? Are we going to learn anything new? Will these experiences be different from what we have heard before?

True, there is a sense in which there is nothing new from beginning to end. One paragraph could say it all and we need not have a book. The end is known. We seek—the reduction of psychological distance between people, the growth in their ability to give leading to parents' increased capacity both to accept and guide children, and a diminution of self-defeating ways of relating to others. But the route of therapy is much analogous to Greek drama, or any great traditional epic of the human race. We can if we wish, summarise events in a few sentences. The Trojan women will become slaves and Hector's son will be thrown from the battlements of Troy. Oedipus will find out about his crime in killing his father and marrying his mother without knowing it just as each individual will in therapy discover the place of his family triangles involving parents without knowing about or referring at all to the term Oedipus complex, with its connotations of regressive attachment to the parent of opposite sex. But we are not concerned here with an abstract summary of events, or an abstract goal or a technical term. The human *experience* is what we seek to understand. We are concerned with the process by which people reach their individual goals and what the process reveals of what it is to be human for each human being. No one has an answer for someone else. Carol has Carol's answer, Jim has his, Ralph has his, though the universals in human experience find their variations in each person's heart. Our explorations of human events will now often be more detailed, the associations to dream images both more concentrated and expanded. The primitive and civilised, the drama of the mind and everyday events will come to us in familiar and unfamiliar ways in the most personal of human equations.

We shall explore further the meaning of admitting feelings ('from ice to heat') and the continuing fight against doing so. We shall look at some of the disproportionate operations of unconscious guilt and needs for retribution which are perhaps the greatest cripplers of emotional life and personal relationships. We shall see the multiple uses of decoys and camouflage by which a person hides from himself his most frightening experiences, his most painful remembrances of deprivation of love. We shall encounter crucial issues of dependency, when a parent is still crying for his infant needs to be met, and see parents grow up with their own children. In two further chapters we shall learn something of the search for sexual identity and a mature sexual relationship in marriage, and we shall grapple with the problems of resolving the contradictions of a parent's hostile indentification with his own hated parent.

It will be neither a streamlined story, nor a conclusive one. But we shall have shared more of what it means to be a person and a parent, when parents are heard.

FROM ICE TO HEAT

At the very bottom of Dante's Inferno in a frozen lake in darkness are those who have by betrayal negated relatedness to kindred or others who gave them trust as guests or benefactors. So, in our human world, the ultimate in unrelatedness seems to be the symbol of ice. 'I have no feelings', 'I don't care', 'I have no friends', 'Cut off relating because it means anguish', 'Be immobilised, frozen; paralysis is preferable if movement means finding a world of hate'.

When violent emotions are the antithesis of ice, fear fights letting in the light to look at self, and allowing warmth, and only slowly gives way to a willing awareness of thawing feelings and acceptance of needs. Gaynor, wife and mother speaks in retrospect of her violent discoveries when she moved from ice to heat and looked at the source of her ice world in her relationship with her parents.

'*A big show*'. 'I felt nothing for my parents—I was frozen. But I put on a *big show*. Once I started admitting them I found my feelings so strong that I hadn't dared look at them. And I found that there was a viciousness and anger and resentment that amazed me. As a child there was nothing but resentment to my mother. I wanted to be close to my father and that meant living up to his standards, which I could never do. My mother always seemed to let down my father's standards and she never seemed to be there when I needed her. My father stood for education and my mother for all that I labelled common and low class. Yet I married a husband who was the opposite of my father. And then I resented it. Then we had a child and I rejected her from the beginning. But I didn't know it. I didn't know I was not ready to give to a child. I only knew I was tired and discouraged. But I put on a big show of loving the baby.'

But Gaynor feels some understanding for her mother by now and is conscious of a new sympathy for her. 'I don't get mad if she says, "Gaynor, you put me in mind of myself." I don't have to have her "neurotic" ways. I don't have to be the cry-baby if I am like my mother. And I don't have to cling.'

But she is still working on resolving an old need for a mother's care, and on looking at the basic feelings that her father's standards seemed to deny.

A dream of rebellion. She tells a dream in which her rebellious primitive feelings come out as a black people's rebellion which separates a mother and daughter. Projection of feared basic feelings on to dark-skinned people and consequent rejection of the dark-skinned people is a feature common in prejudice. Gaynor's personal meanings become clearer as she talks.

> *Gaynor.* I was in a store and met a friend, and spent more time than I should shopping with her. I should have been home and I was supposed to pick Anne up from school and all the clocks said different times and I was panicky I'd be late. And when I went outside there was a black people's rebellion and all the black men had guns and they took me to a ranch and put me in a barn and there were other prisoners there including my friend. I was in a tiny room with just a little screen at the top and it began filling with milk. I had a fight to keep from smothering. Finally they drained the milk out. Then they put heavy make-up on me for some reason. And I was crying for Anne and was afraid she was crying for me. And my friend said they put the same make-up on her but they brought her child to her and that Anne and I would be

reunited. The crying and being separated from Anne were the only depressing part of it. And the feeling Anne would be crying for me.

Therapist. A child separated from her mother.

Gaynor. It was the thought I wasn't with her. My feelings were definitely with her on that point. I can never actually remember being separated from my mother when I was little, not physically. But I could never get close to her. That must be the part of being separated. And blackmen have been in my dreams so many times It's the same deal of this foreign element and it keeps reappearing. Like Mexican Joe and the fascination he had for me. My mother warned me against this group of people that came to my home town. But I was fascinated with all these different races. But I took it as wrong because she warned me. And I took it as warning against fascination for any men especially a foreign man.

Therapist. (Restates the personal meaning for Gaynor of a stereotype.) The blackman, the Mexican, the man who is different, seems different from the idea of your father for instance, not so cultured, not so affirming of education.

Gaynor. That's right. And this business of having no time. We were never in time for school. But the janitor would ring the bell till we got there. He'd see us coming. He was a wonderful fellow. It was Mother's fault that we didn't get there on time because she could have got up earlier but she waited till the last minute because she didn't want to get up. I can remember running and crying all the way to school and saying Mamma all the way to school.

Therapist. A child crying for her mother.

Gaynor. It's the same thing I thought Anne was doing in the dream. And something else struck me. The heavy make-up for disguise made me remember the way my mother looked when she had a headache. Her eyes were sunken and she was least available when she was sick.

As we have seen, dream provides a release in disguise for unwanted feelings. Both fantasy and dream may be wish fulfilments—as an old popular song has it, 'You can't stop me from dreaming.' But the literal content is the surface vehicle for hidden content. The dreamer's wishes and counter-wishes may be played out in the images of different people and events in the dream, like a drama. The more unacceptable the unconscious wish, the less to be talked about, in other words, the more disguised it must be for the dreamer in images that can be talked about. 'I do not have these primitive strong feelings. They belong to foreign outcast people who use force to imprison me in an uncivilised barn. I am civilised and that means I don't have these feelings.' The hidden content of the dream embodies for each dreamer the personal synonyms of his private experience and as he sees their meanings for himself, so hidden conflict with himself diminishes. The more overt the dream's images, the closer is the dreamer to admitting their meaning even though a nightmare seems to be the route.

A nightmare. In the early days of their first class parents hear, 'A parent who feels he can't handle the situation is a parent who rejects', 'If a father feels "my child is a monster" it means that his needs have not been met, not that he's bad'. The new look at words which have frightening connotations helps to reduce the fear and guilt attached to their significance and makes greater initial honesty about conscious feelings possible. But being able to experience, later, needs that have not been met if he himself was a rejected child may come as a shattering awareness to a parent.

Janet, mother of three, was, like Gaynor, frozen in feeling. She said when she first came to a parent group, 'I have no feelings, but I get mad if the kids get in my way.' At the end of the first meeting of a group of mothers she said, 'I suppose my mother did reject me. I haven't thought about it.' Nearly a year later she tells a dream in which her feelings become concrete in the image of a monster.

> *Janet*. I can hardly stand to talk about it. There was this monster which was me and I yelled for my mother in the dream and suddenly she was the monster and I was sorry for her. I got some insight into how I must have felt as a child. I felt I had done something to my mother. She was very black, sort of black around her eyes and face. I put my hands around her neck choking her. Then I woke up yelling her name, and sobbed and sobbed. The dream takes me back to my childhood. I must have felt this hate for my mother for which I turned on myself.
>
> *Therapist*. You felt you were a monster because of it.

A long-denied need is coming to life. Janet is beginning to look. Shortly after in an interview she says, 'Every time I get a bit of feeling

I hang on to it. When I first began to unfreeze, though, I wanted to leave it alone, so I stayed away from the group for six months. Then I couldn't wait to get back. I had to be ready.'

GUILT, RETRIBUTION AND REPARATION

The way that the images and actions of a dream may both reveal and hide (This is my dream but someone else has these primitive feelings, this sexual impulse) is true of many behaviours in the conscious life also. Such compromise behaviours arise from unconscious attempts to allay pervasive feelings of guilt for 'what I have thought or felt and at least in fantasy have done.' In headaches, digestive troubles, and other 'body talk' needs and guilt for the needs may find partial communication. 'If I could be as furious as I feel *and* have my needs taken care of my headache would go, but I am bad, unworthy', 'If I could receive the emotional food I need, my stomach would stop giving me trouble, but I do not deserve this love I'm looking for, nor do I have confidence anyone will care about me in all my helpless angers and desperate needs.' Speech problems such as some forms of stuttering may both hold back in hesitancy and express hostile feeling. In children they may be a way of striking which succeeds in getting worried concern from grown-ups. Similarly, frightened children hold in their feelings and their stool together, yet express resentment, implying, 'I cannot give my gifts if you don't accept me'; but constipation has power both to upset these hurting adults and to bring their attention. In constant colds and coughs a child may 'worry' and 'control' a covertly rejecting but overtly concerned mother and at the same time find an acceptable outlet for the repressed crying which the mother's pervasive anxiety produces in him, symbolically saying, 'The mucous membranes may cry but I may not.'

In sulking, Gaynor discovered she both expressed and denied her feelings about conforming.

Gaynor. I had some comfort from sulking as a child. Going off by myself and feeling that everybody balks me, hates me, and I have been wrong and bad and mean.

Brenda. What's the comfort in it?

Gaynor. I don't know, must be self-punishment of some sort.

Brenda. Maybe the comfort is just an indulging of a feeling.

Gaynor. If I were indulging it, I'd throw things and then society would kick.

Hilda. It seems to me, Gaynor, that sulking was the same thing as conforming.

Gaynor. It is.

Hilda. You're out of your mother's hair to a certain extent and you can't do what you really want to and throw.

Therapist. Compromise. Compromise. Compromise between being what her mother wanted and what she needed to be herself. She wanted to be angry and her mother wanted to get her out of the way. So she put the two together in sulking.

In this way Gaynor also 'paid' for being bad.

'You must pay.' Guilt means 'You've got to be punished'. Such re-definition has power to go beyond dictionary denotation into an individual connotation which strongly implies self-condemnation.

The following interchange in a group setting illustrates the way in which the therapist may use this kind of re-definition therapeutically. A more explicit response than usual can reinforce teaching already given in a previous class. Occasionally even in deep therapy such a clarification, using a person's own cue, enables the therapist to assist insight into a life situation. Re-definition in a therapy context makes personal the meaning of guilt and denial.

Brenda. I'm very scared inside about my father. I've always thought of him as a gentleman and a dreamer, an idealist and so on. But as a child I'm sure he scared the life out of me. He had a terrific hold on reality, I thought. But he's dynamite. I mean he gives you the feeling that he'll explode.

Therapist. That's the way he handled his strong feelings. By denying them. By fantasy and idealism. Idealism's a denial of strong feelings.

Brenda. I can remember sometimes when he did explode. Like when a little boy kicked my bicycle and my father was furious and chased the little boy who was just terrified and escaped into some-one else's house. But I must have been very unhappy in those days. I thought I was just feeling guilty. I must apparently have been expecting trouble.

Therapist. Guilt is expecting trouble. That's what guilt is. 'I expect trouble for what I have felt or lived.'

Anne. (Another member of the group finds insight for herself in this interchange.) I seem to condemn myself all the time.

Therapist. That is, you have the feeling that you will have to pay for this.

'That these feelings of unhappiness are really guilt' is a realisation that can gradually lead to the discovery of the true meaning of the vague anxiety. Awareness dawns: 'This depression really means that feelings I can't bear to look at are threatening to come up and that I've turned on myself for even possessing such feelings.'

Capitalising on guilt. Finding the real source of the guilt, however, is harder than recognising its presence. There are multiple decoys, multiple smokescreens, multiple ways of seeking relief from tension to avoid looking at the real cause of guilty feelings, which is unknown and unconscious. Confession itself may serve as a blind: 'Look, I have revealed myself as an awful person. Isn't that enough?' 'I've been punished. Now surely I've made reparation.' But there is more. Personal meanings only gradually become clear for Elise. First she speaks of a conscious problem. She works in individual interviews and has difficulty speaking her thoughts. She has a confession. A confession is to reduce guilt.

Elise. There's something which I feel most ashamed to say but I've got to get it out. (Long pause.) I haven't said how much I've always masturbated. And still, whenever I'm depressed, I masturbate. I guess it's a form of comfort. They say it is the same as a child sucking its thumb when he can't get the comfort anywhere else. I think I did that.
Therapist. That is you feel you turned to yourself for comfort because you couldn't get it anywhere else.
Elise. That's right.

But masturbation has many more meanings than comfort for Elise. Guilt has many faces too. Her father was a heavy drinker and her mother divorced him when she was eleven. Previous to this he had left the family on several occasions. But even after the divorce, six months later, he came back for a few weeks.

Elise. I wanted to comfort my father. I felt I understood him better than anyone. But he still left. I always tried to be with him. I'd take my homework to his office. But when he'd been drinking he'd be violent. He had a terrible temper. I wanted to be close to him but I was afraid of him, too. Then, after the divorce, I did everything to be close to my mother and when my father came back he upset everything. He started spanking us and I was sleeping in my mother's room and he took that. And then he went again. (Pause.) I feel in intercourse I'm not relating to a man. I'm just a little girl getting close to my father with all the guilt. I fantasied sex with my father and I was ashamed. Sex is getting close. But it didn't seem right that anyone coming back the way my father did had so much power. I wanted him and I hated him. I wanted to take away his power and I think I thought of taking his penis. (Long pause.) Masturbation was the only way I knew how—that robbed a man of his power. But I felt so untouchable I had to prove that I was not. That way I depended on no one.

Therapist. Masturbation was a way of attacking your father and asserting your independence of him as well as asserting you were not 'an untouchable'.

Elise. I can hardly bear to even mention it. What a damned mess! And on the outside I was the model child, doing everything to please my mother. Because it was a way to get what I wanted.

Therapist. Pleasing your mother was a kind of power, too.

Elise. Yes. And, of course, I felt guilty about that. My mother always wanted me to tell her things. She was a nose. And whatever I told her she'd go and spill it to everybody. I could never trust her with anything.

Therapist. You felt let down that way with your mother also.

Elise. I didn't feel I pleased her though she said she was pleased. I know that just before the divorce especially I competed for my father with my mother. When I was nine and ten. I felt she was always talking about *him* and I sympathised because she was always talking about *me*. And then I felt it was my fault when they broke up. And I had to make up to my mother. But I was so rigid and held so much in under the model child behaviour. I felt I should pay. It's true, that's just the way I did feel. And actually I hurt myself; I dig my nails into my body, and hurt myself when I masturbate. And I bite my nails. It's almost as if I'm biting and scratching myself.

Therapist. You feel you're attacking yourself.

Elise. I am and it seems to me that I'm at the biting and scratching stage. And I *hold in*. I'm never more rigid than when I masturbate. (Pause.) I took a nap yesterday afternoon and I dreamed I killed my father and I woke up masturbating. I was horrified and completely exhausted...

Therapist. To see what you were doing so clearly is horrifying to you, and maintaining this conflicted position with your father is an exhausting business.

Six months later she had some other thoughts about guilt and masturbation.

Elise. I still have to hold in. I can't trust to let go. Now I haven't been masturbating as much but I feel I still hold back in intercourse. There's a feeling of guilt all the time. We do have some times of joy but Colin feels I hold back. (Pause). And I've found something else. I masturbate *when I already* feel guilty. That makes it possible to *make* masturbation the *cause* of my guilt. And I do have guilt feelings about intercourse. It's as though I'm looking for a *specific thing* to be guilty about, better than a *vague* feeling of guilt. I give myself something to be guilty about.
Therapist. You don't have to look at the real reason then.
Elise. I feel I can't. It's too terrifying. I don't know what it is. But it seems to me I *need* this guilt.
Therapist. You do feel you ought to pay.
Elise. Yes, that, but also when I've given myself something to be guilty about then I can accomplish a lot, as though I'm exorcising the guilt, repairing the damage in some way. The house is never so clean, the cooking is never so good as when I'm making up for my guilt. I deliberately give myself something to be guilty about so that I can have the energy to accomplish something.
Therapist. You are literally capitalising on your guilt.

Reparation. Guilt serves as the means of retribution, it is the instigator of punishment. Even though each person does not 'act out' in concrete images like Lennie who put himself in the corner, or fantasy as concretely as Carol daydreamed she was a prisoner on parole, yet in fact through the agency of guilt each person is his own punisher—his gaoler and executioner, literally putting himself in the prison of his own sense of unworthiness stifling his vitality, his capacity for venturing. On the other hand, a drive to repair the 'damage of what I have felt or lived' is a constructive healing force. Elise's reparation for guilt derives from a constructive force but as it is part of an artificially contrived smokescreen it does not dissolve the deeper guilt. Similarly she became aware earlier that she got angry at unimportant things because direct anger had been associated with a kind of damage for which she felt no reparation was possible.

Elise. I can't stand the vagueness if I don't give myself something to be guilty about. I don't accomplish anything. I go to pieces. And I can't stand the feeling of something missing.

Therapist. Something missing.

Elise. It's like getting mad. I couldn't get mad at anything that really mattered. I had to get mad at all kinds of little things. Things I couldn't care less about. And that day I got furious with you about payment (fee) if you remember, and called you all the four-letter words. It seemed to be a turning point. I got mad direct. I know I had to make the excuse of payment to start it. I couldn't just get mad with you out of the blue. I could now, of course. To hell with you. (Smiles). I'm better now. And I talk more easily to people. But there are many ways I find it hard to talk here.

Therapist. Finding anger did not bring disastrous results makes it possible to relate to others more easily. But you're saying that the situation here does not make it easier to talk.

Elise. Here I have to go deep. I can't get away with pretence here. It wouldn't help just to be the model child here. I'm moving away from the feeling *everything* is my fault, of course. But I think other people may be to blame, too.

Therapist. You're not blaming yourself, you say. But you are still seeing things in terms of blame. Blaming yourself, or blaming others?

Elise. I resent that. (Pause.) But I have to admit that I am hitting at others. I attacked my sister for being so crummy in the way she dresses and for being so lazy about housework. (Pause.) I still have some of the perfectionist in me. And I'm afraid of rejection. It's not just if I get mad, But I feel I'll be rejected if I care about anybody. And I am afraid Colin will leave me, although I know intellectually he is devoted to me. I think it's another reason why I hold back. And when he's away on business trips I die until he phones me. He has to prove I won't be rejected.

Therapist. 'If I reveal how I feel I shall be cast out, I need constant reassurance I won't be rejected.'

Elise. Well you remember that time when my uncle was staying with us and he was ill for several weeks. I did a lot for him always. But one day he wanted me to make him some coffee and a sandwich and I wanted to play, and I said, 'Oh, can't you wait?' And he never forgave me. Nothing I could do would bring me into favour again.

Therapist. You learned it pays to be on guard against asserting what you need.

Elise. I know I'm guilty about showing my real feelings. (Pause.) I think the something missing is love.

Untrue confessions. Confession has as many faces as guilt. A constant need to confess may well cover a deeper guilt of which a person is not consciously aware. Mary has always believed she was close to her mother but she is making some discoveries that shake her deeply. She explains her relationship with her mother.

Mary. You know that feeling I talked about that if my mother died I would not want to survive her. If she went away when I was a child even for a day I was anxious. And once she went on vacation for a month and we had a housekeeper. I thought I was letting my mother down if I didn't cry every night. I trusted my mother. I could tell her everything because she never blabbed. And I made a point of telling her everything. I confessed everything to her. Every detail of my activities—if I used a swear word, and if I heard sex stories at school. Everything. But I'm coming to realise something that just tears me up. (Sobs and cannot speak for some time.) All these confessions to my mother, all this trust was not true confession at all and it was not trust. The confessions on little things gave me some release. But they were a camouflage to take away from the real confession which I didn't know I was avoiding, but now I know. I wished to get rid of her because she was not my father, she was a poor substitute. And that's why I couldn't survive her death. Because I killed her and must pay with my death. I wanted my father's affection and nothing else would do. So I struck at him by getting close to my mother, telling all my thoughts to her, and never telling him anything. Shutting him out. In reality you couldn't have trusted his tongue anyway. When my mother went away for that month I had to cry because I was guilty. I was afraid she'd get hurt because I'd wanted it. And most of all I resented her because nothing I did ever seemed to make her happy. And I don't think she knew she rejected me. But she was critical and rejecting always underneath. Oh, I had such guilt. I can see it all now. I told my mother nothing. It was all a pretence. But I turned myself inside out to take her into my confidence and to gain her love.

Therapist. You tried in every way you knew to make the peace with your mother.

Mary. But deep down I resented her in so many ways. It wasn't just that she wasn't my father, but because she didn't like being a woman. Two impossible contradictions! But it was so hard to learn to be a woman from her. She tried, she did try. And I do understand she was a deeply hurt person. But she hated housekeeping, and body functions were not to be mentioned. She told me nothing about menstruation. It came on me like a shock and she explained nothing then. She was so uncomfortable with all of herself. I never once saw her naked. Yet she was a beautiful woman. She needed love so desperately and was so anxious to please. This is a tragedy really. She worked so hard feeling so unloved. And my father was the last person to give comfort. He landed an attack that just shot you to the ground if you said anything about the way you felt. Of course, he couldn't face his own feelings, his own needs.

Therapist. You felt your parents did not meet your needs, but you do not want to blame them; you'd like to understand them.

A new kind of reparation. Mary reached out to understand the world of other members of her family, especially her brother for whom she felt deep envy as a child.

Mary. My brother was close to my father and I did nothing but fight him from the beginning. I couldn't get near my father, so I fought my brother. Now I realise how much my brother really meant to me. And I cry for what his world must have done to him when he was so little and everything must have been overwhelming. And he's been very antagonistic to me. He couldn't see my troubles and I couldn't see his.

Therapist. Understanding your own devastations has helped to give you understanding for your brother who seemed to you as a child to take away your father.

Mary. I should not have been guilty. I've gone through all my life condemning myself. But trying to put on a bold face. It was such a hollow show. And I think the thing that tears me up most now is my brother. He doesn't see at all what he is doing and he married a wife who is quite a bit like the old me before I got some understanding. And she can't stand me. She can't stand to see herself, I think. And because I'm freer it seems to be a threat to her.

She's really the ultimate in hostility. I think she feels she has to maintain a position, however false. It is such a suicidal course they are following. She is so afraid to accept affection. They are their own worst enemies. If they could only see. I've thought of every way to do something for them. The tragedy is that she has the children on her side—as if it is a question of sides, other than the human side. They can't be happy if they are lined up against their father. She doesn't know how many times a day she says critical things about him, and, of course, he lives up, or down, to the image. He doesn't know what he's doing. And I suppose he's seeking his own punishments, 'cause he feels he's no good. He's been brutal and he won't own his tenderness any more than my father did. These mistaken guilts of childhood. I should know. They won't accept help either one of them. And I know they're afraid. And I know what it means when you have to fight for your life wondering if it's worth it all the time. Wondering if you're worth it. I went about apologising for my existence. Guilt just that I stayed alive. I remember those horrifying dreams where I was being executed and I didn't know why. It seems if I apologised for my *existence* that included *everything*.

Therapist. Are you saying that you expected trouble for everything that was you?

Mary. It looks like it. I can see why I couldn't sleep when I was a teenager. I didn't know what was going to happen in my sleep. I was so afraid if I let down my guard. And then I got so exhausted I could never get enough sleep. I think I wanted to die even then. Just to escape.

Therapist. That would be more than sleep, wouldn't it? Permanent escape.

Mary. I was afraid of sleep because I was afraid I'd die in my sleep. I had to keep awake to keep myself alive. Because I'd wanted to die and it might come true if I lost consciousness. I might never wake. Then, of course, you're *helpless* when you're asleep and that's the worst thing to be. I was afraid of dreams, afraid of nightmares, afraid of the punishment that would come with sleep, including death. All the blame my parents heaped on us! If only people could see what they were doing to children. I thought of suicide as the only way so many times. I can see I couldn't handle the sense of guilt for every feeling I ever had and the despair of ever finding understanding.

Therapist. That anyone could meet your needs seemed impossible.

Mary is voicing the emotional consequences of deep irrational guilt: it seems impossible to depend on anyone; moreover, one is unworthy in one's own mind to receive such care. None the less, the search to depend continues.

CAN I DEPEND?

If we have not experienced a dependency we can trust, the continuing search to depend takes many forms. 'I want someone to take care of me' means looking in a wide range to have our child needs met—husband, children, friends. Finding that we can trust a need to depend goes as deep as any human experience. Oldest needs go deepest—the needs of the baby, the very young child. 'That I can depend no matter how I feel, no matter how I am' stretches into feelings before words. Devastated feelings of being deprived of love by those where we had to depend come painfully to recognition in the adult. A person fights hard the seeming helplessness and vulnerability of dependency. So he may reverse roles and always externally be the one to take care of others while innerly wanting to be taken care of. So, 'Let me take care of a stray cat or dog or a lost bird' is a safer way to express awareness of these sensitive needs than to ask for oneself to be cared for. 'I am not deserving.'

A feeling of unworthiness means looking for acceptable external reasons to protest a need.

'*He stops me from eating.*' Gaynor says she is annoyed at her husband because he stops her from eating by asking for attention at meal times.

Gaynor. My idea of Jim's acceptance is that he will feel that my desires and needs are important.

Therapist. What you most want is to have your needs accepted, isn't it?

Gaynor. Yes.

Therapist. To have your needs accepted. Your desires should make him give you acceptance.

Gaynor. There it is. I didn't even recognise it. This must have been the way I felt about Daddy. Somehow I looked that my desires and needs might become important.

Anna. It sounds as if you both become two babies at the same time.

When he most wants to be fed, you want to be fed. And you're just howling for each other at the same time.
Gaynor. Oh I can admit that Jim is a baby but I can't admit the fact that I'm that babyish. I have admitted it before, but I hate to admit that I'm a big baby.
Anna. You seem ashamed of it.
Gaynor. You mean I can be a baby at this age and time.
Therapist. You'd better be, or you'll never be anything else.
Anna. If she could accept that she was a baby—I just want it real badly—you've got to take care of me.
Therapist. It isn't very practical. You can't act like a baby. But you can at least admit you feel like one. You can't go around sucking the bottle in public you know. And if we can't depend on our husbands to meet us as babies we can at least admit that we feel like a baby, and it's all right to feel that way. And the sooner you recognise it's all right the less you're going to ask it of a husband. and work on it yourself.

'*Domination is demanding what you want.*' But Gaynor was still resolving her baby needs. She did not like them. Neither did Elise who wanted to be the strong one.

Elise. I'm just controlling everything, especially myself. But I want everybody to do things my way. It's subtle and there are always real excuses. But I seem to have a need for domination.
Therapist. Domination is demanding what you want.
Elise. I hate to think it's because I'm a baby and want to depend. That embarrasses me and I don't trust it. I've always been the strong one. I've always been controlled.
Therapist. You've always handled this thing by control you mean.
Elise. I felt I had to be stronger than both my parents.

Gaynor began to discover that her need to be cared for crept into more than a reaction of anger that her husband stopped her 'from eating'.

Gaynor. I'm mad at him because he won't fix the doorknob and the window. The door just won't shut, and the kitchen window is broken.
Therapist. He really lets down on these responsibilities.
Gaynor. Yes and I've thought about this. I'm mad at him because

he's doing directly and openly what I want to do—he hands over responsibilities, he just lets other people take over. But I hate this wish to be cared for. I'm afraid of letting down completely if I admit how I feel.

Therapist. You're afraid you might enjoy it too much.

Gaynor. But I can see I'm *using excuses* to let down. I had a tooth out and I stayed on the couch all day. But the tooth wasn't that bad.

'*Wanting babies and being babies*'. Looking for acceptable reasons to be cared for finds a most acceptable place for a woman in becoming a mother. Having a baby brings special attention to the one who gives it birth. Also a baby is helpless and gives a mother an opportunity for control if she needs 'to demand what she wants by domination'. Then the baby growing up can be a threat if keeping him dependent is a source of adequacy.

Melanie is disturbed when her baby 'begins to do everything for herself'.

Therapist. She's not an extension of you then.

Melanie. I feel it isn't safe when she tries to cook things.

Therapist. It isn't safe.

Melanie. And she wants to sew. So I have her sitting by my side and helping.

Therapist. You want to hold her to the helping you stage?

Melanie. I'd love to have another child. I envy people with two or three children.

Therapist. That is, you would feel more adequate if you had two or three children. Is that what you mean?

Other members of the group speak their feelings about having a baby: 'I feel deprived because I haven't had another child', 'My husband is so different when I'm pregnant', 'Well, everybody takes care of my needs more'.

Melanie. I can't wait much longer. Perhaps I should forget about age and security.

Therapist. Do it in a hurry. The problem is when you start to think about it.

Gaynor. I feel deprived of another child too. But something happened yesterday. I was holding a baby and the thought crossed my mind that I don't even like babies.

Therapist. 'I don't even like babies.'

Gaynor. No. And it scares me. I thought, 'What kind of a person am I that I don't like babies?' I've always all my life said I wanted a baby, I couldn't wait and I don't think I like them.
Therapist. Here is your statement. You don't like babies.
Gaynor. It's been dawning on me. I know I don't like these baby feelings in myself. I don't like the baby. Me.
Therapist. You both admit and fight this realisation.

Janet was disturbed because she became pregnant. Like Gaynor, as we saw, she was frozen in feeling when she first joined a parent group. Now, as in the nightmare about her mother as a monster, she admits to very strong feelings and needs of her own. Talking in group about, feelings in relation to the coming baby helps reduce danger of a mother projecting her own baby needs to depend on to the new baby.

Janet. I hate all my three children because I want to be taken care of myself. I don't want another baby. I went to bed the other night and I said out loud four or five times 'I don't want another baby. I don't want another baby'. And yet I've got the feeling that I must have wanted to get pregnant again for needs of my own.
Therapist. You wanted to get pregnant to be taken care of yourself.
Janet. To be cared for myself. I'm sure that it's to make me important and cared for.
Therapist. To be important. To be cared for.
Janet. I mean I want to be the baby. I don't want the baby.

Wanting to go back to infancy to be cared for, to depend, means undoing deprivation of love.

'*Proving I'm first*'. Gaynor's need to depend takes the form of wanting her father's approval and puts her in competition with her daughter, an echo of a former rivalry with her mother for her father.

Gaynor. I got hold of something about the way I feel. I want Anne to think I'm efficient. I always thought Mother was so efficient.
Therapist. You want Anne to think you're efficient.
Gaynor. I want Anne to think I'm efficient. I want Anne to think I can do things right.
Therapist. In other words, you want to *prove* that you're efficient and that you can do things right.
Gaynor. I guess I want to do that with everybody.

Therapist. 'I am trying to prove that I can do things well—efficiently and well.'

Gaynor. My feelings don't connect up with Mother. They connect up with Daddy again. I always come back to the same thing. Those damned standards. How can I ever?

Therapist. You're trying to live up to the standards your father set.

Gaynor. And I'm in competition with Anne the way I was in competition with Mother. But Anne's just a little girl. I mean at the same time that there's the desire to let her go, let her be independent, there is always the desire to always keep ahead of her and do things better. She showed me how mad and mean I look, putting on such an expression the other day. I said I was going to spank her if she splashed in the bath tub and she sat there just daring me with her foot out. And I got so mad.

Therapist. 'Who was going to win?' You were playing it out.

Gaynor. Mother was always first with Daddy. (Pause.) But I'm beginning to see him differently. Yesterday he looked like a tired old man.

Therapist. Not so far up there and you down here.

Gaynor. No. His shoulders are all drooped. He isn't as good looking as I thought he was. But I looked and his figure really isn't good-looking.

Therapist. You're not having to look up to him as much, are you?

Gaynor. Not so much, but still some. And I still would like to please him.

Therapist. I would like to please him.

Gaynor. I would still like to have him think I was wonderful.

Therapist. I would still like to have his acceptance.

Gaynor. Yes. But he doesn't look like he did. I think I looked at him for the first time in my life and saw him as he really is.

Responding to trust. As a parent finds in therapy that he can depend, trust in his own feelings takes the place of fear.

Elise's rigid control of her feelings meant inability to talk during large parts of many interviews. Holding in words found a parallel in constipation. 'Not talking in therapy is like a little child refusing to go potty for his mother' was a repugnant discovery for her, but constipation proved to be another means to power.

Elise. But it gives me control of the situation.

Therapist. Not giving what they want of you gives you control of your parents.
Elise. I don't trust giving of myself. I could never depend on their being available to accept what I gave or even to notice.

As she was able to talk of her feelings in therapy, as words came from her mouth without fear, reduced tension allowed bowel movements to take place, too.

Helen tells how her increase in self-trust affected her son. She had been an adored child. 'I was a doll rather than a child. I was taught I needed nothing, because I had all the toys I wanted. I got acceptance by not showing anger. Control was crucial. And then I found all this anger inside and wanting to scream four letter words.'

She is moving now to self-trust and her son in his turn is finding a different experience of dependency.

Helen. I'd like for everyone to know about Dan. You remember I've spoken about him being so constipated and it's been very interesting to me to hear people say they handle their children this way and that way and I feel I have a long way to go but I feel that in working this trust angle out myself that one of my problems has just disappeared. I know I've always been in fear, deathly fear, I've lived in fear. One side of this is sex, and I'm going through this stage of being able to feel adolescent in a sexual manner, which is very comforting to me incidentally. But the other is anger. And I was really I think on an unconscious level and finally consciously taking it out on Dan and I know that the result was that he became constipated and he just wouldn't have a B.M. And I had to give him everything under the sun to make him part with his stool. I finally got my anger to such a degree that I know this and I mean no one can convince me that it isn't true; when I felt sound enough in myself, when I could trust myself with him, suddenly as if a miracle had occurred he started regularly having B.M.'s. And he just has a B.M. every day now. He's no longer constipated. It's nothing that I did *for* him, it's just something that I did in myself so that I feel, I mean I'm just convinced that it does so much with children. I didn't know what to do. Now he just hugs me and parts with his B.M.'s. He plays enema with his toys and so works it out that way.

Deprivation and hunger for love. Demandingness, criticism of others, domination but never being satisfied with anything were key themes in Mary's life until she saw and felt her own hunger for love, an insatiable need. There was no experience more painful than this self-knowledge in a long and painful struggle to find herself. She speaks to the therapist in an interview.

Mary. I've been in a collapse all weekend. You know how upset I've been, feelings of panic and despair, feeling everything was falling to pieces. It's very difficult to put into words what happened this weekend, but I know that as a child I was so deprived of what I vitally needed—understanding and warmth. There was so much tension. My father would threaten to leave us and then he started drinking. And my mother was in a panic—I can see it now—that she would be deserted. 'He'll leave us,' she said. And the look on her face and the feeling of despair I'll never forget. I lived in constant dread. Well this weekend things came to a head. It wasn't vague panic and breakdown in despair because the world was falling around my ears. It was my world inside. It fell. I have been in such need and have felt myself so unworthy of any human love, based on my experience and all. So unlovable, so repulsive. I've blamed other things—in every situation there was something wrong, I blamed my husband. And the point is not whether they had failings—every human has failings logically. The point is that I felt, and the experience was the worst thing, was the worst I've ever been through. I felt my own deprivation. The extent of it. I was so hungry, so in need, that nothing and no one could satisfy me. The thought came to me, not even the Archangel Gabriel. I mean not the most perfect person, no one, nothing. And I would have to find something wrong with them, and really because I couldn't look at how awful I was. Hopelessly unlovable.

Therapist. You saw the extent of your need for love, and you saw how much you had to hide it because you were afraid it could never be met.

Mary. But something else came in here, and this is what has made it possible to look. You once said after something I said to you, 'You find it too rough to be human.' I have felt that. But you are helping me to be human. You are giving me the caring for myself, with no demands, no matter what I'm like. And it's helping me to *give* that love and understanding. I talked to my husband. He's known how upset I've been. After this weekend there seems to have been a turning point. He said, 'There seems to be a different quality about you'. You see I'm not blaming him for anything. And he feels it. Of course, life will have problems and we shall have problems, and I know Tony has deep needs, too, but there will be a different way of seeing them. It has helped that he and I have been able to work on these things together. But if I had not been able to depend on you, I couldn't have found myself. I couldn't have freed myself from all this hopeless hunger inside.

Therapist. You have felt in this relationship that you could depend on understanding, that you would not be cast out; it has met a need

Mary. I went all my life with this heartbreak inside, behaving irritably and explosively and not knowing why. And that was like my father. I have some idea of the heartbreak that went on under his arbitrariness and cruelty now.

Therapist. You're finding in your own experience some deeper meaning in angry and hostile behaviour.

Mary. I thought there was no way out. Now I can see a way out.

Therapist. It seems at least *possible* to be human now.

Mary. At least possible. (Smiling.)

GROWING UP WITH CHILDREN

Children don't grow up all at once, and neither do parents who literally grow up again as they look at and re-experience themselves in the light of a stronger position than the one they held when they were children. Finding different answers from the old ones marks a continuing lessening of the gap between intellectual understanding of 'the way one should be' and 'being that way'. But 'I'm punishing in them what I don't want to look at in myself' can come as a fresh recognition at each stage of growth.

'*Mummy's dolls*'. Gaynor tells her reaction to her daughter's breaking of some figurines.

Gaynor. I was furious with Anne. She just took my figurines and broke them in pieces. I said to her, 'Why did you break Mummy's dolls? Would you like it if I took Anne's dolls and tore the arm off and tore the head off?' And she said, 'No.' And I was trying to make her pay and feel guilty for breaking those dolls. And then afterwards I thought if this is anger, thank God she has the dolls to break. But I just couldn't recognise it. I thought it was just mischief. I couldn't see she was mad at me.

Therapist. You couldn't see her feelings in it at the moment because you were in it.

Gaynor. I'd much rather think that Anne took the hat off the figurine's head.

Therapist. You'd rather think that than that she was mad at you.

Gaynor. Well if she did it that way I had a right to be mad at her. I should like to have a reason for being angry at her isolated from the fact that I should understand her feelings. And not have to say 'Well, why is she doing this? Is she doing this because she's angry or this and that and the other?' I'd like her to destroy things just out of mischief.

Therapist. You'd like to have the freedom to feel the way you feel, about her without having to stop yourself and understand her.

Gaynor. Yes. (Pause.) And that's about everything. Anna hit something when she was talking about not liking people to, not being able to stand it when they tell you something you already know.

Therapist. I want to say this back to you. You have come to the challenge to understand, an intellectual awareness of the importance of understanding before you are ready to, before your feelings are out of the way.

Gaynor. Well, what are my real feelings? I was mad at her. But it was more than just the incident. We know that. (Laughing.) Actually I didn't even like the figurines. Somebody gave them to me and I kept them because everybody had them. It was the thing to do. I think when Anne broke them my feeling was that I'd have liked to smash them myself. But you're not supposed to do things like that. (Pause.) I've got it now. I'm just sick and tired of conforming to what other people expect of me. I'd like to put my feet on the table and squeeze the butter and all the things not accepted by society. But if you're yourself, you're not accepted by society.

Therapist. If you do these things that you feel like you will not get where you want to is your early feeling. If you do them you will not get where you want.

Gaynor. It's an early feeling and I think it's true.

Therapist. If you did the thing you felt like, squeezing the butter, for instance, you would not have got what you wanted. Why was it that you wouldn't squeeze the butter?

Gaynor. Because Mother would have got mad at me.

Therapist. In other words what you wanted was your mother's acceptance.

In such talk Gaynor separates social behaviour from its equation for her of a search for her mother's acceptance, from the standards which have made her feel she could not get her father's acceptance. Her personal synonyms are changing.

The need to punish. Helen is having difficulty with her elder son and finds some new light on 'punishing him for me'.

Helen. Mark's doing everything not to get acceptance.
Therapist. He's testing the limits. He's trying to see whether he has it or not.
Helen. I'm nearly beside myself about him. He'll kick over Dan's blocks. Poor little kid, it's a wonder he doesn't have a fit over it. He'll cry a few minutes, and I'll hug him but I know I should hug Mark. (In the parent education class we heard, 'Love them when they're least lovable. The aggressive child needs your arm around him.')
Therapist. Of a baby you feel the need to protect, the compulsion to protect.
Helen. Dan is wonderful. Of course, he's had different help than Mark. I was so concerned when I first started this therapy. I was so careful to do the right thing. And now I'm ready to choke him when he does things like that. I try so hard you know.
Therapist. I try so hard but in my feelings I'm ready to choke him.
Helen. I was going to hit him the other day and I stopped and thought, 'Ah, I didn't hit him.'
Therapist. With stick in the air, you stopped.
Helen. Or I'll go into the bathroom and I'll start swearing, really cussing, and all of a sudden I'll stop. I'll catch myself.
Therapist. You perceive clearly what you're doing now, when your feelings have carried you away. And the emotion ebbs then, doesn't it?
Helen. It ebbs. Somewhat. I have been a lot firmer with him than I've ever been, that's the point. Sometimes I'm too firm with him. He took some library books out and he kept them out and he didn't get any notice and he didn't bother to take them back. So I said to him, 'Well, young man, you're not having any privileges. You're

just going to use your allowance for your library dues until your library fine is paid up.' And it seems he's always being punished.

Therapist. Let's look at that. You do feel that you're punishing him now.

Helen. Yes, I really am.

Therapist. In other words, punishment is not being firm.

Helen. Well, how do you deal with a child like that?

Therapist. You're being more than firm with him, you're punishing him.

Helen. Yes, I am.

Therapist. (Pointing out a reality for the child.) Can we look at what Mark meant for a minute? 'I didn't feel like sending it back when they didn't send me notice.' What does that mean on a feeling level? 'I want them to take more care of me before I can function.'

Helen. Well, I hadn't thought of it. I'm not free enough to even look at it.

Therapist. That's why it doesn't do any good for me to tell you, you see.

Helen. It really means that, doesn't it? I think I'm just mean. I think I'm just mean.

Therapist. You're feeling mean towards him.

Helen. I know I am.

Therapist. We don't call that setting limits. We know we don't set limits that way. You're just feeling mean to him, that's what you're feeling.

Helen. I am a bitch towards Mark and I never used to be. It never was a sound adjustment anyway. It wasn't sound.

Therapist. Now at least you know you're a bitch to him. That's sound, sound on that basis.

Helen. I could drive him to the library, I suppose, and say, 'Come, let's take you books back.' Instead I just glory in the fact that he's going to have to use his allowance to pay the fine—and feel I'm just being firm with him.

Therapist. You're just enjoying punishing him. And calling it being firm.

Brenda. But you know in your heart that's not going to cure it, don't you?

Helen. Yes, I know.

Brenda. 'Cause I felt that way too.

Helen. How are you going to show a child that he breaks limits like that? It frightens me, though I think it's wonderful he's getting it out of his system. But at the same time—there I'm getting to it now—my goodness this is terrible, he's doing all those things that you can't do you know.

Therapist. In other words you're clamping down on the things that you just can't do inside of you, aren't you?

Helen. Yes. These 'dangerous' things. *That's* the thing that's been solved, that one must be punished for this. Of course, probably I've punished myself for so long for all these things that I've felt indirectly I've done them. And maybe I feel that he should be punished for doing these things.

Therapist. For all the things you ever did.

Helen. Yes.

Therapist. And wanted to do.

Helen. That's right.

Therapist. It puts an awful lot of weight on him to put your own past needs for punishment on a library fine, doesn't it?

Helen. But shouldn't you be punished for breaking limits?

Therapist. (Pointing out a child reality again.) You don't feel that your own feelings of loneliness and badness and so forth are ever punishment enough?

Helen. I never looked at it that way, I guess. He knows he did the wrong thing.

Therapist. (Reinforcing a concept.) Someone should see to it that children do not break limits. But punishment for breaking it isn't the best way to help them understand a limit. If we punish them because of our own feelings then we so destroy the setting of limits that it has no good relationship to the limits that we need to set. But we can set many limits just by our strength and see to it that they are set and carried out. We're already lost and gone when the child has broken the limit and then we do an eye for an eye because he's broken it.

Helen. The way I feel about being punished, about breaking the limits seems to be the way I feel. It has nothing to do with his behaviour.

8 Beyond the Doll's House

The most wonderful thing of all would have to happen. . . . Both you and I would have to be so changed . . . that our life together would be a real marriage.

Henrik Ibsen

The fulfilment of growing up is to become a human person. This means finding identity as a man or a woman freed from the need to punish ourselves in others because in hidden ways we don't approve of ourselves. Essentially we must like ourselves if we are to grow up to be ourselves. We must like ourselves as man or woman, finding adequacy and satisfaction in being man or woman. One man in a parent group said, 'To fight what you are—there's no heavier lead balloon.' Of all the battles we have in accepting feelings that may have brought pain, in being comfortable with body functions if they have brought us shame, there is no more lost battle than fighting our sexual identity. It becomes a focus of all other feelings about ourselves, a central proving ground for relationships between parents and children. If we have learned to like ourselves in our growing up, to find being us is enjoyable, we shall learn our sexual identity and the meaning of love at the same time.

SEXUAL IDENTITY AND LEARNING TO LOVE

To learn to love means to learn to receive as well as to give. And, as we define love now, it means as great a concern for the needs of a loved person as for our own. The two—concern for our own needs, respect for them, and concern for the needs of another—are inseparable. As a person sheds distortions derived from unfinished learnings and from unrealistic expectations, the matching of self-caring and caring for another becomes a human possibility: a possibility, parents discover, in a new kind of freedom. We know that a man will have difficulty being tender towards his wife, being an understanding husband, if he is still, though unaware of it, battling his resentment towards his mother or father, and if he is still fighting his parents in the guise of hostility towards his brothers or sisters. He may feel inadequate as a man, as Andrew Smith did, but assert a pseudo-strength in harshness and assumed indifference. If a man uses sex to prove to himself his masculinity in a series of promiscuous conquests under the rationalisation of free love, he is choiceless, a driven man rather than a free man, and he a part of loving another. If a woman uses sex to get close to a rejected and hated father in the men she meets, to find love she felt deprived of as a child, guilt will tend to drive her to re-enact the broken relationships of her family as part of her self-condemnation—the man will never be the 'right man', even when she marries. And her children will never be quite satisfactory if she tries to prove through them that she can be a better mother than her mother was to her.

A man for a woman—reality. We are concerned here with a growing self-understanding that helps to bring growing discrimination in seeking and achieving realistic goals. But the social roles of men and women change, and it is important to understand that, too, so that masculine and feminine do not become synonymous of false images of what a man or woman 'ought to be'. The anthropologists' studies point out that masculinity and femininity acquire different attributes in different cultures. And in different eras acquired attributes change. In these learned attributes masculinity and femininity are culturally determined. But our upbringing may have taught us false expectations as Helen found out.

Helen. My husband gives me no satisfaction. I was taught that men should do things for you. That it was their role in life to give you things. Michael just doesn't bring any satisfaction. He just has nothing to give.

Therapist. Is it that he has nothing to give or you can't get from him what you want?

Helen. You mean I could be mistaken. Shouldn't a man be there to look after you? Doesn't he owe you anything?

Therapist. Do you feel he owes you anything? That that is his first function? Could a person be first responsible to himself?

Helen. I see. Just as I am responsible to myself first, so is he? Actually everyone is responsible to himself. But my upbringing taught me men were there *just* to take care of you, to do nothing else, practically. If that isn't the case it makes a great deal of difference.

Therapist. You see differently what a husband has to offer now?
Helen. It's a completely new slant. It's just like a big awakening. (Pause.) Now you know that suddenly seems very relieving, very comforting. It's much easier this way. (She feels ready to accept a new way.)
Therapist. It squares with the reality better.

A wide range of humanly possible goals are available if a man and a woman have found a positive sense of sexual identity in tune with the acceptance of self that derives from experiences of self-worth, adequacy and belonging. In such a context housework would not become a synonym for a 'woman the drudge', 'used by men', nor would fulfilling abilities outside the home become a source of conflict in which men and women play out child needs to prove themselves. Helen was finding along with reduced fear of her own feelings and more realistic expectations of marriage, that not only her relationships at home improved, but that she had artistic ability. She found herself enjoying modelling in clay. Life as a whole seemed to be fuller, less guarded.

Envy of men. Laura has always been conscious of an envy of men and has often spoken of wanting to be a man. But she comes to see other meanings in her envy.

Laura. Old feelings come in again—women are underdogs, women are just chattels. I feel that a man has things his way.
Therapist. In other words you equate men with being the master.
Laura. Yes.
Therapist. A man is free.
Laura. I know I am becoming more acceptant of the role of woman though, and I think it's because I'm finding the freedom in myself that I *equated* with men. I had a dream about a rooster chasing a hen, and a bull chasing a cow. And I thought about it and I felt it was me chasing my own femininity. And I am becoming consciously more content at home as a wife and mother. This envy of men has been really a wish to arrange things my way—so that I would be catered to, cared for. Women are underdogs. (Weeps.) Men seem to have much the best of it.
Therapist. I want to be a man instead of an underdog.
Laura. There's something else though—another impossible wish.

I want to be little and dainty like Joan. When you're big and strong the way I am you have to take care of other people.

Hilda. Is it the sort of feeling that you don't want to be a man, you want to be small and little and have someone take care of you?

Laura. Yes, that's it exactly.

Hilda. So you don't want to be a man, you want to be a woman that is taken care of?

Therapist. You want to be taken care of.

Laura. Yes. A man has things his way and can work out his salvation in a world of his own.

Hilda. It sounded to me that you wanted someone to take care of you so that you could arrange it go to along at your speed but with someone to help you, to support you till you got your breath. That's happened in my own experience. I waited a long time but I'm getting out of it little by little.

Laura. Why am I thinking of something impossible? I can't be little and dainty and taken care of the way I want.

Hilda. It isn't impossible on a feeling level.

Love between women. Laura's personal synonym that 'being a man' meant freedom to arrange for needs to be met changed in the direction of a greater reality as she found her own sense of freedom. Other personal synonyms may involve homosexual feelings and fantasies, equated in individual ways to seeking identity with a parent of the same sex. 'This woman is attractive to me' in real life and in the group becomes 'I am finding a liking for myself as a woman'. Janice had acted out a homosexual relationship when she was in college. She is conscious of striking at her father; 'emasculating him'. She expresses some sexual confusion. 'You know I've had these feelings I want to be a penis, but also I have felt I want to be a breast.' But she speaks of deeper needs to find a mother and her own femininity in her relationship with her college homosexual partner.

Janice. My feeling was that I was her baby, and I wanted to suck her breasts. She was my mother.

She expresses in concrete images her wish to get in touch with her sexual identity as a woman.

Janice. I had a fixation on breasts and vagina. I wanted to touch.

A NAMELESS FEAR

Gaynor has difficulty in letting go in sexual intercourse. She discovers some surprising equations.

> *Gaynor*. I went to a meeting on faith healing. I'm both fascinated and frightened by it. I'm afraid of giving up and submitting to 'another power' which it seems to me to be. I'd like to let go but I can't. And the thought occurs to me that it has something to do with sex. I'm stopped from having faith because I'm tied up somewhere down here in feelings of sex. I think that is actually what is stopping me from having faith.
> *Therapist*. Because it represents letting go.
> *Gaynor*. How can I find confidence to trust myself, how can I get self-acceptance?
> *Anna*. Accept your nice primitive feelings.
> *Gaynor*. I feel if I accepted myself where I am, I would lose respect for myself.
> *Therapist*. In other words, you do not respect the primitive instincts and human frailty. You can't respect them as acceptable.

Consciously she wishes for the romantic love of a teenager—'pretty dresses and a beautiful atmosphere, and idealised love which you don't really touch.' But her dreams do get into touch with the 'primitive instincts and human frailty' in the persons of dark-skinned and foreign men. Then one day implied violence against men, denied in idealised teenage love, comes closer to home in another dream. Both an impulse and its denial find expression. The dream gives someone else the unwanted impulse.

> *Gaynor*. I dreamed that a little boy next door was cut up and put in the deep freeze. And it was discovered that my daughter Anne had done it. I was glad in the dream that I hadn't done it.
> *Therapist*. You wouldn't have wanted to have that impulse.

She literally cut this man child in pieces and put him in the deep freeze. Now the door of the refrigerator is open and there may be some unfreezing.

Shortly after this she has another dream. Her relationship with her husband is improving but she has a fear which involves him in a dream.

Gaynor. I want to talk about a fear today, because I am afraid. I can't place what I'm afraid of but last night I dreamt about scorpions. And even when I'm awake the thought of scorpions is just terrible. In the dream last night there was a scorpion and I got out of bed and it was right by my foot and I screamed to Jim and instead of grabbing it away from me he grabbed it and pushed my heel with it. And I was just cursing, just bawled him out. And then Anne cried and I was almost afraid to get out of bed and go to her in case there was a scorpion on the floor even though I was awake. And I thought it isn't right to walk barefoot because there might, there just might be a scorpion on the floor.

Therapist. It isn't right to walk barefoot.

Gaynor. But I went barefoot all my life. I'm trying to figure this out because I walk barefoot every summer and yet I can't understand why my feet are in it at all. But when I got back after taking care of Anne I just lay there and it was the same terrifying feeling that I used to have when I was a child. I can remember being afraid, but I still don't remember what I was afraid of at nights. We'd lie there and it would be hot and yet we'd be afraid to throw back the covers. And it brings back all those ghost stories that I heard when I was a child, especially this woman who told of a girl who heard a noise downstairs and went to see and came upstairs and fell across her sister's bed and her head was cut off. When her father came to find them there was nothing downstairs to hurt her but there was a little trail of blood going upstairs and there was one of his daughters insane with grey hair and the other with her head cut off. And after this story I was so terrified, so terrified to get up and find out.

Well I was even afraid before that. Here was Daddy saying, 'If you hear anything that frightens you, get up and see what it is. It may be a door banging or a moth flying against the window.' But if there's a noise I'm scared to death to get up and see what it is.

Therapist. (Focusing a fear of finding out.) You opened these remarks by saying, 'I'm in a state of fear,' now you say, 'I'm afraid of where it may lead me. I'm afraid to see what it is.'

Gaynor. Yes, yes, I am afraid.

Therapist. Of the thing coming up the stairs and noises in the night.

Gaynor. I've tried to think and it wasn't someone coming up, a man or a woman or a child. It's none of those things. It's something unreal. It's something, a horrible thing.

Therapist. Something you don't have any words for. Something of which you had no logical knowledge but had to put into a shape.

Gaynor. And I know I'm putting this fear, whatever it is, on to scorpions. And I know you can kill scorpions, they are small. (Pause.) So I can't figure out what I'm afraid of. What in the world could it be that is so huge? I've already discussed Mother's rejection of me and Daddy's rejection of me. But it just doesn't fit. I just can't place it. I think the way to get at it is through scorpions because I'm more afraid of a scorpion than anything else.

Brenda. Is it sex? Sexual intercourse that's so terrifying. Is the scorpion a sexual symbol.

Gaynor. I've tried to link it with sex. But it looks to me it should be placed with anger for some reason. Something violent that's going to destroy rather than sex. Something big, and black, and angry. I wish I could place it.

Brenda. I don't think to a child it has to be that clear. You don't think of sex as a child like that.

Gaynor. How do you ever get back to it then?

Brenda. Feel it. The thing coming up the steps.

Gaynor. This is terrible and I was still scared this morning. Scorpions are just in my mind. But what is it about scorpions that I feel is so treacherous? Why am I so frightened? What am I afraid of?

Therapist. What is the noise downstairs that you hear?

Gaynor. I know what it was when I was a child. It was the furnace running. But it wasn't the furnace running to me. It was something more than that. It was horrible. And if the house was creaking when the wind blew it wasn't that to me, it was something coming up the stairs.

Therapist. Something coming up the stairs.

Gaynor. But what was coming up? It wasn't anybody I was afraid of. *Just a thing.* A huge great big blob. I couldn't handle it. There were no words for it.

Therapist. A preverbal feeling.

Gaynor. Fear causes such tension. I remember holding my breath.

Therapist. You were that much on guard.

Gaynor. I thought if anything did come in that door I didn't want to lose control. (Pause.) Can you menstruate too often from emotional causes? I've been menstruating every two weeks instead of twenty-four days. I think there's something wrong with my female organs.

At this point Gaynor goes no further. She has stated her problem of displacement of a vague fear on to one specific source of fear—a scorpion. 'I am disturbed and my female organs are disturbed' is as far as she can go. We can see in her dream how we literally dream up those things we both want and fear. Her own wish to have the lowest part of her in touch with the vague thing she also fears becomes her husband pressing her heel with a scorpion (her wish) and her screaming at him for doing it (her fear and condemnation of her own wish). If she is to go beyond her fear she must find the meaning of her personal synonyms in her way.

STRENGTH TO LOOK DEEPER—NAMING THE FEAR

Meetings in groups or person-to-person interviews become a clearing house for continuing work by each individual to understand the meaning of his own experience, not intellectually but as experience tells its own story. The most frightening experience reveals its meaning when many other areas of the self have been discovered and found good, and relationships with others have greatly improved. But a sense of profound disturbance may greatly increase at the time of looking at the meaning of the most terrifying personal symbols before they, too, shed their fear.

In the middle of the next meeting Gaynor comes back to her fear.

Gaynor. On this scorpion business. I'm trying to think where I first heard of it, because there's no such thing at home (childhood home). And I know now where was the first time I ever saw a picture of one or heard about it. It's Jim's birth sign. He's Scorpio. He was born under the sign of the Scorpion. And that was the first time I ever saw a picture of a scorpion. It was the most horrible looking thing I'd ever seen in my life. And I think this fear of scorpions means I must be afraid of Jim. I actually think I must be terrified of him. (Clears throat.) I know that I'm afraid of his anger. I know that I'm afraid of pushing him too far. And I know that I will tiptoe around and handle him with kid gloves because I'm afraid of his anger and I never realised I was afraid of it. I mean I just tiptoed. I didn't realise why I was tiptoeing. And if a situation comes up where it's his will against mine I will just simply turn away and maybe be resentful about it but I won't carry it on because I'm afraid of what will happen if I do.

I've tried to connect my feelings towards Jim with my father and can remember having seen my father angry only once. Then I was terrified by the fact that he could raise his voice, because Daddy never raised his voice. But when he was angry he never touched his daughters. It was all verbal. And it wasn't loud. And that was for everything. My sister once said, 'None of us snore. And none of us breathe hard.' At that time I thought, 'Isn't she right? Aren't we a lovely family? We don't breathe hard.'

Therapist. Wasn't it wonderful not to show emotion? (General laughter.)

Gaynor. Yes, well, I thought, 'Aren't we refined?' I mean, we're controlled.

Therapist. Refinement. You equate that with not showing emotions.

Gaynor. Yes, I do.

Therapist. And a very high value.

Gaynor. I know these are the same standards that Daddy had because Mother's family was very emotional. They showed their emotions. They cried and they laughed and they sang and they danced. And Daddy, oh the way he felt about her family. He never talked about it but if he did talk about it, the tone of his voice. All those that couldn't make a living and I imagine they breathed hard too. And they had seven or eight kids.

Brenda. And they breathed hard. (General laughter.)

Gaynor. They didn't sleep quietly at night like they should. And when Jim snores I think that he is the lowest class thing that ever lived. It makes me so mad that I hit him in his sleep.

Therapist. You show your real feeling about it.

Gaynor. Yes, but he's asleep. When he wakes up he doesn't realise how furious I've been at him. (Laughs.) He'll turn over and grunt too. Vulgar and low class.

Therapist. Expressions of your feelings are vulgar, aren't they?

Gaynor. Now I realise I feel that way about emotion and about feelings. But how in the world am I ever going to get over it? There's something else I want to bring in here, too. It isn't a nice subject. To me it's horrible but I'm going to bring it in anyway. Evidently it's the same old deal of the smells of the bathroom.

Therapist. Snoring and body smells.

Gaynor. At home if Daddy went to the bathroom or Mother went to the bathroom, that door was locked and nobody was allowed in there, and I can remember being so ashamed of the smells of the bowel movement that I would take a match and light it for fear Daddy or Mother would come in there and smell it because it was so horrifying to me, and I can never remember my father coming out of the bathroom and me walking in it and it smelling bad. I don't, I mean I must have had the feeling that Daddy didn't do such things.

Therapist. Daddy didn't do such things as go to the bathroom.

Gaynor. I suppose that I feel that he didn't. If he did I'll bet you anything he shook shaving lotion or something all over the bathroom. He has the same distaste that I have for things like that. I know I got it from him, this terrible distaste of anything human, of anything that people do that isn't controlled.

Therapist. (Quietly.) Anything that isn't controlled. (Louder and more slowly.) Of anything they do that is not controlled.

Gaynor. Well, it isn't only passion. It's just everything. It's anger. It's anything.

Therapist. It started out with raising voices and losing temper, going out of control. It isn't only passion but you associate passion with it.

Gaynor. Well, passion's mixed up in it. There is so much anger and passion mixed up in me that I can't separate the two. The two are just one to me.

Therapist. Strong feeling.

Gaynor. I guess it's strong feeling of any kind I feel fear and revulsion for it.

Therapist. Dangerous and disgusting.

Joan. I used to be embarrassed by strong body smells, but I'm moving away from that reaction now.

Gaynor. When I married Jim I felt I married him because he was so earthy so there must be a great desire in me to be able to be earthy.

Therapist. That is, marrying him was an assertion, an affirmation of that side of your nature.

Gaynor. Yes. And yet I'm fighting it. Every minute I'm fighting it. The minute I let go with a strong emotion I have no respect for myself. If I get angry, I feel guilty. I feel I'm low class and uncontrolled. It's the same in intercourse, if I go all the way and have a climax, I feel guilty, I feel I'm low, I feel like I'm not a Wrightson (maiden name) any more.

Therapist. You early learned to put down intercourse as low.

Gaynor. But I still have the desire to be a Wrightson. I don't want to be a Harris (husband's name). I mean there's something in me that wants to go to bed with Jim and then there's something else that says 'No, you can't. You will no longer be a Wrightson.'

Therapist. That is if you move over and become naturalistic and a free person, you won't be with your father.

Gaynor. No. And I do love my dad. I want him to love me and I think he respects me, but I don't know if he loves me.

Therapist. That is you are still trying to get your father's love.

Gaynor. I think maybe my father does love me from what he said about choosing his daughters if their mother hadn't got there first. Then I began to think, if he really loves us and can't show it, then what is wrong with the way he feels about it? After that I got more involved until I didn't know what to think about it any more.

Therapist. If he really loves us and couldn't risk showing it, there must be something in that.

Gaynor. I had the feeling immediately that he must have been sexually attracted to all three of his daughters, but I'll never know whether he was or not.

Therapist. But you got the feelings, Because we don't mind whether he was or not. What we're interested in is the feelings.

Gaynor. We had some girls staying with us and Daddy used to flirt with them. But he didn't flirt with his daughters. And I resented those girls. What have they got that I don't have?

Therapist. 'When I can't get my father's interest what's the matter with me?'

Gaynor. Well, what is the matter with me? I try to think about it and can't get any further than I'm neurotic. Now about this fear of Jim's anger, there's fear of something else too. It isn't just anger I'm afraid of something to do with passion in my fear of him. But I know he can't hurt me. We've lived together ten years. I know he's not going to hurt me.

Therapist. It's in you, isn't it?

Gaynor. Yes, it's in me.

Therapist. And not in Jim. 'I'm afraid of something.'

Anna. The big black thing coming up the stairs you were talking about last week.

Brenda. Is it something in yourself you're afraid of?

Gaynor. I don't think so. It's what my actions will bring out in him. What my words or my pushing him too far will bring out in him that I'm afraid of. His mother and I both walk on eggshells lest we might have to handle his anger. And I'll be realistic. I don't think I could handle it. I don't know how mad he'd get, because I've never pushed him that far. Maybe he wouldn't get mad at all. (Pause.) He may not get mad at all. It's me. I'm afraid he will.

Therapist. You're afraid that you couldn't handle what would happen.

Gaynor. Daddy never punished us in our life because Mother wouldn't let him do it. She said, 'If there's any spanking to be done in this family I'll do it.' Oh, I've got something now. She said, 'Men spank too hard; they don't realise their strength; they spank too hard.' So I never really knew what punishment from my father would be like. Physical punishment. Whether it would be hard or whether it wouldn't be hard. And I'm still doubtful about it. (Pause.) I wonder if that could work in there. It came right to my mind, that what she said, 'Men spank too hard.' She gave me the idea all my life that men were rough and were (pause) too strong and men were big and I feel the same way. I think they're too big and too strong.

Therapist. You're afraid of them, aren't you?

Gaynor. I'm afraid. I'm afraid of men. And I'd never even thought. That's why I was afraid of that scorpion. Jim was born under the Scorpion sign so, consequently, he was the scorpion then in my dream.

Therapist. It's masculine for you.

Gaynor. Yes.

'I LIKE MY HUSBAND'

The father who never touched her and did not reveal his feelings to her, and the mother who reinforced the concept of untried dangerous strength ('men spank too hard') produced a terror of men. Now she has invited the 'scorpion' to touch the 'lowest part' of her, symbolised in the dream by her foot, and she has named the nameless fear. Four weeks later she speaks of new feelings for her husband.

Gaynor. For the first time in my life I'm having feelings of *liking* for Jim. Before it had to be an adolescent crush or extreme hate. I'm enjoying him and me. And we went for a drive and it was just as Hilda said if you ask for something in a way that commands respect, expecting to be heard. I said 'I'm hungry. Let's stop and get something warm to eat.' And we did. He's happy to do it. I'm not walking on eggshells any more in fear of his anger—and my own. I feel I accept him now, and I can accept his mother, too

In an interview she contrasts past and present feelings.

'I thought I was getting along pretty well until I came against my first problem—adjustment to marriage. I wanted to sit on Daddy's lap. But that was no good because he wanted to sit on Mummy's lap. There was talk of divorce several times and I left once. But I came back because I was so insecure and I didn't want to tell my folks I'd made a mistake. Now I feel Jim and I will never get a divorce. Death do us part. I could see nothing in my daughter's needs but demands on me. Now I can anticipate her needs without fighting her.'

'*I gave my father back his power*.' Elise, like Gaynor experiences for her husband either an extreme crush or extreme hate. She has fantasied she would leave him at the times she has hated him, but then the feeling of being unable to do without him has overwhelmed her. 'I'm afraid of offending him. I keep some feeling in reserve. I'm afraid if I care too much he'll leave. It will give him power over me.'

Elise. I've been having these extreme ups and downs about Colin. I can't do without him or I want to have nothing to do with him. I'm either in love or repulse him. I'm reluctant to trust him, having felt let down by my parents, I suppose. I think he'll leave the way my father did. I don't trust my feelings.

Therapist. You're reluctant to trust this vulnerable part of you.

Elise. I want to avoid the pain if I lose his love. So I think of leaving him. And after we've been close, with warm feelings, had intercourse, all these critical feelings come up. I don't accept him. I want to get mad at him and I don't know why. I never *say* anything angry to him. I need his approval. I keep myself going by other people's approval. Not only Colin's approval. I'm just chronically afraid of being left and feel I have to be nice all the time, do extra things so that I won't be left. It's not logical.

Therapist. That is Colin, and others, can't be expected to prove you are lovable, but you still find yourself unconsciously looking for that proof.

Elise. I know he can't disprove my father leaving me but I'm still expecting him to disprove my father's rejection and I'm afraid he'll simply be my father all over again.

Then one day she tells a dream of being married to her father.

Elise. I had a brief dream, an amazingly calm and acceptant dream in which I was married to my father. It was just an ordinary setting. And I remember thinking, 'And now I've put myself in your power.' And he gave me some instruction about what I should do just the way he did my mother. And I thought, 'My whole life is going to be swamped with his demands. I shall not have a life of my own.' And then I thought, 'I don't have to take it this way. It isn't domination. It's a partnership.' And I felt my father could be the same person, but I could accept him, and move into being myself. I felt in the dream I was accepting my father's penis, his symbol of potency, and his human potential in every way without taking them away from him, because I had my own potency, my own human potential. We could both realise our potential and enjoy living together without being threatened by each other. Since this dream I've been feeling with Colin much less the little girl and much more a woman. I loved my father in the dream, and it was so acceptant. And he wasn't perfect. He was just the same person. And the feelings carry over. And I'm beginning to feel much less up and down about Colin, and much less on guard.

Therapist. You accepted your father in the dream and now you are more sure in your feelings about Colin.

Elise. I gave my father back his power. I'm not afraid of *not* pleasing Colin now. (Pause).

Accepting a father as a man seemed to be associated with accepting herself as a woman, and trusting her love for her husband.

'I love you because you're you, and because you're a man'. After two years of therapy Hilda's remembered dreams began to increase in amount and to decrease in disguise.

Hilda. Consciously I feel more secure than I ever did before. And for years I've never been able to remember dreams except snatches and just short ones. But last night I had the damnedest dream. It had everything in it. It had murder. It had climbing a rope with only a string to go out on after I got to the top and being unconscious for two years. (Breaks into tears.) In the dream I put on my mother's nightgown after finding there was a strange woman in the house. My mother was in the hospital and I felt I should not wear her nightgown. Then my husband told me that I had been unconscious for two years and he had gone out with other women. After that he and I climbed a rope with string at the top going both ways. In another part of the dream there were three headless bodies and the heads were beside the bodies and were to be used as police evidence. Am I really that unsure of myself inside me? Consciously I don't feel that unsure. I've only had snatches of dreams before, but last night, Gads, the book was thrown at me.
Therapist. I'd just like to respond to you the same way I did to Gaynor. You're just secure enough that you can dare deal with this.
Hilda. I feel the dream took me back to early times I can't remember. The headless bodies are my three older sisters with whom I have no memory of competing. I've had dreams of climbing and being suspended by a piece of string. That seems to me to be holding on to something rather than getting panicky, even though the something would not hold. I wonder if my husband and other women in the dream really mean my father and that it is all right for him to sleep with my mother.

Four weeks later she tells another dream.

Hilda. Since I was six at the very latest, I've absolutely no memory of any affection for my father, any feelings for my father except pain and fear and loathing. Then when my mother went to California, one winter, when I was, I can't even remember, twelve or thirteen or fourteen. I thought my father brushed up against me unnecessarily and I repulsed him. And it occurred to me that at that moment it made it impossible for me to love any other man. To hold him off I cut off all feelings of real love for any man. And, of course, I've been working things through with my husband for a couple of years now and it's gone through different phases. But I hope I'm where I should be. I had a dream.

Someone mentioned a dream about her husband being a maharajah or something like that. Well, my husband wasn't a maharajah, but there was an extremely wealthy middle-aged man and not particularly good-looking. And it seemed that I was in a room with him and my husband was in the next room and this fellow, stood up and he took me in his arms. I responded and he said, 'Now you're going to tell me that you love me like a father.' I said, 'No.' And the feeling I had was that I knew I was speaking the truth. I said, 'No, that isn't it at all. I love you just because you're you and because you're a man.'

A feeling of extreme irritation may frequently accompany emotional change. This is Hilda's experience.

Hilda. The day after the dream I felt extremely irritable and mad with everyone and everything. And then it got time for my husband to come home and it was the strangest feeling. Here I was just furious at everybody else, but I wasn't mad at him. But it's the strangest feeling, I wasn't mad at him. And, uh, there's something about that dream. I loved a man because he's a man and not because I was afraid he might be my father.

Therapist. You were disassociating yourself from that as a feeling, weren't you?

Hilda. Well you see I felt so differently toward Howard. And so often I would get mad for just 'no reason'. I'd just be mad, just before bedtime. (Laughter.) And it's such a funny feeling night after night goes past and I get mad at everything else but I'm not mad at Howard, my husband, and in the dream I disassociated the fear of loving a man from my father, whether I can remember ever having loved him or not. (Long Pause). Until now I've been afraid to use swear words in front of my husband. But now I'm not afraid he's going to be mad at me even though he is mad.

The therapist recognises swearing as a symbol only.

Therapist. You're no longer expecting the rejection of your full expression of feeling.

Hilda. My parents never even let me say, 'Darn'. And I learned quite a vocabulary of swearing. I learned things my father would have killed me if I'd said.

Therapist. If I'd shown my true feelings to my father, he would have killed me.

Later in an interview she tells her experience in therapy.

> 'My life was to do exactly as my husband wanted. I completely submerged my life to him. I had a breakdown. As a result of therapy we have had to re-orient our lives. We are actually closer than when he was everything. That wasn't real. I was too much on guard. Too afraid. I'd given up being a constructive member of society. And if we blow a fuse now we can discuss it. Before we wouldn't speak for weeks.'

'*The little crosses*.' Laura, who had envied men because she found she wanted to arrange things to be cared for, tells how she found a 'new me', finding satisfaction as a wife and mother. The way was not easy. Therapy meant upheaval. Six years of painful self-discovery and change in many areas precede what she says now.

> 'No one carried the word worried on her shoulders more than I. No one had such a low opinion of herself and such an inability to do anything about it. I was worn out, drug out. And it was everybody else's fault, especially my husband's.
>
> 'Then I came to the realisation that I couldn't ask help from my husband because I didn't feel worthy. And when he made a gesture, whatever he did couldn't please me. The trouble was me. And when I finally came to the realisation I was tearing everybody else down because I was subconsciously tearing myself down, I knew I had to build a new me. I started this by allowing myself a few minutes each day, absolutely my own, feeling I was entitled to it, worthy of it.
>
> 'When I was a little girl and anybody asked me what my ambition was, it was to be a good wife and mother; but when I got to the wife and mother stage I just wasn't there. No one could have convinced me six years ago that I would feel very adequate and very satisfied in the role.
>
> 'If things bother us we talk it over now. We are free enough to say, "I wonder why?" I used to leave the cupboard doors open all the time to annoy him subconsciously. He's making the shelves in the kitchen now different from what I said. I know it's his unconscious reaction to his mother. But I'm learning to get along with the little crosses a lot better. We've found a new love and it's a lot better for the kids.'

'*I often felt I was on trial.*' Helen also thought she had an 'unsatisfactory husband'. Her marriage, too, was 'on the rocks'.

> 'It was the problem of simple basic things, the whole problem of basic feelings and the problem of control. I'd just turned on myself. I'd get acceptance as a child only by not showing anger.
>
> 'When I got to the parent class our marriage was hanging by a thin thread, and everything was Michael's fault. He is the last thing I would have married. I was doing him a favour to live with him, I thought. He said, "I often felt I was on trial."
>
> 'I criticised his table manners, the way he walked, the way he talked, the way he ate, handled the children—but everything—the way he dressed, his means of support, what he did for me.
>
> 'And now I'm completely devoted to him. It's just like night and day. I have my moments of anger which are just like that. (Snaps fingers.) If we get angry we understand and say nothing.

'THE MOST WONDERFUL THING OF ALL'

At the end of Henrik Ibsen's play *The Doll's House*, Nora leaves her husband because she does not want to remain in a 'let's pretend' world of unself-realisation, a doll in a doll's house. At the time critics accused Ibsen of encouraging women to break up their homes. But Nora, when her husband Torvald asks her to stay, says at the end, 'The most wonderful thing of all would have to happen. . . . Both you and I would have to be so changed that . . . our life together would be a real marriage.' We can't go back and ask Ibsen what he really meant—if Nora's words spelled hope or despair. But we have shared what it meant for more than one woman when 'the most wonderful thing of all' did happen and she and her husband became so changed that her life with him did become a real marriage. Where Nora ends these women begin.

Where husband and wife share a growth experience in groups or in interviews with a therapist, they change together and find new means of communication and insight. Where one goes further than the other after an initial class they can still work together. It is harder to find a real marriage where one partner does not accept the need or the meaning of the kind of growth experience we have followed. Then we have the situation of a wife or a husband rejecting not just the idea of change and the process of change, but a partner who has changed. But overwhelmingly the increased ability of even one member of the family to listen and relate, is a leaven for the attitudes of others, bringing all closer, if the philosophy of husband and wife is one of commitment, 'Let us stay and learn together', rather than, 'it doesn't work, so let's break it up'. When they first came to the classes, every one of the women whose deeper journey into self we have shared was ready 'to break it up' because 'it didn't work'.

Parents should be heard was our early thesis. We have heard them and their parents in them, and the hearing that leads to the deepest change, leading to a real marriage. Perhaps there is no more appropriate way to end these chapters on the deeper self-journeys of parents than with the journey of one parent whose deepest change affected most profoundly her relationship with a child in an experience which gives pause to look back at the routes we have taken and to answer some yet unanswered questions.

9 *A Mother Learns to Study—a Problem of Hostile Identification*

Now they dare not to hunt your savage dream,
O Beast of the heart, those saints who cursed your name,
You are the current of the frozen stream,
Shadow invisible, ambushed and vigilant flame.

Allen Tate

From the beginning we have assumed that if parents should be heard, we listen to the individual human person in his needs whether he is alone or in a group, whether he speaks in a single interview or in several interviews, and in listening we offer him a choice of taking responsibility for change in his ways of seeing and doing. We have followed his choices in initial classes, in interviews, in unstructured groups of varied occupations and levels of education. We have journeyed in depth with a few.

But how old may people be to change? Is there an age limit? The parents of young children whose words we have heard have been in their twenties and thirties. But there is no age limit. We listen to people irrespective of age. The philosophy of prevention, as we have seen, would aim to reach parents of young children, to reach young people even before they became parents and would not wait for breakdown but aim to help family relationships from the beginning. However all is not lost if parents do not seek help until their children are teenagers or even older. Our experience shows that people can change ways of looking at their worlds at any age if they respond to the quality of listening we are concerned with here, whether they are eighteen or eighty. The individual himself chooses how deeply he travels into self. And Virginia Peters who first came for help with a teen-age daughter at forty-five chose to journey deeply into herself.

Like Mrs Green and Mrs Murphy, whom we met earlier, Virginia's immediate external situation was a harsh one. Her husband had just died and at forty-five, with no special professional skills behind her, she had to go to work to support herself and her thirteen-year-old daughter, Vera. She obtained training and a job as a typist, but she had difficulty making ends meet even in a small low-rent apartment. And Vera had health problems. She was born with a cleft of the lip and the palate and was subject to bronchial and ear infections. There were always outstanding or impending bills not covered by insurance for medical treatments or periodic cosmetic surgery. Speech therapy, too, was still an important item for Vera who needed to remove the remains of cleft-palate speech, and it was in fact the immediate reason for Viriginia seeking help. When she found herself in a relationship in which she was the centre of concern and not the object of advice she told her difficulties and wept.

Virginia. I don't know where to turn. I just feel I'm fighting a losing battle. I'm so upset I keep making typing errors and I'm afraid I'll lose my job. I'm supposed to have above average intelligence but I just failed an intelligence test for another job.
Therapist. You know what it feels like to have emotions get in the way.
Virginia. Yes. But I don't know how to find solutions. I'm desperate.
Therapist. Here we believe that parents can find their own solutions that talking helps.

From then on 'Emotions that got in the way' were the focus. The initial interview was the first of a series of interviews in which she chose therapy to help her handle the stress situations in her life.

THREE STAGES OF THERAPY

We have talked about a shift in emphasis as therapy proceeds from a first stage in which a person stresses external problems, to a second stage in which he explores the internal aspects of the problem—'the way I am seeing my world'—and finds a way to changed perception. But with growing awareness of the real origin of emotional stress and increasing discrimination of response in dealing with external situations of potential stress, there seems to be a third stage associated with the end of therapy. This is when a person literally lives strongly resisted emotional experience and it becomes part of relating in a new way, as Gaynor lived her fear of men and then began to like her husband for the first time.

Virginia's experiences illuminate each stage. Particularly clearly, too, her difficulties cast light on the meaning of hostile identification with a hated parent and the recognition and re-assembly of scrambled elements in her relationships leading to a new identification.

Looking at the problem—first stage. On first entering therapy she told her problems—in the immediate situation and in her childhood which she remembered as nothing but harsh.

Virginia. I hated my mother. She always called me stupid and ugly. She made my father give us whippings, just waited and lined us up when he came home. She cut a switch and put it there waiting all day. (Pause.) I don't want any part of being a woman, anything that would mean being like my mother.

Therapist. You'd like completely to eradicate your experience with her.

Virginia. It was hideous. She was some kind of a she-devil. And I was determined I was going to do a better job with my children than she did. Then when Vera was born she was disfigured. But I remember her there on the pillow and I felt full of love for her. Then my mother said it was a punishment to me for everything I was that the baby had a cleft palate. I felt defeated from the start.

Therapist. Even your child seemed to be a source of punishment.

Virginia. Vera had to have early surgery for the cleft lip and the doctor told me I had to make her cry if necessary to stretch the lip for twenty minutes a day, so that it would be mobile. I had to hit her to make her cry. It killed me. Then, because of the cleft, she had difficulty feeding. Those days were a terrible nightmare.

Therapist. All the stripes seemed to be against you.

Virginia. My mother said my father loved me. But I can only remember his punishments and that I could never get close to him. (Pause.) But every week I attended a ball game with him just to be near him.

Therapist. You did try to get close to your father.

Virginia. But I never did. And I felt so hideous, so hopeless that I could never mingle with people, that I daydreamed all the time.

I still do. I'd fantasy the mean things I'd do to people, and I'd fantasy that I wasn't ugly. My mother stood over me at times of home study and said I was stupid and crazy. I believed it. And she made me wear hideous clothes, especially as a teenager. They never fit. I loathed myself.

Therapist. You found you were living your mother's evaluation of you.

Virginia. I think that's why I failed the intelligence test.

At first in therapy Virginia waited for authority to give her the cue about what to say and do as she had with her mother. 'My life has been coerced by authority.' After a few sessions of finding that her initiative was what mattered most in finding her own answers, she said, 'I now look to myself and I also work things out between sessions.'

Finding me—second stage. Now moving in the second stage of therapy, Virginia began to take responsibility for her attitudes.

Virginia. My fear of mingling with people is because I'm terrified of going out of control and showing my feelings. In reality I'm not as ugly as all that, but I feel ugly. (In reality she was physically pleasant in appearance, but her face was tense and drawn when she first came for therapy.) I'm so full of hatred I *have* to daydream. It helps me to keep going.

Therapist. Daydreaming gives you both a release and a protection against real contacts with people which you fear will bring you pain.

Virginia. I've been terrified of people. And I've had no confidence in expressing myself to any kind of authority. Coming here I'm getting some confidence that way now. And for the first time I've been expressing my feelings at work in a self-respecting way. I can say what I think, and I'm not mad and people pay attention. I always had a chip on my shoulder before. I was so aggressive, expecting everyone to contradict me.

Therapist. You find that what you expect people to do makes a difference to what they actually do in response to you.

Virginia. Well, I am finding I can enjoy being with people. But there's something else. They do have their problems. There's a woman at work, she's always bitching about something. And she's mad at me because I've always picked up mistakes in the office. She made a couple of errors in one of the memos and I found them.

Since then she's gibed at me. Calls me a perfectionist busy-body. She's very threatened if she makes a little mistake, thinks that's the end of her job. But I find I can throw off her criticisms, and others'. I can recognise their needs for the first time. I don't have to go into a fit of self-blame.

Therapist. You recognise the experiences that make a person want to hit out.

Then Vera became very ill again and Virginia was faced with medical bills for an ear infection and with expenses to pay for cosmetic surgery for her daughter.

Virginia. My feelings of loathing are coming back. I've just been feeling all week I want to get rid of all responsibility, give up completely. I've wanted to end my life completely—just let the gas take over.

Therapist. That is your need for someone to take over, to help you, to lose this load, is so great you'd like to lose yourself.

In the next weeks she spoke of desperate needs to be taken care of and of rejecting her daughter. As she brought deep needs to depend into the open she gradually developed more confidence in handling her everyday problems, and in giving to her daughter. Then Vera's time for surgery came.

Virginia. I feel I'm more available to her than I've ever been. This is the first operation she's been through that I haven't been through the suffering with her and I caught her looking at me in a very funny way, a questioning way; I think she felt the difference. too.

Meantime other changes were taking place.

Virginia. I've been obsessed with the idea that I have to account to authority—for everything. I was ashamed of my body. My hands were slapped for everything—everything could be a mistake. If I made an error in my homework. If I touched my body. My mother was obsessed with finding out if any of us masturbated.

Therapists. Errors of learning were associated with your body as well as your books.

Virginia. Yes. But I'm feeling more comfortable with my body these days. I can even say, 'I'm feminine', without feeling revulsion.

And someone the other day said, 'You look nice.' And I could accept it. And I'm getting recognition. They made me editor of the organisation paper at work. Another thing, at home I'm putting fewer pressures on Vera. There's much less coercion. I thought she listened to the most awful television programmes and I was always riding her about it, making suggestions about what she should listen to. And she always kicked and went right on listening to her choice. Then I stopped criticising and suddenly she was listening to the programmes I'd suggested. She said, 'You never gave me a chance to choose. You were always trying to make me do what you wanted. I liked the programmes really but when you kept trying to make me listen it made me want to fight you. There seemed to be no other way to fight you except with the programmes. I had to do something different from what you set up.'

Therapist. She wanted acceptance, didn't she? Before she could make a real choice. You saw clearly the components of teenage rebellion around a choice of television programme? (Vera was now fifteen.)

But there were two areas where Virginia had felt most painfully her 'mother's slave' which remained uncomfortable: housework and study. Housework was especially associated with woman's work and her mother had hated it and made her do a great deal of housework from as far back as she could remember. Study, too, was associated with pain and coercion. She repeatedly recalled how her mother had placed a high premium on intelligence, stood over her when she studied and called her stupid and crazy and wrapped her over the knuckles when she made a mistake. Because Vera had missed extended periods of school because of illness and hospitalisation, she needed help with her studies, and Virginia wanted to help her.

Virginia. But I can never work with her in any form of learning or study without becoming filled with anger. And all this involuntary name calling comes up. And it's the same in housework. Whenever I do housework I go into hostile fantasies about all kinds of people of my acquaintance.

Then one day she told a dream which she felt showed a deep readiness even a deep wish to be a girl, to identify with her mother, to be comfortable with her own sexuality, and with the basic functions of her body. She felt she was at the same time finding a new parent and giving birth to herself over again—the dream was a rebirth.

> *Virginia.* I was going to have a baby and it was going to be a girl. I went to my mother's and my mother and I were going to deliver it. I felt no antagonism to my mother. In the dream I went to the toilet to urinate and there was peanut butter smeared inside the toilet bowl. I felt something slipping. It was the baby's head. The thing I was glad of in the dream was that there was no antagonism to my mother. I can remember a time when a dream like that would be a nightmare.

Two months later she said her feelings about housework were greatly improved. She had displaced on to housework pervasive antagonisms to her mother. With these antagonisms dissolving, housework looked different.

> *Virginia.* I am keeping housework up without getting angry at people. But study's another matter. I just feel this uncontrollable rage in the study situation with Vera. She was asked to leave a class because she couldn't learn. I wanted to say, 'You're stupid,' like my mother. I equated fear with learning. Why did I swallow this evaluation of my mother?

A month later she said she saw more and more clearly how she was really like her mother.

> *Virginia.* I have made a conscious effort not to do as my mother, but despite all my efforts my identification with her came through. I was like her unconsciously. She so completely dominated everything. And she was not a person to be sorry for.

Living me—third stage. The third stage of therapy, living a deeply denied experience, was vividly exemplified a month later.

> *Virginia.* I've been miserable all week. There's been a sense of deep and disturbing discontent with myself. Until today, when I did some creative writing. That was a release. I know I have ability. So many things fascinate me. But I have a feeling still that in some area I don't want to be myself. I've had several nightmares. I've felt that I didn't want any part of myself and the feelings of

well-being I've been having are a cover-up and a fool's paradise, and there's a nasty me sitting inside glaring.

I've been thinking about my mother. I'd swear vehemently I'd never do what she did when I was grown and the manner of teaching the child would be one thing. But the minute Vera and I study there's this terrific anger I can't control. (Pause.) I've found it abhorrent *knowing* I am like my mother. (Long pause and evident emotion without words.) You know just then, for the first time I *felt* I was like my mother—and a lot like her. It wasn't knowing; it was feeling. As though I *am* my mother. (Pause.) For the first time I felt her anger in me. Before I felt a rebellious anger *against* her, but not an anger *like* hers. (Pause.) Now for the first time I feel a deep pity for her.

Therapist. You feel compassion for her now.

Virginia. (Pause.) I think I've finally cut her down to size. Before she loomed like an ogre.

Therapist. You see her not as an ogre but a rather pathetic person.

Virginia. She was so afraid herself of being a woman. It was so terribly frightening to her. (Pause.) This is the first time I've ever thought of her as being frightened over anything. You know now she's fighting off the remembrance of our childhoods. She can't remember so many things that happened and I think she's afraid. She is too frightened to face the whippings she made my father give us.

Therapist. The havoc of her own hostility.

Virginia. This is one reason they can't face my sister in the sanatarium. They say, 'Buck up'. They are both afraid, both terribly afraid that if they face my sister's problems, they'd be wide open. I couldn't stand my girl being punished. I know now it was their guilt. I couldn't bear any reminder of what they had done to us. But of all the things I couldn't forgive my mother for, I couldn't on learning. She queered the pitch. To me that was the worst of all. To me that was unforgivable. (Pause.) It seems strange to think of her as being so small.

Therapist. To see her as she is instead of the way you felt.

Virginia. I wonder how many creative urges she had that she could do nothing about—except her piano playing.

In subsequent meetings she spoke of continuing new warm feelings to her mother and a little over a month later she told of a discovery.

Virginia. I've been finding I've lost the old tensions associated with learning and I can study with my child for the first time. Vera and I did eight hours' study together. I typed seven long papers which she had done. And I didn't get angry once. Boy this is new! And Vera glowed through it all. I gave *no advice.* (Emphatically and laughing.) I don't see how I did it. At the end *she* asked questions. (Seeking her mother's help voluntarily in matters of learning was new.)

Week after week the new study habits seemed to hold.

Virginia. We enjoy studying together. I spent my life covering up. I thought what a monster it would be if I uncovered myself. I was afraid of finding I was like my mother, even exactly like her. Rather than find that I'd rather learn nothing at all.

Vera and I studied together. Then she had some make-up assignments, and I left her alone. I was able to let her do on her own what she could and what she couldn't let it ride.

Therapist. You are getting free of your mother standing over you with a stick to wrap your knuckles.

Virginia. And it's a pleasure now to stay home. Housework is no longer a burden. Things that used to get me so involved aren't doing so. I think I'm coming around to a much easier way of living with myself and others.

At the beginning of therapy she had wanted to eradicate the experience of a hated mother. Now she had done so by unexpected routes. At the end, in dissolving a hostile identification which she had consciously denied as part of her angry counter-rejection of her mother, she learned to love both her parents and to give love as a parent in a new way.

WHEN IS THE END OF THERAPY?

In the work described here, as a person chooses the beginning of his deeper journeys into self, he chooses the end—when he is ready. Readiness is, of course, discussed with the therapist and termination is scrutinised for defensive elements. (We have already seen that avoidance of looking at feared feelings may be rationalised by using excuses to stay away.) Regularly scheduled meetings until voluntary termination cover on the average one to three years. However, in some cases, cessation of a regular series of meetings may not be the end of such meetings and the next chapter looks at some implications of the open door philosophy. Therapy does not normally come to an abrupt end. Meeting less often for a transitional period is not infrequent—every two weeks, then every month, for example.

Virginia terminated of her own accord at the age of forty-nine. She had not missed an appointment in weekly interviews over a total therapy period of three years and four months. She was strongly motivated. In a city of cars she had to rely on public transport and even when there was a bus strike she walked each week six miles so that she would not miss an appointment. At the end she said, 'I know now I do not need to come any more.' Two years later at the age of fifty-one she wrote to the therapist. She quoted Karl Menninger: '. . . The best thing that psychiatrists can do for their patients is to light for them a candle of hope to show them possibilities that may become sound expectations.' She added, 'I feel you did this for me. I am so grateful.'

10 An Open Door

Love bade me welcome.
George Herbert

Therapy begins by opening doors, and, when it ends, the door for return to therapy remains open. This is an essential strength. A child is more likely to make responsible choices and find autonomy if he does not feel shut out by his parents. Similarly, at the end of therapy, the open door paradoxically enables a person to move on in his emotional growth knowing the door is not closed if he needs to return.

Large numbers of people leaving with an open door behind them do not return but find they can use resources within themselves to handle both expected and exceptional demands in their life situation. Such was Virginia—she did not return. Occasionally over the years, however, when regular therapy is over, at times of unusual stress, a return to one or two interviews proves a constructive resource, reinforcing and enlarging the emotional learning of therapeutic experience. It is possible, too, for later therapy which a person had previously been unable to accept. Therapy does not abolish the incidence of disruptive events in life, nor the problems to be solved. It aims to help people to handle them realistically by reducing those sources of psychological disruption which spring from personal perception of events, rather than from the events themselves.

PROBLEM SOLVING FOR PROBLEM PANIC

'*Innocent and yet attacked.*' Margaret had spent two years working in an open group which met once a week. She had left the group for one year when she returned one day. Her experience illustrates well the way an occasional return may provide an insight to diminish a peak of emotional turmoil. Margaret recognises that merely seeking reassuring counter-experience in social situations with friends may be a means of denying the deeper personal difficulties precipitated by disrupting events.

Margaret. On Saturday I was attacked by a woman who accused me of snatching her husband. She made a public scene. I went home recognising she was insecure and it was futile to argue. But though I didn't feel guilty I just had to get down here because I reacted so violently towards it there must be more in there. But I have been accused of things in the past where I have felt innocent and I have been forced to apologise; I have been placed on the defensive a good many times in my life by my mother and by my family situation, I think. And this thing aroused all of this in me. As far as the situation is concerned it's just out of proportion.

I think I could have worked it out with my husband (both have been in a parent group) if he'd been at home but he was away on a business trip. He wasn't home to take this load off me and whilst I had some very dear friends around me yesterday to put me socially back, after all that's the sort of thing you can't work out with your friends.

Therapist. You were accused. You've been accused in the past where you did not feel guilty, as yesterday.

Margaret. Yes, I felt free of guilt. My mother made me apologise twice to some girl for something I didn't do. And it sure did eat into my soul for a long time. It's part of the same pattern I mean. I always felt innocent and yet attacked. And I think that that is part of my feeling I've got, an innocent baby and yet not wanted. I think it's part of that rejection. Now of all the things that I've said to myself I've never said quite that before. (Pause.) That's why I came down to find the thing that I couldn't get out by myself, on my own.

Therapist. You don't want to say it again, do you? That was different from any thing that you've ever said before?

Margaret. I've always felt innocent and yet I've never attached the innocence of a baby being born into the world and yet not wanted as part of my response.

Therapist. A baby is very innocent when it's born. It's not responsible. I think that this is where the rejection comes in. It means a great deal if one is held responsible for what one is not responsible for.

Margaret. (Pause.) So now I can extricate my past reactions from this present one. (Pause. pondering,) That brings a new light. (Pause.) I feel better.

She is able to respond so quickly because of many previous hours of working through feelings of rejection which stemmed from being an 'unwanted' child.

'*Tuning in on myself.*' Alison chose therapy as a result of experience in a class in attitudes and communication and went far enough to find glimpses of a more comfortable life with herself and those around her. She had turned her need for love into a drive for material possessions and status. She had resented her mother running her life, she said, but felt closer to her father. Her husband fell short because he was not like her memory of her father, 'supporting and kind', and because he did not meet her ambitions for success and money. She had not wished for a child and rejected the role of mother when her son was born. When she terminated regular therapy, by no means all problems were resolved, but she was conscious of warmer feelings towards her son; and her husband told the therapist she was a warmer and more understanding wife. Family get-togethers at holiday times such as Christmas used to be times of dissention and Alison was depressed by her 'less than ideal house and family'. But she had discovered more realistic expectations of herself and others, and the year after terminating regular therapy she reported the first enjoyable Christmas at home. 'Even though we were short on things we were long on love', she wrote of one family gathering. Then two years after her termination of therapy she was more than usually upset by her son suddenly leaving home to be on his own and by a business reversal of her husband. She asked to talk to the therapist. 'I've been thrown back to my old self,' she said. The therapist's aim was to help give Alison clues to work on the problem herself and to reinforce reality.

Alison. I think I must have been more of the possessive mother than I realised. Now, when Julian (son) comes to see us I'm in a turmoil. His leaving home at this time means I've failed. I'm mad at him but I don't tell him. I want him to stay *and* I want him to go. For good. I had it all set up that he'd be home at least for the first two years of college. His leaving caught me completely off-guard. He's just an ungrateful stinker.

Therapist. He did an about-face from what you had set up for him, didn't he?

Alison. Yes, that's what he did. And I didn't know I was really running him to that extent. He will have to work out his own life. I realise that. (Pause.) But what I mostly want to talk about is Derek (husband). I'm more concerned about him. I can't stand the way he does things. I thought of going off for a few days because I'm so mad at him because he doesn't assert himself enough. I'm sick of pushing him and shouldering everything myself. I'm after him all the time because he just won't make the effort to talk to the right people. I tell him he's to blame for the limited life we have and the slum we live in.

Therapist. That is, your experience of you where you live does not satisfy you so you call it a slum? And you feel Derek is responsible?

Alison. I've taken a morning job. I suppose I could go full time to help the finances, but why should I? When he takes it easy? You've got to push. (Pause.) I get through my morning job as quickly as possible and then I go home and watch television. I want to just sit and relax. I don't feel like doing the house. I just let the dust collect.

Therapist. I can hear something here. You say you're mad because Derek takes it easy. But you're saying you'd like to take it easy too. Are you mad at him for something in you? Is he your scapegoat? Are you blaming him for what you are?

Alison. Mm. The way you put it sets me thinking. (Pause.) But he'd get somewhere if he'd follow my suggestions and push. (Gives many examples of suggestions not taken by Derek.) (Pause.) He doesn't assert himself, but the more I tell him the less he does.

Therapist. You started by saying you were angry because he didn't assert himself; but you stress he should be doing what you suggest. Does this seem contradictory? We have a situation like a child with a parent. One girl said 'My mother was always riding me for having no backbone, and when I did assert myself, she knocked me down.' The way you tell it, Derek's asserting himself in resistance. He's saying, 'I don't want to do this.'

Alison. No, he doesn't.

Alison came for one more interview the following week. She was smiling.

Alison. After last time I went home and listened to myself. I didn't check myself in anything I said, but just listened to myself. I didn't check myself at all. I knew I was dominating. But I tuned in and he was literally the baby in a high chair getting his food from me. I don't know how he could assert himself. And he was asking me what to do in everything. What he should wear, where we should go, everything was what I said. So I stopped myself. And when he asked me, I said, 'What do you think? You make a choice.' And he came home at the end of the week and said he'd been talking to his bosses about leaving early on two days a week for a refresher course. He told them he wanted a new interest. He's even applied to do some work for a higher degree. I was amazed. And this all came from you.

Therapist. That is, you began to see how much you were making his choices for him and then blaming him because he didn't make his own. Now his initiative comes as a surprise.

Alison. Yes. And now I have to work out a balance about voicing my own opinion. I can't just not have an opinion.

Therapist. That is you want to work out a way to be you and allow Derek to be him, without trying to change him.

The process of therapy always involves confrontation—with 'What I am really doing in relation to others and the real world' and with 'the inner self and its needs'. We know that this confrontation must go at a pace at which people can absorb its meaning and make use of it. Even so, it can be a disturbing experience and, at times, may seem to be a disabling one; a person may feel much worse subjectively before he feels better. Alison's encounter with herself had been extremely upsetting. Criteria for terminating therapy are not absolute and she had at that time gone as far as she could in the direction of improved functioning. She was able now to use therapy as a resource to handle a crisis, to help her clarify its real elements and its emotional projections, and to renew her resources for working on problem situations without inner collapse.

Involuntary name calling. A combination of debilitating illness and a family crisis brought Teresa to a state of turmoil eight years after termination of regular therapy. She had been a gifted but deeply deprived child who had described her own insatiability as 'a starving dog inside me ready to eat or be savage'. At a time when she (Teresa) was recuperating from hepatitis, her mother was hospitalised as a result of a car accident and for a time her mother's life was in question. Her father, and a sister who lived in the same town as the parents, did not tell Teresa of her mother's accident. She heard of it by chance when a neighbour of her parents wrote to wish Teresa herself well. Then she telephoned her sister who said they (sister and father) did not want to worry her as she was ill with hepatitis. But Teresa saw the reason given as a rationalisation on her sister's part (disguising what she saw) as her sister's continuing bitterness towards herself. There had been a childhood rivalry between the two in which each saw the other as more favoured—Teresa felt displaced in her father's affections by his attentions to her younger sister, while the younger sister felt constantly trodden upon by Teresa's demands. (We see a parallel with Andrew Smith and his sister, whom we met in Chapter 2.) Teresa's sister has had no therapeutic help. Now, while Teresa talks, ambivalence and extremes of reaction find free expression as she verbalises without concern for logic or transitions. But an objective self listens and comments too.

Teresa. (Weeping.) I'm just going to pieces. This thing is breaking me up. It isn't just the fact that my mother might have died without my knowing it, and she is still very ill, but just that my family didn't see my needs at all. I know it was because I was ill and helpless and weak; I was as vulnerable as any baby and that brought all these old feelings up. I know I shouldn't go to pieces like this, but that doesn't make any difference to my feelings. It's futile and stupid to want them to help me. And what's more to want them to do things for me to prove I'm liked. But I've found more insight than ever in my life before into how *involuntary* feelings are. It's stupid but I'm crying. It's illogical but I'm sobbing my heart out. Because they haven't done what I wanted and needed and they can't. But I just long for some kindness from them. My mother is badly hurt but I can face the reality. It's just all the rejection and cruelty in my family that seem increased at times of need like this and, of course, in having to rely on them for information about my mother, I was literally dependent on them for something vital to me, which is like my childhood. And my sister knows I have been ill but she hasn't sent one word of sympathy or a get-well wish. But to hell with explanation. I just want to let the words pour out as they come. I'm not feeling at all loving. I know all about my sister's problems. But the only thing that comes to my mind is that she's the worst bitch I've ever met. I hate her. I'm getting all these feelings that I'm ugly and that no one could possibly love me, that there's something wrong with me. And you know how I just had to see you in the old days, just to give the lie to all the despair—that I was so ugly, just the sort of person that no one could love—a stimulus for other people's distaste.

I hate my family. I'd like to dump the lot. They're so stupid. My sister's husband is nice enough but all I can think of is that he's a bore. I can't be bothered by such fools. I'm just so furious. They all make me sick. And here I sit crying because of them. I'd like to cut them off. That ragbag my mother. The bitch I'd like to cut in pieces and stick with nails my sister. (Pause.) I think now of your warmth, your kindly humour when I've called you names. You have a deep laugh from the heart. I don't like being around my family. They've nothing to give. They're like vultures. Or leeches that suck you dry. A bottomless pit. You go on giving and get nothing. And to have to deal with all that irrationality is more than I can take. It flashes across my mind that I'm being irrational and doing this to myself now because I'm looking for help to my family who can't give it. But that's not the point. I'm not here to be logical. I have some needs too. I feel desperate. I don't care. Let them get themselves to the hospital. Let them die. I'm saying all these things and yet I can see with another part of me what it means. All this disgust is my only defence. They make me hurt so horribly. I seem to switch between words like 'Forgive them, they know not what they do' and 'Love those who despitefully use you' to hate and anger. All of the anger helpless which makes it worse. I want to avoid my family, have nothing to do with them. Cross them out. Just kill the lot. Dump them in a common grave. I think of children who kill people in their play. They make those things which hurt them impotent. It seems a desperate thing to kill what you most would love. My father is a nothing. A violent uncompassionate whimperer. My sister a jumped-up hussy. You can't win with her. Nothing you ever do is right. I hate everybody especially my family. Then I can hear what all this means. I know that that kind of total hostility means total devastation and I can't bear it. I know it's a guard against total collapse. It's not events but non-events which are the trouble. What happened? Nothing. You just went hungry. So you've *nothing* to worry about. A glorious piece of dramatic irony. But that's the way people talk. 'It's all in your mind', they say. 'You've nothing to worry about. Nothing's happened. Look at all these other people and the calamities that happened to them.' (Sobs.) Nothing's happened! How can people be such fools? Is *no* food at all better than poison? How pathetic this flimsy armour of anger is. The heartbreak's all too visible.

Everything I've said means something else. I want to dump the old ways of reacting, put them in a common grave now and for all time, kill the lot. I can see this so clearly. Kill the power of these people to *kill me* is really what I mean. And I had thoughts about my sister getting in at the kill and feeding on my parents' bodies. But that only tells me of my need for help and caring brought on my my own illness and then this seeming indifference from my famly. And this thought about my parents' bodies was also a need for bodily closeness like a baby as well as feeding like a baby that came in there. But eating my parents' bodies, the picture that came was just that. Almost like young animals feeding from their parents' body, but in this case it was eating the body.

I have been disturbed. But I haven't been at all disturbed by all this involuntary name calling, just letting it come. Not trying to control it. I must be free enough, secure enough, to do that. It teaches me something about my own experience. I let it tell its own story. And I can allow myself to be just where I am. In reality I'm not taking it out on my family. I'm not cutting them off. But I've freely said these things to myself and to you. All these opposite feelings—I've let them come. And the end moves towards compassion and calm. Because you are the good parent and I know you love me for myself. All the opposite and devastated feelings I can say them without thinking to you; because you know what I mean. And it makes it possible for me to find what I mean myself. I could hardly believe the bewildered crushed lostness thinking suddenly that my sister became my mother and I had to get to my mother through all that trauma. The past all over again. The baby past. And I remember that my mother did shut me out often after my sister was born, and I banged on the door sobbing to get in. I thought in this last thing that I've had enough of my life being torn in shreds by my family. I collapsed over this last crisis along with my own illness. But I hardly know whether I was crying for them or myself. It was all one. You don't stop feeling if you understand. Your heart can be torn to see the suffering of others and the tragedy of indifference. Like a picture of Jewish women running naked to the gas chamber and the guards standing

> grinning. There is heartbreak. If one feels. But the rages of a young child, I feel this is what I've been through—an infant needing reassurance and nourishment. You have to understand that in yourself as well as in your real child. Finding tenderness and love to yourself is the answer. And then loving those people who give you nothing because they need love so badly themselves.

Shortly after speaking these words to the therapist, Teresa visited her parents' home and found a more open and direct relationship with all her family than ever before. She said she found from the beginning of therapy a crucial experience for change in what she called the 'warmth' of the therapist, the 'kindly humour when I've called you names'.

DIALOGUE WITH SELF

We have seen how three people's immediate reaction under pressure was to seek the therapeutic frame of reference as a way to enlarged choice in the very nature of their own emotions. In choosing to take responsibility for whatever feelings emerged, they found a greater freedom. The power of the external event decreased; and there was increased flexibility of response to other people.

The manifest signs of an inappropriate response to situations are familiar ones: over-reaction (Margaret); pressurising someone else to change (Alison); involuntary and continued anger and derogatory labelling of others in the face of disappointed need (Teresa). Not only Teresa, however, but Margaret and Alison too are confronted by the strength of their involuntary reactions. Margaret sought from the beginning to deal with the problem of over-reacting to 'being wrongly accused' by looking into herself; Alison came to see her own contribution to her husband's apparent inaction. Teresa allowed involuntary feelings to take over in a personal dialogue in which she saw the way she equated not being fed information by her family with not getting the emotional food she needed as a child. All tuned in on themselves. Pushing under hating feelings meant pushing under loving feelings, too. Admitting hate meant allowing love—all strong feelings could exist. Hate lost its destructive potency and love could accept the necessary limitations of others.

The therapist within—a new identification. There is a sense in which therapy never ends. Teresa's dialogue while the therapist listens in silence particularly illustrates the way in which a 'therapist within the person himself' takes over. He internalises the therapist, the new parent. New spontaneous responses result. Teresa and others find at times of stress, if old reactions return, they do not persist as long and seem to dissolve through dialogue between the person and the invisible therapist within him.

Taking time for meditation, taking time to write 'with the therapist in mind' have been used helpfully between therapeutic meetings; parents and others have used these means when actual meetings with the therapist are over. While a combination of unusual stresses may make any person regress to the stage of non-verbal, infant crying for comfort, involuntary verbalisation can provide increased understanding of non-verbal needs. The therapeutic self, which incorporates the invisible therapist, the 'good parent', listens and heals.

In the child's search for self-worth, adequacy and a sense of belonging, murderous urges, incestuous fantasies, aggression and hate reveal profound personal synonyms. People have found, after the kinds of experiences we have shared in this book, that they are able without fear to verbalise destructive impulses. And speaking them, even alone, with 'the therapist within', discloses their deeper personal meanings and dissolves their power.

We carry the impulses and needs of all the ages of a man's life within us. All the potential acts of other human beings are potential for us too. Feelings continue to be facts. They do not disappear. Receptive recogniton of them when they do occur increases the ability for free but responsible choices. Here lies the paradox again before us—in inviting feelings, looking at them and not denying them, we can in a sense choose them and not be chosen by them. With the centre in ourselves we are not waiting for someone else to make the first move to change our world.

11 *The Parent in the Child —the Therapy of Play*

I was angry with my friend:
I told my wrath, my wrath did end.
I was angry with my foe:
I told it not, my wrath did grow.

William Blake

Words which come unbidden yield images which reveal a person to himself. Saying them and expressing the feelings they convey is a safety valve and provides a route to insight and change. But speech is not only word symbols; it is a *form of relating* and embodies the whole context of attitudes and feelings with which we relate to others.

Speech is also a *form of behaviour* and as such it is a derivative of behaviour as a whole. Gestural language becomes symbolic and more finely differentiated in verbal language, but speech and other behaviours remain fused as one. The behaviours of body postures and tensions speak as do skin changes in blushing or pallor, and the covert signals of the autonomic nervous system, with its overt signs such as 'butterflies in the stomach' and inability to eat. Behaviour then has its language without words responding, as speech does, to many aspects of a situation and expressing simultaneously many meanings. The child in his play merges the language of words and the language of action.

A child learns by play. In the sensory experience of play, he comes to know the nature of the materials of his world. Then as he experiments with materials and discovers how they may satisfy his senses, he may accidentally 'make something'. But of course, it may not mean for him what the literal adult mind sees. The child who tells the story in Saint-Exupéry's *The Little Prince* has a very low opinion of the adults who cannot see that his drawing number one shows a boa constrictor digesting an elephant, and tell him that it is just a picture of a hat. We will not help a child to get to know the raw material of his environment, or give free rein to his imagination, if we impose literal, visual interpretations on his image of what he sees. Intuitively he interprets his own discoveries. How can a row of straight lines be a balloon? The continuity of a balloon gets into those straight lines, the stretch of a balloon makes itself felt in those straight lines, synonyms for a balloon that get lost in the single equation of a balloon's shape. Given freedom to explore the feel and look of finger paints, a child may begin to make arrangements of form and colour, and express his sense of wonder as designs emerge from his developing awareness.

Play is a child's language. He makes his own unfettered creations and learns the limits of his world in play. We need to understand his symbols. Becoming more sensitive to children's behaviour means becoming more sensitive to their play. Parents learn, 'Parents who belittle their children's play, miss the power of it.' In nothing more than a child's play does he tell us the way he is negotiating his identification—being a boy, being a girl, the feelings he has learned about his important adults and their attitudes to him. In the behaviour of play he communicates his deepest needs and his greatest fears, even though he cannot verbalise them. Are his feelings safe or must he be guilty about them? Must he condemn himself for existing, because any part of him may bring pain, or does he discover he can without fear be the self he was born with? Does becoming a social being mean that he has to conform at the expense of inner strain with difficult internal conflicts always threatening to provoke random and illogical behaviour resulting in further external battles? Or has he learned that even when he may not hammer his mother's dishes, or put paint on his father's car, or tear up his plants, he has things of his own he can hammer, blocks he can build with or push over, and a place of his own to dig in the garden or the sandbox?

Play incorporates, then, a means of emotional learning as well as a means of acquiring specific skills and knowledge. And, where a child's relationship to himself and others has become one of strife, play may become a route to emotional re-learning. Play therapy reaches the underlying conflict which gives rise to the outward manifestations of emotional difficulties—bed-wetting, learning and behaviour problems, speech inhibitions. The therapy of play offers the child both the possibility of release and of re-experiencing himself.

We have heard Helen tell us how her son, Dan, began having regular bowel movements in the context of her improved relationship with him, when her terrors of her own strong feelings diminished and she was less 'held in' herself. 'He plays enema with his toys,' she said, 'and so works it out that way.' Helen was able to accept his surgical play, understanding his needs to find a safe place for healing the old trauma. She could offer him a relationship of trust, an uncondemning climate for his communication in play. To this extent she was offering him an essential aspect of a parent-child relationship utilised in play therapy; for play therapy is essentially relationship therapy and results in improved interpersonal communication.

Play therapy for the child is analogous to talking therapy for the adult, and the same principles underlie the therapeutic process. Play therapy offers the kind of attitudes in which children may become free enough to express themselves honestly and achieve feelings of self-worth, adequacy and belonging. The climate of play therapy is permissive as is the climate of adult therapy. That is, any feeling is permitted existence and there are greatly extended freedoms beyond the normal social setting in the means of expression. But there are realistic limits—the limits of the room space and the therapy hour. The goal is recognition of feelings and channelling them, not literally acting them out. The room is equipped with toys and materials appealing to different stages of growth and different areas of potential conflict. The therapist tells the child at the beginning that he may do as he wishes in the room except hurt people or damage valuable property. But there is no restriction on what he may say, or on symbolic play expression. Dolls, puppets, animals give him opportunity to re-enact family relationships. Sand, clay, water, finger paints or crayons provide less structured messy activities. They also offer a means for the creation of people and things upon which hating or loving feelings can be projected; people and things which can be destroyed and made again, killed or brought to life as the child plays out his personal synonyms. A nursing bottle may elicit feelings about a child's baby brother or sister, or make it possible for him to meet his own baby needs; in play, he can negotiate soundly a stage in growth he may have felt pushed beyond before he was ready. Sucking and blowing on balloons may serve as another outlet for baby activity. (Balloons are among the easily dispensable items in the play room and so may be a convenient recipient of aggressions.) Non-mechanical toys are preferable to mechanical ones because they give a child more latitude to make them move at his pace. He can make his unique feelings propel the bus, the truck or the car that he must push.

As speech is symbolic, the language of play is symbolic. Thus, a child may speak of flooding the world, and play at doing so in the 'ocean' of a cup of water. In this way he learns to test and discover realistic limits and find all his feelings may exist and find safe outlets. The therapist is a sympathetic perceiver-listener who aims to convey understanding of the child's inner world without criticising. At the same time the therapist represents environmental reality—the limits and the protective and enabling sanctions of the social order.

IN THEIR OWN GOOD TIME

Like adults, children must make their own choices and take responsibility for their own emotional development. But they can only admit each part of their hidden selves when they are ready to do so. Growth cannot be forced. Various forms of denial of emotional need may precede the expression of the need. *Freedom may seem threatening because it entails recognising and exposing painful areas of experience.*

Denying the need. Michael's mother told how she 'beat him well' for his mess when he had an 'accident' and related a bitter scene when she found him smearing faeces on the wall of his bedroom when he was twenty-seven months old. She had wanted him clean and had attempted toilet training at five months; she was at her 'wit's end' because he still wet the bed. Michael's play showed his need to feel adequate as a boy in relation to his mother, but also a need to come to terms with his baby activities. Denial immediately finds expression when the therapist tell him he can do as he wishes with the materials in the room. He expresses anger because he has a woman therapist, and asserts, 'I'm too big for this baby stuff.' He is now seven. He is to come for play therapy twice a week.

> *Michael.* I don't play with dolls. What's all this baby stuff? I don't want to play with a girl. What do we do? What's the time?

In a room with a woman who may turn into his mother and disapprove of his messy activities, the room itself becomes stifling.

> *Michael.* I can't stand this stuffy room. (Pause.) I'll play with the clay. I'll make an elephant. That's enormous.
> *Therapist.* You'll make something big.

Michael. (Asserting another masculine symbol.) Now I'll make a snake. (Rolls clay.) I'll make a bull next. (Makes a bull.)

Therapist. You want to make men's things.

Michael. Now I'll drown the doll. (Fills toy bath tub with water and puts the minature doll in it.)

Therapist. That got rid of the girl.

Michael. Yes. I don't like girls. (Looks around. Seems to be more relaxed after his assertions have been simply received.) Oh, I didn't see the crayons.

He spends some time drawing a yellow house under a spreading green tree which had two red flowers on either side of it—a use of colours which seems to suggest both tender and strong feelings.

Michael. You make something with clay.

Therapist. What would you like me to make?

Michael. A man. (Therapist rolls body, head, arms and legs, following Michael's instructions.) Now I'll make a hat for him. (Makes hat, and then makes eye and mouth holes for the model.) Now I finished the man. Let's make a woman. (Makes a woman, adding eye and mouth holes as for the man.)

Therapist. A man and a woman.

In play children kill the symbols that seem frustrating, and bring them back to life in a resurrected form more to their satisfaction. Michael drowns the girl but when he has made his own man, he makes a woman. But he has to find a sense of security with this new mother therapist before he can approach the concerns of the little boy, above all the messy little boy. Will his gifts be accepted?

In the next session he plays a while with puppets and then becomes engrossed in other activities.

Michael. I'll make a chemical. (Dips straw in a bottle of water and adds small pieces of clay. Then he rolls the clay using a toy rolling pin.) This is an apple pie for you. (Gives it to the therapist who accepts his gift.)

He spends the rest of the time making darts from paper and cardboard.

Michael. What's the time? I *don't* want to go.

Therapist. The time goes quickly when you do what you like.

Play in the third meeting includes more activity with clay. He uses the washable floor.

> *Michael.* I'll make another pancake. (Hammers clay on the floor and then cuts it in pieces with toy scissors. Spills water on the table and tries to stop the drips with clay stuck on the end of the table, then lets water drip.) It's raining through the fence. (Makes small puddle on the floor which he spreads over a wider area with toy hammer. Moulds clay figure of a man and squeezes neck to make it long.) He's under the ocean and wants to come to the top. (Michael too wishes to 'get out from under'.)

Testing the limits. During the fourth meeting play includes pouring water on the floor and then washing it all over with a sponge. During this and the next three sessions he tests the limits of behaviour and finds he can talk of his feelings of wanting to attack the therapist, to 'mess up' the therapist, even though in reality 'We do not hurt each other'. He can also hit Molly the Mother puppet (his name): 'I'll cut off her head.' During this period he several times asks if he can take things home. Asking for things is synonymous with asking for love, but in themselves they would not provide it any more than things gave Mrs Green what she needed. The experience of being understood, of having someone tune into his world without judging him, cannot be measured by things. To allow him to take things would leave insatiability untouched. Michael can find a sense of self-worth in the experience he takes with him from the playroom. Things are secondary symbols. One of the realities is the rule that toys must be left in the room, to be used in the room. Also there is the reality that other children share the toys. At times he appears anxious as when he spills some water on the floor and wants to leave. 'This room stinks,' he says. (Reminders of messy accidents with faeces and urine stink?) He learns then that he may leave but he cannot come back that hour. He is learning limits and that they are consistent. He is learning, too, to channel his feelings in symbolic ways. For almost one whole session he blows bubbles calling them bombs. He first names capitals of countries as their targets and then drops 'bombs over the world, only the Empire State Building escapes'. (Will this phallic symbol—himself?—be powerful enough to survive a holocaust?) Then the bubbles are rockets with a thousand men in each. Bubble bombs hit 'that guy' and 'another guy' until he gets rid of all the people in the world he doesn't like.

Ensuring trust. There is one small truck among the toys which he chooses for his own. He wheels it around during the sixth meeting.

Michael. I like this. I'd like to keep this. I'll put it in the female box and then no one can have it. (Puts it in cardboard box.)
Therapist. You think your truck will be safe in the female box, Michael.
Michael. Yes.

In such ways he reaches out to ensure 'my male things are secure with and in this female'. In the eleventh session he wraps two carbon crayons in a piece of paper and ties them up. As he cuts the string with the edge of a toy rubber knife, he says, 'This is the knife I nearly killed you with. Remember? I like you. I like today. I'll bring you a carrot. I'll bring you a cabbage you can clean. Will you keep this packet? (Giving carbon crayons.) Put it in your purse. It means a lot to me.'

The crayons are examples of the way things may be used symbolically and become important in therapy. The therapist keeps the symbolic packet. At the next meeting he says, 'Do you have it? Let me see. (Looks.) I don't want it today. Put it back in your purse.'

He seems reassured that this piece of him is not lost or broken, but is in good keeping. His new mother appears to care for him, to protect him so that he can discover his growing self in safety. For the first time he seems to be relaxed in making a mess. He wets some hard clay in a small pail of water. Then he makes what he calls a 'hammer bomb' by putting soap powder in a bubble pipe and throwing it up. After this he sprinkles soap powder on the floor and uses a wet paper towel for washing it over.

Michael. This is a commercial for Axon's soap. (Stands up and sees blue jeans smeared where he has been kneeling, tries to wipe off the smear. Parents are told washable old clothes are desirable for play therapy.)
Therapist. You want to get rid of the dirt? (Michael stops rubbing, slips and sits on the soapy floor, gets up, dances up and down, and slips again.)
Therapist. That was an accidentally on purpose one.
Michael. Yes. (Smiling.)
It is the end of the hour and time to go.

Therapist. You made a nice mess today. And you slipped twice. (Michael laughs.)

He spends most of the next hour (the seventeenth meeting) playing with clay in messy ways, stirring clay and water, getting his hands in it, then wiping his hands, and then going back and getting his hands and arms smeared with clay, seeming to enjoy himself.

Therapist. It's good to be dirty sometimes.

Children offering their gifts for acceptance, is tantamount to offering themselves, whether the gift is the faeces of regular bowel movements that makes Mother happy, or his 'mud pies'. He may learn then the socially acceptable ways of depositing elimination but still feel comfortable with messy materials. For Michael the clay becomes eventually frankly 'pooh-pooh' water 'pee-wee' but it is not until the twenty-fourth meeting that he seems comfortable with his labels. However, he appears to disown the 'consequences' when he spills water on the floor. His new parent must take responsibility, be like him, make it all right.

Michael. You did it. You pee-wee'd on the floor.
Therapist. I did it?
Michael. Yes.

He takes clay powder and wets it; then he asks the therapist to mix it.

Michael. You do it. This pooh-pooh is yours. (Appears defiant now.)

He is playing out the most painful areas associated with bed-wetting and drawing with his faeces on the wall. He asks the therapist to smear some wet clay on the wall.

Therapist. You'd like me to do the smearing. (Follows his instruction and smears some clay on the washable wall.)

In such ways Michael discovers a parent he can identify with, and can seek a more comfortable identity for himself. 'Here is someone who makes messy activities completely acceptable, and so makes me acceptable.' he seems to be saying.

In the next meeting he shows no sign of anxiety and smears the 'pooh-pooh' himself.

Making a new self. Meantime there are other areas in which he is asking the therapist to take an active part in re-creating himself and his experience. Little boys imagine making children with their mothers as well as seeking love and identity in shared activity. Adults, the parents of children, speak of a sense of being re-born in finding a new self, a new way of seeing as a result of therapy. Children may play at re-entering the mother (as Michael put his truck inside 'the female box'), going in as a baby to grow or to make babies with the mother. Little girls play at 'losing their tails' inside the mother and identify with being feminine at the same time. Michael's two carbon crayons remained tied in paper in the therapist's purse week after week where the therapist remembered to put them before each session. Seven meetings after he gave them to her, in the eighteenth meeting, he asks the therapist to roll the clay.

Michael. Roll it an inch long. Now smooth it out. Don't leave any cracks. Now make it longer. Now make it into a rocket. (Therapist follows instructions.) Now do it so long. (Showing.) Now smooth this part till I tell you to stop. That's wrong. Do it well and I'll give you a red apple. Screwball. Are you a screwball? This is good. We made this together—*you* and *I*. (Emphatic. He is really pointing out what therapy is—a joint creative venture to make a new self. While instructing the therapist he has been mixing clay and water in a toy bucket. He wants to transfer it to another bucket.)

Michael. You do this. You do the dirty work. Now blow a balloon and tie it.

Therapist. You want me to do all the things you wish.

Children have their ways of understanding the sexual relationship of their mother and father. In wanting to give his 'man thing' in play to his mother, Michael wants to be a man for her, and at the same time to identify with his father.

Michael. (Lies on the floor and holds his clay rocket.) It goes up and up and up and it can't land except in a crevice.

Therapist. This man's thing lands in the female crevice. (Using his words.)

Michael. (Sits up. Look at some straw in packing box used for play.) I don't want the packet. (Referring to carbon crayons in therapist's purse.)

Therapist. You want me to keep on taking care of your things.

Both aggression and regression may be expressed by messing. Anger can be generalised (destroying all the people with bubble bombs) or specific.

In the twenty-fifth meeting Michael draws a picture of the therapist on the blackboard. (At this time there are reports frrom the parent counsellor of strained relations between the parents.) He projects his feelings about his mother. The dynamism of displacement is evident—he displaces his attack on to a substitute for the real target of his anger as he draws.

> *Michael.* That's you. You are a witch with a long nose and a big mouth. You and my mother, you both take the words out of my mouth. (Pause.) Now I'm going to invite you to a necktie party. (Takes string and doll and hangs the doll.) I'm hanging this man. He's a stinker.
>
> *Therapist.* You're getting rid of a stinker.
>
> *Michael.* You next.

At the beginning of the next two meetings he hangs the man again and leaves him hanging.

> *Michael.* He stole fifty thousand and killed five men. You take a lot of killing. (To the doll he has hanged.)

In the thirtieth meeting he says the therapist is the guy who is being hanged. (The sex of the therapist may become male or female as the child projects his feelings.) At the same time he brings the man-woman back to life. (He has killed both unsatisfactory parents and now seeks reparation and reassurance from a re-created satisfactory parent.)

> *Michael.* Untie him. It's you. You stole yourself. Money from the bank. It wasn't the guy, it was you.
>
> *Therapist.* It wasn't the guy, it was me.
>
> *Michael.* He wasn't hanged anyway. (Pause.) May I see the packet? (Looks.)
>
> *Therapist.* You want to be sure I keep safe the things important to you.
>
> *Michael.* It's important to me. (Me remains cared for no matter what his feelings.)

The next meeting he asserts he can make his own clay, but he spends some time playing at feeding the baby, turning the therapist into the baby.

Michael. Here's a baby bottle for you. Will you do something for me? Suck on this nipple. (Therapist pretends to suck. Then Michael asserts aggression in ways children often assert sexual aggression, a fantasy of sex with a parent.) I'll run my rocket ship into you.

Assertion of maturity and regression to infancy seem to run together. He shoots water from a squirt gun into his mouth and says it is milk; he puts water in a balloon.

Michael. This is you. (Referring to balloon with water in it. Makes a small hole so that water squirts out.)
Therapist. Milk? (Michael nods yes.)

He squirts water into his mouth and then bursts the balloon. In such activities, children in play seem to feed from and attack the breast and the mother herself for not being a satisfactory feeder. In projecting his fears and needs on to the parent-therapist, Michael continues to find a new parent and a new self.

In the fourtieth session he spends the whole time playing with four toys—a tank which he makes tow a toy bus, a small truck and a wagon. These are his 'man things' and he seems pleased and sings as he plays. Another of his repeated games is to get in a box, which becomes his bed or hideout. 'Shut me in. I have problems to attend to,' he says when he uses the box. So the box becomes a special place of his own where he wants to solve his problems and take his special things. At the forty-first meeting he plays with the four toys again, then gets into the box and asks the therapist to hand the toys over.

Michael. Now don't peek or you're a dead duck.
Therapist. This is your world and you don't want people to look unless you want them to.
Michael. Don't peek. (Getting behind the box, he sings as he plays.) Oh, you can peek. I was setting up a garage.
Therapist. Now you have your own place for your things.
Michael. And I want my drinking fountain balloon. I want my drinking fountain and this box and these four trucks every time.

Michael, in his struggle towards emotional growth and maturity, plays out openly, with diminishing fear, infant interest in wetting and messing. If a child is angry, urine and faeces may be weapons as well as gifts. Bed-wetting for Michael has seemed an effective way to engage and upset his mother and it has been a way of dominating her, demanding what he needed. It has been a way of forcing participation, too, for then his mother had to do his 'dirty work'. Play therapy reflects his need both to attack (with 'pee-wee' and 'pooh-pooh') and to have his mother share in and accept his baby ways. He is also concerned with finding security in his sexual identity. His dominating play, giving orders, precedes less defensive and less defiant play in which he is more contentedly himself, setting up his 'own garage' and singing as he does so.

MATCHING APPEARANCE AND REALITY

The major faces of need which emerge in play therapy seem to involve three major socialisation and training areas. First, infant feeding and weaning associated with the deepest dependency needs become part of being a baby again, finding a secure dependency in these baby needs before moving into greater autonomy in caring for the self, and in motor and creative activities. Second, the area of elimination and toilet training becomes associated with issues of control in all other ways, with feelings about dirt and being dirty, and a child returns to unstructured messy activities to find greater comfort with himself in these often taboo interests which have made him feel an outcast. Third, a child's sex, identity as boy or girl, present a crucial area in negotiating a place, finding maturity in the social world. And here the child's sexual fantasies and play, overt or disguised, present another repeatedly taboo area and so one for confusion and uncertainty as he looks to find himself and his role with others. And at all times a fourth and pervasive issue needs to be resolved realistically—the issue of aggression and tenderness, of hate and love, the interplay of seemingly opposite strong feelings, and their co-existence in ambivalence.

In play therapy a child may go back and negotiate each stage in growth, as he responds to a climate of trust where he can genuinely make his own choices. Then with increased inner security and self-esteem, regressive behaviour diminishes, as Michael's bed-wetting problem clears.

The aim is a real maturity and not simply its outside appearance, not a seeming conformity which covers confusion or rebellion.

A seeming adult. There are children who spend much of their time with older brother or sisters, and with parents, and seem to develop an adult point of view, but in fact these children remain innerly confused about and even threatened by the labels they seem to use with such confidence. There is really no such thing as a child having an adult viewpoint. He is still a child and may retain excessive infant needs and fears under the façade. Such a child is six-and-a-half-year-old Gary. His mother describes him as a 'sweet boy who is no trouble'. But he has developed a stuttering problem also, like Michael he wets his bed.

Gary's father, from being an absentee father often away on business, has left the family—Gary, his older brother, seven years older, and his mother. She has divorced the father. In talking to her own therapist she reveals ways in which she is using her sons, and finds insight into some devouring needs for love in herself which, as they reveal themselves in pervasive criticism and demandingness, tend to drive others away, including her husband. Gary's brother she says, is a bully and a whiner, but she comes to see that she is rejecting him because he is 'like her', the aspects of herself she does not want to admit, her own 'whining'. She says she puts all her affection on to Gary. But the older brother is one of those older children who finds ways to strike at the baby who seems to obtain all the love: he teases Gary even though he invites for himself more rejection from his mother. However, in therapy she says, 'I can see this (teasing Gary) is a way to get my attention as well as to punish me.' She also gains insight into the way she is, under the appearance and name of loving Gary, in a reality dominating him and keeping him dependent on her as a baby—trying to meet her needs through him in fact.

Labels may become important in reducing fear in a child. Thus the therapist's acceptant verbalisation, or acceptance of the child's verbalisation that messy matter is 'pooh-pooh', a balloon a breast, rod-like material a penis he wants cherished, may bring both relief and clarification. Attitudes are all-important. Attitudes that become attached to the label are more important than being able to use the labels. Gary has ready labels and an adult vocabulary, but he is uneasy. His labels seem to be more than the names of things; rather they seem to be a way of expressing the areas of his confusion. He repeatedly talks about a penis.

Gary. (Getting into a box under the table.) This is my boat. I'm in charge.

Therapist. You're the captain.

Gary. Yes. Now I'm shooting the man. (Shoots with toy pistol

at picture of man he has drawn on blackboard.) I shot his penis to pieces.
Therapist. You shot his penis. (Simply recognising acceptingly his label and his action.)
Gary. What an awful penis he has. (Goes and looks at his picture.) What an awful penis. All stretched out.

He attacks both the mother and father in the guise of Mother and Father Bear, and plays at cutting off their heads. Much of his play consists of cutting and stabbing. (A penis is a weapon as well as a means of relating.) His father in a sense, too, since he has left, is a 'missing piece' cut out from a whole and Gary feels the deprivation.

Gary. (Draws a house.) This is my house.
Therapist. Who lives there?
Gary. I do.
Therapist. Who lives with you?
Gary. My mom and (pause) oh, anybody.

Later in the hour he fills the nursing bottle with water and sucks it.

Gary. I'm a baby. (Sucks.) I wish I was a baby.

In the next meeting the same polarity in play occurs between violent aggression and helpless infant needs. Wanting and attacking his father come into play. He equates breast and penis as something to feed from. Both parents are potential sources of succour.

Gary. (Crouches near box and sucks.) I'm sucking a daddy. (Gets up and picks up a toy hatchet.) Now I'll break this guy.
Therapist. You're really mad at that guy.

Early in the next meeting he sucks on the bottle again.

Therapist. How's the baby?
Gary. I like this.
Therapist. (Restating and accepting his perception.) It's good to be a baby and be fed.

As his mother gains insight into what her needy and 'devouring' attitude might mean to him, Gary in his play reveals how a child internalises the bogeys of his parents. He seems to identify with his mother's attacks on his father and to join the attack.

Gary. (Making eye-holes and a mouth in a cardboard box with his toy knife.) This is a man. Now I'll kill him. (Stabs the box several times.) The mother wants to get rid of this daddy.

In attacking the 'awful penis' he reduces his father's power but also expresses his fear that he himself may be attacked. On another occasion he expresses his fear openly in a fear of castration by a 'she'. 'A monster, she took my penis.' In his play he is both the attacker and the victim.

Six meetings later his play seems to be repairing many injuries. He has many times beaten and kicked both the Mother and Father Bear, tied them together and bounced them together on the floor—a violent yoking of his actually separated mother and father. Today he puts them to sleep together in a cardboard box.

Gary. They are sleeping together. This is what they should do. A bomb falls while they are asleep but no one is hurt. (Turns to clay and makes clay family. Then makes a fishing rod to put in the father's hand.) It's his fishing rod. (Makes chair.) This is a chair for the momma to sit on. She's tired. I used to be mean. Now I'm not. (Rolls a flat piece of clay.) This is a hot cake for the poppa. The others can wait.

In such ways, alternating between reparative and aggressive play, messing the room and cleaning it, Gary works through his problem areas. His mother reports that his stuttering and bed-wetting gradually disappear. At the same time, she, in her therapy, finds inner resources to handle his temporarily greatly increased aggressiveness as, she says, he sheds the 'sweet exterior and seems to find an inner security', and 'not just a surface adult point of view'.

I'm the toughest. Six-year-old Jack's mother seeks help because he 'seems unusually scared of play equipment like the swings and rollercoaster which boys usually like'. His first verbal expressions are opposite of his frightened everyday behaviour. They also test the therapist's capacity to accept, and even dare disapproval.

Jack. I like to fight. I like to hit my friends on the head with a hammer. I like to beat people up.

Therapist. (Responding to underlying feeling.) It feels good to hit out. (This response recognises Jack's desire, expressed in his extreme symbol, to be more positive in his expressions, instead of the fearful child he actually is.)

Then Jack identifies with the frightened little child vicariously by referring to another little boy at home. He is testing the therapist's capacity for acceptance in another area now.

Jack. Everybody beats up Lenny. He isn't tough. He's just weak and scared.
Therapist. When a boy's weak and scared, everybody seems to beat him up. (The therapist uses Jack's symbol to convey understanding of how it feels to be beaten up.)

But Jack is not ready to accept openly his own sense of smallness, inadequacy, fear. His ideal self-image seems to find more acceptable expression in the violent assertion of his verbalised fantasy.

Jack. I'm the toughest kid on the block.

The therapist says nothing as Jack then sits and says nothing. There is neither approval nor disapproval—feelings are, they exist, they are not good or bad in themselves. Jack follows this non-evaluative reception by modifying his statement that he is the toughest kid on the block.

Jack. Well, I am not really the toughest. Dick's the toughest.

For five meetings his play is predominantly aggressive. 'I'm the big shot.' He has mock battles between 'good and bad guys' as he draws pictures and tells stories, as he manipulates small trucks and cars, as he plays with puppets. He pounds clay, occasionally makes a model of a person or animal, but destroys his model quickly. He expresses some dependency needs when he asks the therapist for help in blowing up balloons even though they have been previously inflated to make it easy for him to do it for himself. He fixes clay on the ends of the balloons to hold them down so that they will 'not get away' from him. On one occasion after puppet play in which he shoots and kills one person, he locks people up in a clay gaol. In such ways he plays out disapproving and punishing feelings for the unacceptable parts of himself as well as permitting their expression. Similarly he shifts from 'big guy' play with the toy guns to baby messing by smearing little pieces of clay on the guns; but he quickly cleans them. 'I don't like them dirty.' He is touching gingerly on areas that are much more difficult to come to terms with than the aggressiveness that can be expressed in structured activities and more acceptable 'masculine play'.

In every encounter with the therapist, there is implicit testing, of a new parent both for attitude and response. But, as all children and adults may do, he proceeds cautiously in exploring 'helpless' and therefore what seem to be more vulnerable parts of him. At each stage he has to find sufficient security from his experience in this new relationship for him to risk opening up. Each person, child or adult, has his own most difficult-to-express feelings. He can only acknowledge them as his when he is ready. For Jack 'baby business' elicits the most difficult-to-handle conflict. Here he reflects the parent in him. His mother has discovered he is in fact a replica of herself in conflicted and hesitant social behaviour. And she has been fearful of his going out away from her but, as we have seen, has censured the result in his tendency to hang back in baby ways and to be 'scared' of the 'swings and roller-coaster which boys usually like'. Jack's baby self, then, calls for sound negotiation, and his aggression needs to lose its protective defensiveness.

After four meetings of vigorous verbalisation he is again silent in the playroom. He spends nearly half an hour doing nothing but sit, looking drawn and anxious. When he does speak his conflict finds symbolic expression. He seems pre-occupied with 'cops' and 'dirt'. Guilt and its attendant fear seem to limit his play.

Jack. My *dad* can get away from the cops. (Will there be a parent who can reduce the danger of punishment?)

As is not unusual when troublesome feelings are pushing to be heard, fearful behaviour increases. He plays in a desultory manner with clay. At previous meetings he has rushed to it.

Jack. The clay's dirty. (Puts it down.)

Therapist. (Simply accepting his immediate expression.) You feel the clay is dirty and you don't feel like playing with it today.

The next meeting Jack's activities are much less structured than at other times. He is able to express hostility directly to the therapist, an important test of a successful relationship.

Direct expression of hostility to the therapist may arise from a growing security as well as be the *first* defensive reactions of a child. To be mad at other people and things in dramatic play and not find condemnation is a healing experience, but to be directly mad at an important adult and still be liked by that adult is even more crucial for a child's emotional growth. An understanding reception of angry feelings by this important adult aids in increasing security in handling angry feelings so that a child is not overwhelmed by the frightening omnipotence of fantasy. For it is important that containment accompanies understanding so that the adult represents a sustaining strength which will protect the child from himself as he internalises his own controls of behaviour and ways to channel his feelings. His adult is not a punishing parent then, but a parent limiting and guiding in reasonable and loving ways.

Sometimes it is in a group rather than in individual therapy that children find a quicker route to the expression of hostile feelings to the authority. They seem to derive security from the group in 'ganging up' on the adult: 'I don't like her (him),' they say to each other as they talk of the therapist. In such cases an element of denial may become evident, as though the child is really saying, 'I don't want to let on how much I like and want the liking of this person I can get mad at without being afraid.'

Jack, in individual therapy has been able to test the therapist in many areas and found a growing security. His open hostility is a reflection of a growing confidence.

Jack. You'll get wet if you don't watch out. (Splashing water on to table towards therapist.)

There are some new dolls among the toys. (New materials are from time to time introduced in the playroom.) Jack wets the baby doll which is wearing a diaper. He is smiling and seems pleased. Moreover, he takes responsibility for his action. He doesn't pretend its someone else.

Jack. (Emphatically.) I *helped* him mess himself. (Then the echo of cultural condemnation, but lightly spoken, without manifest anxiety.) I'm a naughty boy.

Therapist. You mean messy boys are sometimes called naughty boys. (Recognising both cultural label and the possibility of another more accepting connotation.)

Jack. I'm not supposed to play in water—and I *did*. (Emphatic.)

He squeezes drops of water from the baby bottle on the toy dolls and animals and says, 'I'm flooding everybody out.'

The next meeting he wets the doll some more, and with a smile and with energy rubs its face in the small puddle he has made. (He is allowed one cup of water each time. His floods are symbolic ones, or verbalised fantasy.)

Three weeks after the doll-wetting, Jack crawls on the floor of the playroom, leans against the therapist, closes his eyes and drinks from the nursing bottle.

Children frequently place the feelings they are doubtful about on to make-believe figures as Jack did on to the doll, before they can admit them as their own, dare to dispense with disguise. From Jack's structured aggressive play it is a big step to become preoccupied with baby business even in play with a doll. It seems that the unjudging reception of his silence and depression evident in a whole therapy hour is a necessary precursor to his regressing to infant play which he adopts as frankly his.

Paradoxically when he is playing with the baby and being the baby in therapy, his mother is reporting more mature and outgoing behaviour at home; the correlation is usual. Such is the power of going back and negotiating unfinished learnings from the infant world, to enable a child to grow emotionally. Jack's mother in her counselling is finding an outgoingness, parallel to his developing in herself. 'I surprised myself,' she said, 'and Jack surprised everybody because he seems to have lost his shyness.'

THE FACES OF PLAY

Play therapy has its adaptations. A child may draw pictures and tell stories about them; he may tell stories about structured or unstructured pictures which the therapist presents showing familiar child activities (mud pies or playing ball) and family situations (feeding the baby, Mother in the kitchen, Daddy going to work). Finger painting, modelling in clay, creative dramatic play in the child's own person or using puppets are all variations of play therapy. So is free talk. A child may tell his fantasy, his daydream, or he may recall a dream from his sleep. A child's story tells of the ways he sees himself and his life situation.

In everyday life, as in play therapy, if he is not able to distinguish between his dream or fantasy, and reality, he is not lying. He challenges us to read his feeling and to understand our own. Thus, Don really does not know when he tells his mother Aunt Mary says his mother ought to leave his father, that he is voicing feelings he has picked up from his mother herself and made his own; but they are too frightening to admit as his, so he unconsciously censors them and puts them into Aunt Mary. If his mother can hear, she can look more honestly at her own feelings rather than joining the attack on Aunt Mary. Norma is not lying when she says she lives in a green house with the boy next door; her dream is her reality, her wish finding its own fulfilment in fantasy. Discriminating between real events and fantasied ones becomes increasingly possible when play and talk find safe places to be.

Parents are told when children are in play therapy not to question them about what takes place but to allow them to tell if they wish. Respect for the child's private world is of paramount importance if there is to be a climate of trust in which he can take responsibility for his own growth. Play becomes an externalisation of his private world and he will not readily tolerate indiscriminate prodding or watching. 'I don't want people to watch me playing,' says six-year-old Juliet. She wants a curtain pulled over the small window of the door to ensure privacy. Jimmy, a four-year-old with a retarded speech problem is just beginning of play more freely. At the end of the hour he motions the therapist to stay in the room and appears to put on a placid mask when he goes back to his mother to leave the building and go home. Back in the playroom again next time he becomes the baby, or aggressively gives orders to the therapist. But again he shuts his door on his secret world when he leaves, and assumes a placid mask.

Our brief excursion into play therapy and its greatly extended boundaries of freedom as a context of emotional re-learning show the possibility of reducing the inner confusions and blocks in communication where the self has not found the attunement necessary for security in relating to others. Techniques of play therapy may vary as we attempt to enter the world of the child and understand the meanings of its symbols for him. We have shared, in these records, approaches which are in keeping with the philosophy of this book. More important than techniques are enabling attitudes. And parents find they can share the insights of play therapy in the way they receive the child's expressions. Their own classes make meaningful the possibility of recognising feelings rather then denying them in fear, the possibility of losing prison walls of self while finding enjoyment in mature and abiding relationships. In offering similar attitudes of recognition to the child even while limiting his behaviour, parents discover an enabling climate which helps him to incorporate and accept the constraints of social reality while moving in the direction of greater self-realisation and maturity. They discover that the angry, needy child who has not been able to find understanding to meet his emotional hunger will be the one who uses later situations for self or social destructiveness, while the child who has found his feelings safe in their expression in words or symbolic play is the one who is able later to see other people's points of view, get in their shoes, make reasonable attempts at problem solving.

Essentially, if a child's parent has been his friend or if the healing experience of a therapist has given him a new parent-friend, he does not have the hidden accumulation of feeling which tends to feed a growing poison tree. In the words of William Blake:

> 'I was angry with my friend:
> I told my wrath, my wrath did end.
> I was angry with my foe:
> I told it not, my wrath did grow.'

12 *Epilogue: Adventure in Maturity*

When that I was and a little tiny boy,
With hey, ho, the wind and the rain,
A foolish thing was but a toy,
For the rain it raineth every day.

But when I came to man's estate,
With hey, ho, the wind and the rain,
'Gainst knaves and thieves men shut their gate,
For the rain it raineth every day.

William Shakespeare

LOOKING BACK

We began by sharing the experience of people looking into themselves for the first time and finding that if they admit their previously feared internal world, little by little it changes—it becomes less restricted, more confident. We have found that this internal changed world gives a new perspective on the world without, even though external things and people do not change.

We have seen self-fear asserted in unwilllingness to accept help, and self-distrust finding its defence in dislike of others: human relationships must be kept at arm's length—'Leave me alone'. Then with inner exploration defensiveness and blaming others gradually gives way to warmer, outgoing communication. We have seen deep antagonism towards parents dissolve in a widening compassion not just for parents but for all other people. And with changing attitudes, behaviour changes. As pervasive criticism of self and others seems to lose its relevance, pervasive acceptance of people emerges, as well as concrete awareness of the needs of others.

Emotional honesty and reduced fear in the inner world may bring it seems, a sense of adventure in the external world, a new taste for familiar things. It becomes more possible to distinguish real problems in the family or the social environment, from those emotional problems which arise from inner fears and guilts about the body and its functions, about basic impulses and needs. When such inner bogeys are projected on to people and situations in the external world, that world becomes a frightening place to be and people seem threatening. Inevitably they arouse dislike or the defence of indifference, 'I don't care', 'You have no meaning for me.' When inner feelings lose their frightening aspect, the imaginary menace around the corners of the outside world tend also to disappear.

Fighting self by denial (the attempt to keep unwanted feelings outside awareness) is an exhausting business. With its correlative of fighting the world outside, it is also a losing battle. Energy released from fruitless self-war can marshal resources for solving problems in the real world. Parents can accept the limits of both their normal and their handicapped children and give them realistic help and guidance. Husbands and wives see each other's worlds more authentically when stripped of the distortions imposed by their own unrealistic demands and derogation of each other. We have seen people lose their defensive burdens in work and play and find new zest.

Following the implications of our preventive philosophy, we have looked in play therapy at the child's world as he reflects that of his parents'. We have discovered that as he finds a parent who can both love and limit him while he seeks his own identity and relates to others he begins to build an investment for his future confidence and for the release of his abilities. The drama of the child's play has shown most clearly how the experience of secure relationships with important people in the outer world, gives rise to a secure inner world where feelings are no longer frightening.

Perhaps there is no more appropriate way to end our journey than by listening to the words of students, young and old, as they look at their current problems. These are all variations of the basic problems which assail all men at all times as they attempt to meet human needs in relation to others. These students found themselves in a communication class concerned not only with knowledge but with the prevention of communication breakdown and the promotion of personal growth. Here each has an opportunity to learn about himself by listening to himself, and in doing so finds a greater understanding of his world and its challenges. The students speak of parents as well as themselves as they look at politics, minority movements, prejudice, social violence, the meaning of drugs in the light of their own development and personal philosophy. Of the generation gap one speaks for many when he says, 'reducing psychological barriers in communication with oneself opens doors to communication with others and makes the generation gap an illusion. Basic human relationships are no respecter of generations.'

THE PARENT IN POLITICS

'It was so easy to read the books and to analyse everybody else; even in a sense to analyse myself. I was this way because my father was strict and the people around me rejected my family. Because we were immigrants we were treated like outcasts who didn't belong. And I'd had to apologise for my existence and so I was in a turmoil of hurt and frustration inside. But I didn't really know how very mad I was. And I didn't know how much I was putting my personal needs into these political movements. I was seeking a deeper private redress than I knew through public justice. And I was rationalising my wish to hit and to blame. I just thought I wanted to improve course offerings, or to protest the injustice of the government. Then I began to see. I had these fantasies, when I joined that extreme group in college, of being on the barricades, emerging in a kind of thrilling revolution. I needed an escape from this prison of me that I felt with my parents and these people all around who never liked us and let us know it. I remember once some kids threw stones at the window when I was doing my homework. Another time they tipped garbage on our lawn. Their parents supported it. We heard the mother of one of them saying "I don't like any of them", meaning my family. And these people were your neighbours. It was a senseless world for a child. Just because you were the kind of person you were, people didn't like you. You didn't know where to turn. You could cry or kick, but it didn't make any difference. You were still caught. And you just became so disgusted and vicious you were full of it. Getting into politics at college gave me a break. *I felt I was doing something and that part of it was constructive.* And it gave me somewhere to belong. But there's no doubt about the exhilaration of rebellion. I needed it. It was a source of life for me. An out from depression and hopelessness. Quite apart from wrongs to be righted. And there *were* wrongs. That's why student politics made such an ideal cover for my personal anger. I could always make it acceptable because on the face of it everything I was doing was to help the underprivileged. To give to the poor. Help needy children. Get more educational opportunities for minorities. And I could truthfully identify with them all. Because I was all these things in effect. The deprived. The downtrodden. But this joining the group that gives the acceptable outlet from personal despair, an opportunity to attack authority at all costs, this won't resolve your wrongs. You can do the right things for the wrong reasons.'

The good band-wagon. 'Joining the Christian churches or the political groups for social justice can just as much be a good band-wagon for one's own ends. I don't know why this should cause surprise really, to find so much narrow self-interest in the altruistic movements. The better the band-wagon the more convincingly evil can take the cloak of good. Church or politics. And you have a chance for self-righteous hostility, to judge others. Under the appearance of being intelligent about things, I'd always used opportunities to be critical, even vicious. I'd been like that right from high school. My frankness always had a knife edge. But how little self-righteous one is underneath. When I think of my immaturity and all my needs that most surely would have been put into anything I'd try to run. I know I'd have been as bad or worse a tyrant than these people I was attacking for their militarism or their economic exploitation. I'd have had to have everything rigidly my way. I'd have had my own kind of bigotry because I was just terrified at the possibility of having my inadequacies revealed. It was a shock to find that even my pacifism was a way to deny murderous destructiveness in myself—I mean I wanted to drop all those bombs in my child mind that still went on living in me. When I found myself caught in a war in a foreign country, it was anguish to see happening just what I had wanted. That's what it was. I know that now. But at the same time I didn't want it. I was so mad at those people in my home town. They didn't do one kind thing to me. I wanted to kill them all. And of course I wanted to get rid of my parents. A good reason for not wanting to go to war or hold a gun. But I was only saying I really wanted new parents who'd themselves stop fighting and give me what I needed. Destroy the old and bring in the new seemed to be an obsession with me. And it led me to revolutionary politics. The government as well as the college had to be new parents. I was really saying, "Let my parents take care of me better, make me important." Destroy the old and bring in the new? Of course I'm saying, too, that I want to lose my old self, to make myself over again. I'm a better reformer of wrongs in the world since I've understood these things.'

ACTING OUT—THE POLITICS OF PLAY AND SEX

Taste of freedom—college as play therapy. 'I can see in my own experience and talking to others that it isn't the Black Studies Programme or a course of Mexican culture when violence erupts in a situation where such programmes and courses *are* being formed in fact. By the very token of having received an opportunity to forge his own future the student has a privileged position. And he'll want to try and use it to try and meet his needs which haven't been met before in all kinds of places from the beginning of his life. He'll use any situation to hand. Just like those people from places where they've been repressed and discriminated against, sold short on education and everything. They'll come to a city or a college where they've greater opportunities and freedoms and that's the city or the college they'll attack. Even best efforts to help them will seem to be tokenism because needs are so enormous.'

'It's just like a child in play therapy. He uses his freedom to get out his anger for the first time in his life. And he does it to someone who's being nice to him. It has to be so. It's the only way he can be safe. The taste of freedom takes the lid off. And if he's in a position of privilege as a learner it doesn't mean he's going to stick with the assignment from the book. In fact, after all my efforts to get to college, the books meant nothing to me. They fell so short of my need. You'll have to expect a student to try to learn in ways that mean something to him. Like a child he's not really clear what's driving him, but just like a child he'll use all the old magic thinking. "Destroy the bad authorities and all will be well." And the magic of labels. Bleeding heart Anglos, as Mexicans call "do-good Anglo-Saxons", pigs, niggers, hippies. It's easier to lump all the other side together. Then you don't have to make distinctions. And you can tear things down. But a child in play therapy or in any play where he has a parent who can meet his needs, has someone to limit him, as you've said, in reasonable and loving ways. So he doesn't destroy himself and those who feed him. All these programmes and courses giving recognition to people and groups in our society meet a necessity. And a student voice in university government may also be vital. Silenced voices are no part of the partnership of education. But I haven't met a single student who insists on demands being met to the letter and then steps up demands when they have been met. I haven't met one who hasn't a child's buried hunger for love inside him. Like people who keep adding to their property and never seem satisfied. Same reason.'

Free love as free hate—The Politics of Sex. 'I think I used sex as a kind of anaesthesia. To numb other kinds of feelings—tenderness, caring, needs for love. I thought I was free but I was driven. I had to keep getting into these affairs that always terminated. I didn't want any responsibility. That's one level. And I didn't want to get close to anybody. That's another. It isn't surprising that young people who take extreme positions build promiscuity into their political religion. It's part of denunciation of the father, of the establishment. Punish parents that way. You're rejecting their kind of sex relationship and you're rejecting law if that's what law means. You're doing good in general ways so you feel less guilty. But the politics of sex is pervasive. You strip those in charge. Free love begins to look very much like free hate. Power and manipulation become the issue rather than love. Who calls the tune? Who is the authority? But you mustn't get emotionally involved. This rebellion isn't so untraditional after all. It's just a variation on Don Jaun with all his suicidal drivenness. But now it's built into a socially acceptable framework of free sex. Relating to all but relating to none. It's still the cry, "I'll reject you before you can reject me" of these self-hating but love-hungry. Sex without involvement means you're afraid of your feelings. I was panicked by mine. But killing them meant killing myself as a human being. Intimacy of body but no intimacy of heart is a tragedy of denial hardly matched by our forefathers who tried to deny the body.'

THE PROTECTION OF PROJECTION

'Whenever I "just dislike" others it has become so clear to me I'm seeing in them some reminder *in some form* of those things I don't want to accept in myself. And these others are only ordinary human beings we must live with if we are to live with ourselves. And we can never live at peace with others unless we can live with ourselves. It's a murderous kind of revenge story when we keep on blaming others for us because we just don't want to listen to ourselves. And when academically trained people listen literally to the words of students, they don't recognise their own limitations nor their own projection. Teachers are like parents and if they don't see their own immaturities in dealing with students or with social issues, or in judging each other or the administration, they'll victimise students and each other. Not least, if they create a following. The students who can only perform in dependency on a teacher will never really grow if the teacher finds satisfaction in their dependency. If we don't recognise our own prejudices as teachers we'll listen literally when students' prejudices match ours. I don't need convincing that projection is the most powerful part of prejudice—I've felt it. I remember a black student accusing one of the most accepting professors I've ever known of discrmination. But in that particular class the student had a chance to find out that the professor liked him and that he was projecting his own discrimination against himself on to the professor. And that he was making his own antagonism to the professor into the professor's antagonism to him. It's the sort of thing you read in the books. But the power of it needs some experiencing. It happens all the time and you aren't aware of it. But here we can see whole races as victims of mass projection. Whole races made into scapegoats—because of our inadequacy to come up to scratch for our parents, our guilt about all the aggression, all the feeling of being unclean, just plain dirty, the sex we learned to be ashamed of despite our freedom, all of ourselves we learned not to like. We can just get rid of it all like that! Put it on to others and hate them for it. It's hard to allow these things to come into conscious awareness when you've gone to such lengths to put them out of the way. I catch myself now, when I'm irritated and things seem to be going wrong. I'm just full of irrational disgust against poor people like Mexicans or poor whites. I feel like stepping on them. I can't stand them. And more than once when these feelings come up, and I'm ready to blow up and also, I might say, to cry my eyes out, I've thought about it and it's so plain that I want to step on my own feelings. And I can't stand these people asking for their wants to be met and getting nowhere because that's me and my parents. And people think I'm affluent. Some students of one black professor complained he was too conscious of being black. We should help them to ask, "What is it in me that I am so concerned about this? What am I trying to deny in myself?" Some people lose their jobs, as literally others have lost their lives because other people's projections are interpreted literally.'

'We should hear their hidden fears of themselves behind what they're saying. In fighting our so-called enemies on so many fronts, we're fighting our denied selves. It's like a witch hunt with the bogeys in us planted in any convenient person that society will approve. Gets us acceptance and notice and other people support us with their bogeys. How many black men were lynched because of the unconscious projections of women who were in effect saying they wanted sex relations with black men? They'd be expressing their wish and condemning it at the same time by bringing charges against him. And they'd be listened to by men who'd raped or wanted to rape black women. This is, of course, the final social horror—literally killing others because we want to get rid of our feelings which we put on to them. Kill what we *see* in them. Not what they *are*. And the black men hit back. They have their human problems too. I completely identified with a black rapist this weekend. I saw a white woman in a store. White hat. Everything pure white. And her daughter, probably fourteen, well heeled. To me they had a sneer. Whether they had or not I don't know. I didn't care. To me they were self-righteous, or anything indifferent and cold which at that moment the whole white race stood for. Superiority and indifference and everyone else dirt. And they stood for despising me. Making people anonymous. People fight not to be anonymous. Not to be reduced to nothing by being overlooked. It isn't just rejection. It's not being noticed. Pure hatred for this woman surged up in me. The white bitch. The great white dominion. Who does she think she is! I've caught my own sneer as I say that. But I wanted to tear off that white hat and that expensive hair-do, and the clothes and tear her flesh and rape her. Break that smug expression. Make her look. And I wanted to tie up her daughter and make her watch. Make them *feel*. *Make* them relate to me. It's this indifference that makes me sick. Make them hurt so they *can't* shut you out. Do to them what they're doing. Leave *them* in the gutter. The statistic says there's a female rape once every seven minutes in Los Angeles. That screams the extent of a human problem.'

'But, my God, what this tells us about what we learned to feel about ourselves. Our parents' problems perpetrating social prejudice! But when you put it like this it isn't hard to see how extremely projection is protection. Against looking at this "awful me" which somehow our parents with their problems or our lack of parents had made us feel about ourselves. And you think of the destruction of the Negro family, the series of deserting fathers and the exploited mothers, the violence as a way of life. And the smug rich society surrounding it all, giving nothing but charity (that isn't charity at all) in welfare that never goes round. The feeling that nobody cares and how can you break the iron wall of indifference? Unless people are to die without a word—as they have, and they have been murdered—they've got to kick.

And far short of literal murder, we have the ordinary murders o. everyday living in families and outside them. "I don't like *you* because you're the kind of person you are" shouts "I don't like you because *I'm* the kind of person *I* am and I don't want to look at me so I prefer to dislike you." So parents don't like their children, people don't like people. We've got to break the vicious cycle somewhere. The way we're handing down in families, in social groups, this reactive scapegoating, so it's always *them* and not us who must change first. But I'm trying to begin with myself. As a teacher, as a parent, and wherever I meet people I'm trying to meet myself honestly. So that I can meet them.'

'They are us.' 'We don't want to look at what the students reflect of us if they rebel. Us the parents, I mean. But I'm ready to admit now the reflection of us in our son and daughter. Didn't we seek instant gratification? Didn't we say, "I've got to get a divorce. I must have this sexual affair." And all in the name of freedom we pursued our relativistic way. We gave lip service to loyalty. We rationalised our way out of commitments, including commitments to our children. And when they want instant gratification we don't like it. We questioned everything that didn't seem convenient to us. We gave the kids no solid floor of limits or values. But we hate it when they call us in question. They say we're hypocritical, and, of course, with our profession of principles and promises we haven't been able to keep, we have been hypocritical. The worst kind of hypocrisy—unconscious hypocrisy. And the young people strike to free themselves from us; But so often they repeat us in a different form.'

'Our social problems begin to look like one big parent-child relationship.' We don't like it when a minority group becomes violent. We blame them. But we have shown them how in the sense that attitudes are caught and not taught. They reflect us and our society. We'd like to bury out of sight like the unnamed bodies of black men drowned in the southern rivers this effrontery that dares show us to ourselves. But we and they must look to ourselves if we and they are not going to hand on this gap between principles we say we believe in and our actual practice. These young people are us. So are the minority groups. If we stay on the level of blaming them, we're saying more about us than about them. And they'll fail as we did if their assertions of self remain on the level of protest against us. *Whether they assert their*

independence and identity in a teenage marriage or in a separatist minority. If they continue as protest, continue scapegoating us, they won't get beyond us.'

'I saw through it.' 'I want to tell you about the way the class helped me this weekend. I thought my friend was annoyed with me. She seemed cold and would hardly speak when I spoke to her. And I felt more and more frustrated. So I went away and sat down and started to think things through. I asked myself, "What is it in me that I'm getting so upset about this thing?" And I came up with the conclusion that my friend wasn't mad at me at all, but I was mad at her because she wouldn't do what I wanted. So I left her alone to do what she had to do, study and everything else. And the atmosphere improved Come meal-time she was talking to me and everything seemed relaxed. I saw through it. The way I was pushing her because I was feeling left out. I stopped pushing. The problem was in me.'

MIND EXPANSION

'Listening to you sets me thinking. In alcohol, in drugs, we can seek release from the burden of this imprisoned self into an expanded self. Mind expansion with its breaking of reality boundaries. Alcohol the great dissolver of guilt, the release from yourself, the great substitute for tenderness-hunger. I know. I tried alcohol. I could never go to a social function without plenty of it on tap. But I've thought what a much truer release it's been to expand my world through this class. So that I took steps to know myself. Another kind of mind expansion. And this was real, not hallucination. And it lasted and didn't leave disaster behind it. And guilt did dissolve when I found how unrealistic it was.

'I was always trying to escape. From my family, of course, in drinking or men. I thought of the girl who started smoking grass. She didn't like her family at all. She wanted to get away from them. So she did the next best thing for her. She switched to speed so the yelling of her family didn't bother her. She could turn them off with speed. I think what a different kind of invulnerability you begin to get this other way. A strength inside because you've invited yourself to *be*. Not hiding from what you don't like, and taking stuff to help you hide. But taking a look and getting behind the frightening front, of yourself and others. You're constantly breaking through to an expanded world. The shift in seeing does hurt. It's only one aspect of what we've talked about—the paradox of suffering because it leads to insight and greater comfort. As you've said, it can hurt but it can heal at the same time to let in the light.'

CHANGING THE QUESTION

Our commentaries show again and again the question posed: 'How do I handle myself and the world and meet human needs?' Some aspects of the human condition do not change. Birth, growing up and death are always with us. There are handicaps and illness still. Storm, fire and flood occur—the wind and the rain are perennial. Problems continue—personal and social. The kind of response to the continuing human condition can make the difference between a sense of battling an intractable world and resilience in problem solving. In dealing with the problems that recur, finding the right question seems more important than finding the right answer. Changing the question in matters of human relations seems to be a route to finding solutions not 'How do I get rid of these difficult people?' but 'How do I change my reaction to them?' and 'How do I understand their needs?' The questions themselves suggest that the solutions are never a finished issue. They presuppose a way of life continuously revealing its own answers in response to needs.

'I heard on television about the battered child syndrome. All kinds of horrors. One little boy was forced to swallow an electric light bulb. Another had meningitis and he was beaten for not getting out of bed. He died. One mother held her girl's hand over a flame. One of the discussants said, "We must find ways to punish the parents." Now that seems to me a wrong answer because it's a wrong question. Change the question. Not just, "How can we punish the parents?" but "How can we help them?" In talk about conditioning, it's easy to lose sight of a human person by concentrating on his behaviour.'

'Punishment can be an incitement for people to continue to be rotten parents. Punishment can *make* criminals, produce crime. It's really a crime in itself as tragic as the original human damage that resulted from punishment. It can only tear deeper the wounds that lead to ill-treating children. I remember my father hitting me till I was gashes all over. Just to get his frustrations out. And I remember thinking, "I don't care if you kill me. I'm not going to let you know I have any reaction at all." *And I didn't have a reaction*. All denial. No one denied a need for my father's care more than I did. That, of course, is why I'm sure I've just cried and cried as though there couldn't be an end in this therapy. The tears I didn't shed then. But my father was a beaten and desperate man. He didn't need more beating. We must protect the children. But we must find ways to help parents be people, help them be parents. As we did so many times in the groups. There were times when we all wanted to torture or kill our children for making us feel so helpless.'

Freeing the waters. In the traditional story of the Holy Grail, a knight in the quest of the Grail has to ask the right question to restore flowing water to a land of drought and to cure the king's sickness. His question which frees the waters seems to be a question concerned with understanding: 'What is the nature of the Grail?' Water flows, and land and king may lose sterility and become healthy and fertile as an indirect result of the right question. Our experiences of 'freeing the waters' of insight in human persons are analogous. When the 'right question' was asked it brought its own answer, and aridity gave way to *spontaneous* flowering. For parents, growth in unexpected places seemed to occur where nothing came of former *effort*.

We remember the discovery: 'If you're trying, you haven't found the answer. When you're there you just do things differently.' In other words, *when you become the kind of person who can ask the right question, the answer follows* in a different response without conscious effort. So an answer is not a prescriptive recipe, but a new way of seeing derived from changed attitudes which result in changed behaviour.

Children's tales. 'I don't have a physically handicapped child the way a lot of parents do. Candy isn't blind, or deaf or spastic. But she does have a slight limp. You'd hardly notice it. But I've built it up in my mind and been so touchy about it. But there are signs I'm improving. Candy came home and told me how her friend's mother had talked to her about how well her little girl was doing in dancing. And Candy was depressed. "I wish I could dance like June." The first opportunity I'd have burst out at June's mother: "We don't want to hear how well June's doing at dancing. Candy can't and you know it." I'd have gone on about the interfering busybody my neighbour was. My question would have been: "What's the matter with her? Why can't she shut up about her daughter's achievements?" But this time I was more ready to ask *myself*, "What in *my attitudes* has made Candy so depressed about a small limitation?" I'd noticed she had a way of letting one little mishap or negative cloud everything else and that's the way

I was and I hadn't seen it. Now I'm accepting myself better.'

'This time I just recognised Candy's feeling. I didn't criticise or approve either. Just said, "You feel bad because June can do something you can't do as well." But then I did say I'd learned to enjoy things I could do like swimming even though I wasn't very good, and that I used to be so upset because I had big ears, but I don't mind any more. I just accept it and feel pleased I'm reasonably good to look at, as my husband says. Then Candy said, "I think Mrs Smith wanted to say something nice about June because she hadn't done very well in English and she was telling her mother that I was top of the class." The number of times I've down-graded June. I've been so concerned about the shortcomings and unfairness of others. I never stopped to think how my irritations might hurt them.'

Heart and head. 'We were driving Jack's business partner to town. Katie, our four-year-old, and Gillian the six-year-old deaf child, were in the back of the car. Suddenly Katie hit the deaf child and shouted, Mommie, and I was able to meet the situation spontaneously. No panic. Really with *heart and head*. First I had to get some first-hand information. "What is it, Katie?" I asked. "Gillian has my best slip," she said. She pushed Gillian again and burst into tears. She'd just caught sight of the slip as Gillian leaned over the back of the seat. So I did two things for Katie. I just accepted her feelings with complete respect, and then I pointed out reality. "Katie, maybe Susan didn't know when she was helping dress Gillian." Susan, the older girl, always helps the younger ones. "And I know you don't like Gillian to take your things without asking you. But there's nothing I can do about it right now. Why don't we wait till we get home and we'll ask Gillian to exchange. Is that all right?" Katie sniffed and was quiet. I find so many times if I can accept the children's viewpoint, they're able to wait if I can't give them what they want right then. And they've learned to trust me. They know I keep my word. Then Gillian pushed at me after Katie stopped pushing her and I was able to take her hand so she could see my face. "I know you're mad at Mommie," I said. I smiled and said, "O.K.?" I was relaxed and she seemed to relax. I couldn't have done what I did that day if we hadn't built a background of communication at home.'

'If all is well with your relationships and you know your own mind, specific situations seem to take care of themselves. I never ask now, "How can I stop this behaviour?" I'm saying "How can I understand it? How do they feel?" And then I recognise their feelings. After that I simply state the limits, the practicalities, the rules. And they're kept. Changing the question has made everything so much easier. But then I couldn't have done it if I hadn't come to know my own feelings. I can accept theirs now.'

LOOKING FORWARD

The explorations in this book are really only a glimpse of the problems and solutions of a human life-journey. Solutions are not techniques but an outgrowth of ways of perceiving and relating to others.

The masks. Whether we share the experience of a mother calming the screams of a child while showing him the limits and demands of the real world, or hear a girl telling how she took a dangerous drug 'to turn off' the screams of her family, whether we enter the world of a young man who turned on society through violent political movements, or of a 'more respectable man' who turned on himself and failed in business, unable to function with confidence in his own powers, nothing has been as insistent as the many assertions of the need to receive and give love. Seeking for admiration, for power, for possession of things, money or people, subtle or gross forms of aggression, sexual promiscuity without involvement appear as masks. These behaviours may be labelled either as socially acceptable or as anti-social, but in either case on closer inspection they reveal themselves as masks which disguise the search for love.

If he has not found his world secure, the child will use disguise and decoy to build his defences against what he estimates will be his hurt. And nothing appears a more searing source of hurt to him than his own emotional needs. There he is most vulnerable if he dares to depend on another. So, deep and pervasive as his love hunger may be, the masks he wears into adult life indicate the many faces of resistance to admitting this real hunger. Therefore, all his substitute foods leave him wanting more—admiration, or power, or possessions. And he is still hungry. Plentiful sex leaves him empty. Plentiful alcohol does not bring the forgetting he seeks. He is still anxious.

To strengthen his resistance, he uses the powerful but self-crippling ally of guilt. 'I am bad for the very feelings I possess.' He enacts variations on ways to make his own life hard. Again and again he uses the events of his world to reinforce his conviction that 'needs make you a victim'. 'Even television and car repair outfits take you for a ride if you depend on them. And the ill and the old are the easiest victims of all for they have the greatest needs to be exploited by ruthless interests.' In such ways his feelers go out to the replicas of his love-hungry childhood parents whose needs drove them to 'exploit' him. He lacks the experience of his dependency needs being accepted, so he does not trust them. They are 'bad'.

But he must live in relationship with others. Even in the denial of attempted isolation ('I want to be left alone') he is expressing in reverse his real need for belonging and togetherness. And he is expressing his lack of confidence that he can ever be worthy of either.

Each person in his 'punishing them for me' reveals mistaken ways of trying to get close to himself and others: the mother who puts the weight of her own past punishments on to her son's library fine, the brilliant girl who cries her need for her parents' acceptance by constantly criticising her teachers or the limitations of her fellow students, the nagging wife or husband, the black man who tortures and rapes a white woman, or the white man who tortures and rapes a black woman, even the murderer. All are using mistaken—dysfunctional—ways of getting close to their own feelings and to other people. 'Punishing them for me.'

The good authority. Our focus has been parents—understanding our parents in us, ourselves as parents. We have used existing situations—parent classes, seminars in communication—to implement a preventive philosophy that all can gain from the kinds of understandings explored here. The social implications of our approach to parents and families made themselves felt, early in our journey, beyond the immediate family circle: a man's relationship to his bosses, the human being in his social groups. We defined freedom as freedom from fear, from internal stress which hampers choice. Responsibility implies, as we defined it, both the freedom from conflict which diminishes choice, and taking responsibility for attitudes as well as behaviour—owning them as ours. It really means telling the truth to ourselves that what we feel we feel; it means being willing to discover what we feel when we have pushed it out of awareness. By that route of discovery we take responsibility for change. From the responsible parent seems to emerge one possibility of a responsible community. Our respect for the individual, no matter how different he may be from us, has the flavour of the kind of attitudes embodied in the Bill of Rights and ideals of democracy. Our philosophy of the good authority who cares and guides, loves and limits, is both law and mercy, seems in keeping, too, with the philosophy of the good governor who was the subject of treatises in renaissance times when Sir Thomas Elyot wrote *The Governor*. In this way man may re-think his symbols, render them new; merely introducing a new label does not re-new the substance.

Matching inside and outside. We have been centrally concerned in all our work with closing the gap between principle and practice, but even more between attitude and act. Work with parents showed that academic education was no guarantee of maturity. Intellect, knowledge of science and abstract concepts could be an escape from self-knowledge a means of resistance to it. Verbal use of concepts does not mean understanding their personal implications, as we saw when we shared Mr Metcalf's objections before he gained insight into the specific purpose of the parent class: 'It's a frame of mind we're after.'

Our method of teaching and learning takes into account the person as he is and thus enables him to grow beyond his own stalemate. That is, he lessens the gap between his own attitudes and the concepts he believes in. ('The principle says, "Love your neighbour". But I hated his guts.') Thus he comes nearer the Bill of Rights for his family or his neighbours. As he grows emotionally he tends less to overload his marriage partner, his children, his social groups, with his own unrealistic expectations.

We have seen however the multiple faces of resistance to emotional growth, to admitting self, whether in aggression or tenderness. Seeking status through education may be as much a mask as those of power and possessions, or of non-involvement, and all may attempt to hide the small child's need for someone to depend on, someone who cares.

Commitment to values. In making our purpose a route to change which brings people nearer goals of meaningful interpersonal relations and self-realisation, we have at all times implied a system of values. We have not worked in a vacuum to express feeling. Protective and enabling limits have been as important as permissiveness. We have been concerned that parents accept their children, that a husband or wife learns to live with rather than attack or get rid of a partner. Where people do begin to find themselves in our sense of taking responsibility for their deeper selves, they becomes more able to love. Having truly put themselves in their own shoes, they are better able to put themselves into other people's, and loyalty and committment inevitably become part of their lives. ('Death do us part,' said Gaynor.) Sex is not t mechanical mastery of techniques without involvement. Other peopl are persons and not objects to be used and cast off. The expanded family rather than the exclusive nuclear one becomes part of the expanded self whether all members live under the same roof or not. But we do remember Lorraine who found her mother-in-law an intolerable part of the household because of a childhood rivalry with her mother for her father. She sought the ability to live with both husband and mother-in-law, and learnt to say a realistic no to unrealistic demands while accepting her mother-in-law. She became able to love, and to live with both her husband and her mother-in-law.

Talking out, and in some instances playing out and channelling feelings symbolically, has been the alternative to acting out while finding a way to changed communication in attitude and behaviour. We have been concerned with communication and improving it, with correcting mistaken personal synonyms by means of new self-experience. Breakdowns in communication—the person with himself, the person with others—may destroy society as well as the human being; as great civilisations of history have fallen to the enemy within rather than the enemy without. If 'limits set, needs met' is a key to the communication of the good authority of a parent to a child, it seems to be true of a good authority in other settings, too, of those in charge of large or small groups of human beings. A continuing condition of interpersonal communication seems to be an ability to put oneself in another person's shoes—without criticism, with understanding of how he feels. This is most difficult to do if we have so little come to terms with the child in us or any of our most tender feelings, that we hate another's needs because they mirror our own.

The Challenge of peace. Closing the gap between attitudes and actions, between attitudes and words (not saying darling through clenched teeth) is a central challenge for parent-child relationships where the all-important ingredient is what a parent feels rather than what a parent does. It becomes, too, a central challenge of peace—in the family and larger communities of human beings. As parents found, peace does not mean simply talking peace but living the meaning of peace. It implies not an overt absence of conflict in a cold war ready to become hot, but a positive sense of enjoyment in commitment and accomplishment.

When we cease to force others into our image, we see them clearly themselves. Falling in love may seem to make all well, but it turns out to be only an apparent solution for ills because unrealistic demands leave other persons always inadequate to meet them. As Elise and others found, consuming needs could mean that 'being in love' emerged as an up and down of extreme attraction or extreme repulsion, in which nagging criticism obscured the unsatisfactory partner who 'didn't do what I wanted'. The greater discovery seemed to be finding the meaning of love for a husband or wife for the first time. Mature love, we have seen, means as great a concern for the other person's needs as for one's own. The challenge of peace in the world as of concord in the family is essentially to find the meaning of mature love.

'I was painting a bookcase on the porch yesterday, and suddenly my boy opened the door and let in the dog and it sent the unthinned paint can flying. What a mess. But you know I didn't yell. I sat down and I looked. And the first thing I thought of was, "Isn't the nature of paint interesting?" The sun glinted through the window and there it was spread out brown and thick and shining. I thought, "Now if this hadn't happened I wouldn't have had the privilege of seeing this sight." Privilege. That was the word that came, just as spontaneously as anything. There was a time when I'd have screamed at Michael and stayed screaming. But I didn't; and it wasn't because I sat on myself. I didn't want to scream. I think it's just that I feel more adequate inside and many things that happen don't come as a threat any more. I felt in control of myself inside and the situation wasn't difficult to control. I even took time to look at the rock Michael wanted to show me and I said that I'd look at it more carefully after we had cleaned up. We've been collecting rocks and I said, "Think before you rush at me when I am busy." He's actually been much less on edge with this new me.'

As we end the story of our journey, questions open out into a continued adventure in maturity. Starting with parents and exploring family life we encompass all human endeavour.

'Know thyself' was the salutation meeting Greek worshippers at Apollo's temple at Delphi. Athenian philosophers of more than two thousand years ago found in Apollo's motto a challenge for their interpretation. More recent twentieth-century existentialist philosophy asserts that all despair is really despair about not being ourselves. The kind of knowledge each person chose in his encounters with self led him into a sense of being himself, which moved away from despair and into a new apprehension of freedom. After such experiences people have expressed a sense of wholeness which is the literal meaning of health. Such wholeness or health presupposes capacity for functioning fully. A sense of freedom in use of powers arising from the integration of unconscious forces admitted into the personality leads to redefinition of familiar concepts.

'At the time of his trial and death Socrates conveyed that misunderstanding is a form of evil. We have found that misunderstanding of ourselves is a primary source of the destructiveness of the human person—which is what we mean by evil in our human context. But it has been implied in everything we have done that there *is* a choice. There *is* a will, with a new meaning. We're not just victims hedged in by the unalterable determinism of our infancy and childhood. We can change if we *choose* to give ourselves a new experience in a relationship we can have faith in. Then this taking responsibility, this choosing, is our freewill in a much deeper sense than before. It involves the whole person in an authentic response. The old kind of will often meant an assumption of behaviour belied by our attitudes. It could mean that we felt compelled into confession that wasn't real because we didn't know our deeper sources of guilt. In that predicament the will was paralysed. Now it is freed for deeper choice and takes creative wings. The implications seem far reaching for becoming able to use our potential and find good.'

Eastern philosophy, following Buddha, suggests that when a person is able to have compassion on all living creatures he is noble. For East or West, for the antiquity of Greece, or the twentieth century or beyond, perhaps in our context we can adapt an ancient concept: 'When a person achieves compassion on all others, then he is mature.'

But first a man must find compassion on himself.

Spoken after six years of struggle to escape from a strait-jacket of childhood rejection, and of self-blame for parents' unhappiness the following words look back and forward as compassion and forgiveness take on a fresh perspective:

> 'I saw my own inability to forgive. I really think I've been living a very petty revenge, mostly against myself. I condemned my husband for not doing what I wanted. But he couldn't please me. Now I wonder how he could sit back so patiently while I was so contradictory in every way.'

As we have looked in summary at the defensive masks with which people hide their need for caring and love let us finally remember the mask of 'caring for them for me'. For parents this may be a more compelling disguise than 'punishing them for me'.

> 'I have always been the one everybody could rely on to get together a dinner at short notice. I'm always entertaining. Whoever drops in I'll have something ready in no time. But now I know I've taken care of everybody else on the outside because I so desperately needed to be taken care of myself. It's the same thing the way I looked after all those lost cats. Now I can still care but there's a different quality. Less strain and not the same urgent need to prove my worth, an urgency that was never met the old way. Now it's more truly caring for them, because I haven't got my own survival staked on what I can do for them. And I wouldn't *let* anybody help me before. I had to do everything myself. I needed help so much that I couldn't admit even a tiny bit of help. Now I can relax and accept the giving of others because I can give of myself.'

Whether we hear a husband or wife overworking to give to his family, or a student giving up his studies to join a political movement to provide for the underprivileged we may catch the hidden communication of personal need in 'caring for them for me'. Our route in knowing the parents in us has been to meet the hidden need so that we may become more able both to give and receive.

Today we have moved far away from the kind of stability and predictability associated with a task-oriented family where each member had clearly defined jobs in sowing, bringing in the harvest, spinning, weaving. It is not our purpose here to analyse our complex urban society and the ways in which human beings protect themselves by tuning out a barrage of stimuli, even it seems, the awareness of their own and others' needs. If we have become detached from our own sources of affection and caring, and become, as it were, non-members of a lonely crowd surrounded by the impersonality and accelerated advance of technology, our explorations here reveal one way to reach sources from which we may become human and find enduring relationships with others.